ALBERT ELLIS

ALBERT ELLIS

Passionate Skeptic

DANIEL N. WIENER

PRAEGER

New York
Westport, Connecticut
London

Library of Congress Cataloging-in-Publication Data

Wiener, Daniel N.
    Albert Ellis, passionate skeptic / Daniel N. Wiener.
        p.   cm.
    Bibliography: p.
    Includes index.
    ISBN 0-275-92751-2 (alk. paper)
    1. Ellis, Albert. 2. Clinical psychologists—United States—
Biography. 3. Rational-emotive psychotherapy—History. I. Title.
RC438.6.E45W54 1988
150'.92'4—dc 19
[B]
87-22495

Library of Congress Catalog Card Number: 87-22495
ISBN: 0-275-92751-2

First published in 1988

Praeger Publishers, One Madison Avenue, New York, NY 10010
A division of Greenwood Press, Inc.

Printed in the United States of America

∞
The paper used in this book complies with the
Permanent Paper Standard issued by the National
Information Standards Organization (Z39.48-1984).

10 9 8 7 6 5 4 3 2 1

Contents

List of Photographs

Foreword

It is a pleasure to write a foreword to this fascinating book, both because of its intrinsic merits (personal interest and scholarly value) and because the two persons involved, author and subject, are psychologists for whom I entertain a high regard and warm feelings. My acquaintance with Dr. Wiener goes back a good deal farther than that with Dr. Ellis, as I first met Dan Wiener in a section of biometry in 1939.

We have talked a great deal over the years about both clinical and scientific problems, and I have also had occasion to refer patients to him. It is gratifying to reflect upon my longtime acquaintance with a full-time clinical practitioner who has developed and articulated his views about helping troubled persons over his years of clinical practice in an objective, scientific, scholarly way. His self-concept as a practitioner has never once led him, in my extended experience, to attack or defend theoretical or therapeutic positions with disregard for critical habits of thought or the available state of the empirical evidence.

I think it is important that a biographer of somebody like Albert Ellis should be the kind of clinician and scholar that Wiener is. In examining the life of such an unusual person as Albert Ellis, whose "life" is the life of the mind, I cannot conceive a biography that would be even descriptively accurate, let alone perceptive and interesting, being done by someone not technically knowledgeable about psychology and psychotherapy.

Furthermore, the controversial character of many of Ellis's views and practices, and the ideological polarization that unfortunately still exists among psychotherapists — one so profound that therapists of some persuasions can hardly engage in a rational and friendly conversation with some others — means that a scholar-practitioner writing about Ellis (simultaneously about his ideas, movement, personal life, and values) should share some of Ellis's intellectual passion and be able to identify with it without being a "solid gold convert" to RET.

Dr. Wiener, like many psychologists of my generation, was influenced as a graduate student and young clinician by two schools of thought, the Rogersian and the psychoanalytic. But, like myself, being reared in the University of Minnesota Psychology Department, he was never a doctrinaire subscriber to either system. One thing that made it possible for people like him or me to appreciate the merits of Ellis's work at a time when few people did (and hardly any in the "academic establishment") was that our mentor, Starke Hathaway, was practicing an early form of RET before Ellis.

I have always found it irritating and sometimes downright insulting when psychologists speak slightingly of a major contributor like Rogers, Freud, Ellis, or Skinner, saying, "Well, of course, most of us have been doing that for years, we just didn't bother giving it a special name." The plain fact is that most remarks of this sort are quite unwarranted, because those who make them have not been practicing Rogers, Freud, or Ellis at all. But Hathaway really was a forerunner of RET.

My first extensive contact with Ellis was in 1954, at a special conference held by the Minnesota Center for the Philosophy of Science, on problems in assessing the scientific status of psychoanalysis. Ellis's paper was an attempt at formulating the principles of a scientific psychoanalysis. Since then I have had irregular contacts with Ellis. Although my own pre-ferred psychotherapeutic mode at that time was psychoanalytic, my training led me to be open to the kind of intellectual empha-sis that Ellis began to develop in the early days of RET. No Hathaway student was likely to dismiss a cognitive, philo-sophical therapeutic tactic out of hand as intellectualizing and defensive. Some is defense, some is not. Ellis seemed mildly pleased that we regarded him highly and wanted to hear his ideas.

When an innovator combines radical departures from the received doctrines with a personally aggressive style, it is hard for most persons seriously interested in the domain to remain objective. This combination of content and style tends to elicit a reflex defensive response, and in a minority who are deeply dissatisfied and "searching," a sometimes exaggerated conversion to the new doctrine.

On the other hand, it is difficult to write interestingly about a person like Ellis unless one is in some important sense personally engaged by the issues, which is why I doubt that a biographer who was not a psychotherapist could do a good job. My friend Ed Bordin summarized the proper mental set of a psychotherapist as being a suitable mix of "curiosity, compassion and detachment." I rather like this; something similar might be said about a biographer, and is impressively fulfilled in Dr. Wiener's case.

It is obvious from both content and style that Wiener is fascinated by the man Albert Ellis, by what he has to say about psychotherapy and, even more perhaps, about rational living. Yet it is worth noting that while Dr. Wiener, like the late Starke Hathaway and myself, is listed as on the Institute for Rational-Emotive Therapy's board of advisers, Wiener does not generally label himself as being an RET therapist, and he is as close to being fair-minded and evenhanded in his assessment of the RET approach as a psychotherapist could possibly be.

While biographies of the living are attended with dangers less present when writing about those long dead, the opportunity to have (and tape-record!) extended conversations with Ellis about the development of his ideas, as well as his personal life in its most intimate aspects, offers tremendous advantages. I think it testifies to the integrity, the inner coherence of Ellis's view of life and mental health, that he has been so forthcoming about delicate matters of personal history. I concur wholeheartedly with Wiener's assessment that here is a man who genuinely works hard to practice what he preaches to his therapy clients.

I think reflective readers who have not been brainwashed into accepting some dogma about how everybody should live (it is remarkable how bigoted some psychotherapists can be) will find it fascinating to read about Ellis's daily life. One mark of liberation is that they be able to say, on reading Wiener's account of Ellis's life-style, "Well, it wouldn't do for me, but I can't think of any good reason why Ellis should act otherwise."

I find very little critical to say about this book, and what few complaints I made were gracefully accepted by Dr. Wiener. Perhaps I still have a little complaint that he didn't push Ellis harder on the matter of ethics. The only "justification" that I have come across in Ellis's writings, correspondence, or conversation that permits any underlying semantic legitimacy to moral words is one familiar to moral philosophers but today rejected by them:

If I persist in breaking certain moral rules, it will redound to my disadvantage. First, people will not trust me. Second, in the long run, I will find myself living in a world in which people do not rely on others. Neither of these arguments is considered by most contemporary moral philosophers to be a sound reason why, where obeying the moral law is of considerable disadvantage to my interests, I should do so.

As regards the generality of RET, and its probable future, a history of psychotherapies suggests that they share a property with political and religious movements: that a charismatic leader and fairly small group of devoted followers can engage some deep factors in us, which helps greatly in the healing process. In his 1916 lectures, Freud invokes the power of the positive transference and explicitly says that "we heal by love."

It remains to be seen whether RET will begin to run out of gas, have a lower success rate, and take progressively longer to help. Freud's early analyses were frequently two- and three-month affairs, including some of the early training analyses.

Non-RET therapists have objected to the element of RET that is "influencing the patient's values." This is somewhat intellectually dishonest because the patient comes in voluntarily, can accept or reject what is said, and can terminate the relationship. Nor was Ellis the first therapist to do this kind of thing explicitly, since we find it fairly openly in Adler and perhaps slightly less so in Jung.

Finally, it is clear that one of the main bones of contention between the biographer and his subject is the relationship between intellect and feeling, or "reason and the passions," as Hume would have said it. If one adopts a conceptual framework like that of Plato or Kant, one sets "reason" or "intellect" and the "passions" against each other, and asks which does or should prevail. But as Hume saw it, reason was, and ought to be, the slave of the passions, by which Hume did not mean some miserable rationalization of hidden motives but, rather, that the passions drive the machine, and that what the intellect is about is calculating means-end instrumentalities for satisfying them.

It seems to me that in this respect Ellis is much closer to Hume than he is to Plato. There is the possibility that some passions may push a person as regards his means-end thinking in an irrational direction to such an extent that he or she is ineffective in achieving the aim of some other "passion," especially long-run motivations. If I understand him, this is exactly what Ellis is talking about when he says that RET attempts to help people to be more rational. Of course this cognitive instrumentalism is distinguishable from "being passionately intellectual," where the need for cognizance is a person's master sentiment, as is surely true of Ellis.

With Dr. Wiener's permission, I have granted myself the privilege of expounding some of my own views in the course of writing an introduction to this fascinating book. I am confident that RET is here to stay and that the important modifications of it will not involve challenging its basic notions but will be alterations based upon research that has not yet been done.

It is perhaps more important for Ellis to push his main points at the risk of oversimplification than to try to put everything together — for instance, Freud plus Pavlov plus Ellis plus Skinner and goodness knows what all into one integrated package.

I believe that Albert Ellis will go down as one of the major contributors to applied psychology of my generation, and I am proud to have been one of the first academic psychologists to realize that. I am pleased to have this opportunity to recommend this book. We should be grateful to Dr. Wiener for his enterprise and intellectual discernment in having produced it for us.

Paul E. Meehl, Ph.D.
Regents' Professor of Psychology,
University of Minnesota
Past President, American Psychological Association

Preface

The story of how my friendship with Albert Ellis began may not be entirely true, being based upon my current memory. But I have found no contrary facts in my search for confirmation.

In the early 1960s, as a junior and off-campus member of the Psychology Department faculty at the University of Minnesota, I was asked to introduce the first speaker for an annual lectureship just endowed to honor a notable retired professor, Donald G. Paterson.

The esteemed guest was to be the notoriously outspoken but intellectually admired psychologist Albert Ellis, who was famous primarily as a sex educator. He had also described and begun to influence his profession toward a new form of psychotherapy he initially called Rational Therapy.

Why was I chosen for this distinguished occasion? Partly, I believed, I was asked because more senior members of the department had jaundiced reactions to Ellis's unconventional notions about sexual freedom as well as to his vulgar vocabulary, which always produced startled reactions.

My own apprehension seemed to be reflected in the faces before me in the packed auditorium. Senior faculty sat in the front row, headed by the prototypical New England puritan who had founded the department and chaired it for over three decades, Richard M. Elliott.

Ellis did not disappoint us. He flaunted his bold vocabulary and outspoken sexual rationality without concern or apology. He was an eloquent, forceful, and well-organized speaker. Despite occasional midwestern discomfort with his New York accent and speech patterns, Ellis found a warm welcome: his methods were so practical, so sensible, so eclectic, but with the imprint and language of good theory.

The two leading therapy theories of the day were psychoanalytic and nondirective, and Minnesota teachers of therapy were not devoted to either. They liked Rational Therapy, however; indeed, the head of clinical psychology at the university, Starke Hathaway, wrote and talked along similar lines when he could be prevailed upon to teach about therapy at all. Ellis organized his theory in clear, consistent concepts rather than let it float here and there according to eclectic notions of what worked. He was practical, committed to rationality, and clear about connecting methods and goals.

Since the late 1950s, Ellis has devoted himself to enlarging the scope and following of what he renamed "Rational-Emotive Therapy." Each year he delivers hundreds of talks, interviews thousands of clients, teaches scores of students, consults with dozens of colleagues and other professionals around the world, and publishes numerous articles and at least one to three books. He has been consistent in purveying his theory, practicing it, and living it.

Ellis has become perhaps the leading therapy teacher, theorist, and practitioner in the world today on the basis of the size of his audience, output, and influence. His Rational-Emotive Therapy provides methods and inspiration to those who want to utilize the human power of reasoning; to seek ways to avoid pain and achieve pleasure; and to contribute to a peaceful, humane society.

He also is an eminently open, objective, consistent person, one of those rare ones who is, I believe, what he appears to be. If Ellis has hidden anxieties, deceptions, or perversities, they are well controlled. He is living an ultimately rational human life for our time. He was readily accessible and cooperative without insisting that his opinions prevail in this biography.

Yet many think he is abrasive, cold, sexually loose, obsessively hardworking, gaudy. He has acted in all these ways — stories abound, but they do not truly capture him and are usually produced by those who don't know him well. They are warts that do not typify the person.

It has been especially difficult to subtitle this book, to capture Ellis's main features in two or three words. He is a swashbuckler, as Freud characterized himself, a great adventurer in search of a grail worthy of his fondest hopes and capacities. He is a "passionate skeptic," as he himself suggested. He is a rationalist, seeking always to make his recommendations sensible in moving one toward well-considered goals. He is a humanist, believing in the most good for all humankind. He is a hedonist, committed to seeking long-term pleasure and avoiding pain.

Can one find two or three words for a subtitle that would capture Ellis's spirit and body of work? Above all, I think, he is a problem solver who depends upon the intellect to achieve results. He is not romantic, emotional, earthy, warm, or idealistic. He is impatient with fools and stupidity. He wants to wipe irrationality from the world. He wants everyone to learn to think clearly about how to solve problems, as he has done: by learning to live equably with what he cannot change, to change whatever he can that diminishes unhappiness, to conduct a steady life productively, comfortably, and efficiently, and to practice humane values.

I will try to describe how he got this way, and his place in the world of theory and practice of psychotherapy. Writing about a living person has major advantages. The obvious disadvantages, in limited current perspective and unrevealed secrets, is compensated by the opportunity to capture the dynamism of the subject from firsthand experience of him and his friends, colleagues, employees, and adversaries.

The death of his brother Paul, whom I found an invaluable alter ego to Albert, as the manuscript was being finally revised sharpened my awareness of the losses that inevitably accrue for the author as time passes. Written documents are one vital resource; personal recollections are another, uniquely precious, that can provide future biographers with the sensate life perceptions that file research cannot capture fully.

Acknowledgments

Invaluable materials and corrections have been provided by Albert Ellis without strictures on their use. He did not agree with all of my text, but he unfailingly responded to all questions promptly and in good spirit. He gives special advantage to this biography by personally correcting errors only he could detect. I am grateful that he was available and willing to do so. He also wrote his own version of his relationship with Janet Wolfe for quotation in this book.

Paul Meehl has also been of inestimable help by scrutinizing meticulously the manuscript for philosophical perspective and rationality, something he does better than anyone else I know.

Janet Wolfe gave generously of her time and sensitive perceptions. Jonathan Wiener, a historian, provided steady, proficient technical aid, especially to a review of Ellis's F.B.I. file. Phyllis Wiener encouraged the project from the beginning and was always a wise critic at crucial points.

Vital information has been provided by Manny Birnbaum, Ray DiGiuseppe, Paul Ellis, Karyl Greco, Robert Harper, Rhoda Russell, and many others, as indicated in the text.

Special gratitude is due George Zimmar, my editor at Praeger, who, with his grounding in psychology and critical eye for theory and research, as well as for professional writing, made many significant suggestions.

1

Albert Ellis Today

In 1982 three journals published studies ranking Albert Ellis's importance in psychology: *American Psychologist* (D. Smith 1982), *Journal of Counseling Psychology* (Heesacker, Heppner, & Rogers 1982), *Journal of Marital and Family Therapy* (Sprenkle, Keeney, & Sutton 1982).

In the first publication, Ellis was ranked by colleagues as the second most influential psychotherapist in the world today. In the second, he was the most frequently cited author in professional journals since 1957. In the third, he was the fourth most influential theorist. As therapist, theorist, and writer, he has reached a peak of influence unequaled among living clinical psychologists.

Ellis has published approximately (he will add others before this book is printed) 49 books, over 400 professional articles, and over 200 popular pieces. He presents about five dozen lectures, workshops, and seminars around the world each year. He is almost surely the most prolific practitioner of therapy alive, conducting around 90, usually half-hour, individual sessions weekly, leading a half-dozen therapy groups, and directing seminars for his students and staff. At 74 he shows no sign of stopping, or even of slowing up significantly.

He's about 5 feet 10 and 140 pounds, as he has been most of his adult life. His graying hair, combed straight back, recedes high in front. He is hawk-nosed, with a long, narrow face, long curved back, and long thin fingers. Typically, he sits in a reclining chair in his office almost all his waking hours, sallow-skinned, bony, angular, in dim illumination, eyes often closed (sensitive to light perhaps because of his diabetes), as he conducts individual

1

therapy. In winter, a heater runs at his feet much of the time because of inadequate heating and somewhat impaired circulation, also from diabetes.

Ellis speaks of what he wants to do in the next 30 years: to act as an ongoing adviser to research in his field, to extend mass methods of applying RET (Rational-Emotive Therapy), to further group developments, to facilitate greater infiltration of RET into the education of children and youth, to train corporate personnel, and, of course, to continue his present personal schedule. As long as he can, he will read voraciously in the professional literature, respond promptly to letters, and try to cover all bases that will advance the influence of his theory, and controvert all slights and challenges to it and himself.

He works an 85-to-90-hour week, kept on his toes by the continuous flow of clients, staff, and students through his office at the Institute for Rational-Emotive Therapy; the endless stream of books and journals he reads; and the flood of writing he issues ceaselessly. He leaves the Institute and his schedule only to lecture around the world; his views and his person are in growing demand. There is no room in his life for loafing, pretending to work, or what most people consider recreation. While reading and writing, he listens to classical and light music.

Except when sleeping, Ellis is visible to someone at practically all times in his huge, dark, second-floor office at the Institute and in his sixth-floor apartment, where he visits with his companion, Janet Wolfe, eats, and sleeps.

Others with such a schedule and visibility might glibly be called workaholics. Many would assume that these were driven people, frantic or at least burdened by self-induced pressure to work constantly to make their mark in the world as soon as possible. Yet no one who knows Albert Ellis well believes he works under stress. He navigates through his life like a freighter, plowing through seas of ignorance, trouble, and opposition fairly unperturbed, argumentative, abrasive, charming, dramatic, his sharp voice and vivid delivery even more commanding than his fluid but inelegant writing.

Ellis considers himself humorous, but it is easy to overlook his occasional banter in his torrents of serious ideas and criticism. And he has become more serious with age. He has no time nor energy to waste in delivering his cargo of enlightenment to humankind, without fanciness.

He lives in his Institute for Rational-Emotive Therapy, which combines the public service and professional training that two separate institutes were originally founded to provide. Within it he travels by elevator between his home and his office. [It is the luxurious former home of the Woodrow Wilson Foundation.] The building is dimly lighted, a bit shabby and dingy, though its basic elegance is revealed in such details as its gracious winding stairway, decorative woodwork, and high ceilings. Its furnishings, however, reflect the parsimony, and neglect of material luxuries and style, that characterize Ellis's life.

Ellis has had occasional lapses into mod clothes and haircuts, but they are conspicuous in their rarity and discrepancy from his usual appearance. Most commonly he wears nondescript clothes, drab and basic. He owns no car, he wears no ornamentation, most of his meals consist of peanut butter or cheese sandwiches. He is a friendly but spartan host. You can indulge no hedonistic or sensual desires in his place even though he claims to be dedicated to pleasure-seeking on a long term basis — but only in nonmaterialistic ways.

Yet he is wealthy. He has investments he knows nothing about, managed by his brother until his death in late 1986. His yearly earnings are a quarter of a million dollars or more, from practice, lectures, workshops, and publications, but he handles and spends practically none of it. It goes to the nonprofit Institute. He lives on his Social Security income, his housing furnished by the Institute in return for his being available to answer the phone during off hours and to do other tasks when the Institute is closed. He has few financial wants — none for luxuries except for handmade shoes for his often sore feet. He lives a truly austere life. His pleasures lie with his work, with Janet Wolfe, his companion, and with maintaining basic physical comfort and health.

Ellis begins work at 9:00 Monday morning, and from then through Friday, labors until 11 P.M. with two half-hour breaks. Because of his diabetes he eats frequently, often while talking with clients and others; he dines at 11 P.M. with Janet. He practically never goes out socially, and his live-in companion must go alone to visit friends and attend entertainments. Yet at professional meetings or the rare parties he visits, he is usually a lively conversationalist until he gets bored, at which point he goes silent or leaves.

Ellis has not always been so equable. The purpose of this book is to tell the story of how he achieved his present measured, productive, satisfied, influential, physically and emotionally fairly imperturbable state. There are important lessons in this accomplishment for the public and for the profession of psychotherapy. I know of no other living professional person, whose goal is to help others solve their personal problems, who has so fully described his own satisfying personal philosophy and habits, and the process by which he achieved them.

He has his share of adversaries, competitors, indifferent listeners, unimpressed clients, disgruntled ex-employees and students, critics ranging from mild to severe. Yet they are not extraordinary in number or expression, considering his once radical proposals, his often abrasive manner, his frequent irritability, his prolific output, his outspoken presentations — and the fact that he engaged the formidable professional and social opposition in New York of psychoanalysis, and forces of sexual inhibition.

His manner is mellowing, his views gaining in popularity, his opposition softening, his importance in his profession being recognized. Grudgingly in some cases, textbook writers are obliged to include Ellis as a landmark figure in psychotherapy. He has growing numbers of enthusiasts in the public and of followers in the profession, as his ideas are incorporated into the mainstream of professional and social thought and practices.

To be rational and a long-term hedonist are his twin goals for himself and for all humankind. Yet people persist in dodging these goals — and annoying Albert Ellis. To him, being rational is the same as being scientific, which he considers the proudest achievement of mortals. We should always analyze our problems just as we would establish truths: scientifically. We should be as objective and accurate in our observations as possible, devising solutions by using our intelligence to the maximum, determining and applying what best solves our problems and advances us toward our goals — just as we would do to find a vaccine for polio or an antidote to economic depression.

Hedonism in the long term (in the short term it is trivial and ultimately often unsatisfying or even self-defeating) provides the most reasonable measure of satisfaction in life. If we don't consult and depend upon ourselves for the achievement of pleasures, we will often be misled into accepting other people's goals and their "shoulds," which don't fit us.

Ellis has said: "I think that RET is relatively neglected for the same reason that Epictetus and the Stoics were neglected. That is because they're sane! Sanity has never been very popular in the world. The mystical philosophies . . . which are very nutty for the

most part, have many millions of followers."* But sanity, rationality, comes very hard to humans. Irrationality often appears to be
more acceptable to some deep inner desire. Often we want to
believe differently from what reason dictates. So Ellis has many
dragons to slay, in religion, philosophy, and psychology; in their
views of the human fate; and in their aptitude for seeing the world
as they wish it to be.

In *Sexus,* Henry Miller wrote: "The great ones do not set up
offices, charge fees, give lectures, or write books. Wisdom is
silent, and the most effective propaganda for truth is the force of
personal example. The great ones attract disciples, lesser figures
whose mission it is to preach and teach" (1965, p. 426).

Ellis has, as usual, tried to cover all bases. He has purposefully
set an example, but also has done all the rest that Miller
mentions. He has set up an office, charged fees, given lectures,
and written books. He has surely not been silent, despite providing
the model of his own life. He has used his voice and typewriter to
the maximum to spread his message. He has explored and
preached on almost every issue anyone has raised about his works
or about psychotherapy in general.

One reason for his copious writing is that he has tried to
answer all questions raised, each criticism, every attack, and to
encompass in his theory any exceptions, additions, or
modifications made or that he interprets as having been made to
his views. Thus he says that RET incorporates all important
developments in the newest popular denomination in
psychotherapy: Cognitive (Behavior) Therapy.

Perhaps Ellis's major modesty is to slight his personal life as
a model for others to emulate. Not that he has neglected
discussing it, and in great detail. He has personally laid out his
life for others to view more than any other major psychologist has.
Others have gone a way toward doing so — Skinner, for example,
through his autobiographical volumes — but never in such
specific and earthy detail as Ellis: his hour-by-hour schedule, his
sexual troubles and development, his relationships with his
partners, his enormous and sometimes vivid correspondence. He
has held back very little.

But "the force of [his] personal example" has not yet been fully
and objectively explored. Besides his exceptional candor in his
biographical comments, Ellis's self-descriptions have sometimes
been distorted by ignoring deficiencies, overlooking alternative

---

*Albert Ellis 1985: personal interview.

explanations, not acknowledging goals abandoned because of deficiencies. He tries very hard to present himself fairly and fully, yet discrepancies occasionally appear in his thinking, writing, and behavior that belie what he says he thinks and does.

A minor example: At a party he several times asks to use the phone and mutters about his failures to reach his partner — although he states that she is free to do as she wishes, as is he, when out of town, and that he is never anxious about it. (He says his anxiety was probably about reaching her at the agreed-upon time.)

A larger example: He denies ever feeling nurturant toward any one, and asserts, rather, that his interest in and service to others is based entirely upon what pleases him or attracts him scientifically. Yet, like many other therapists, he has responded to a call in the middle of the night to counsel an ex-wife in her misery — and try to help almost anyone else in trouble who calls on him.

Ellis's most important professional contributions to the field of psychotherapy begin with his assertion that people become troubled by what they think about their problems, and not by the problems themselves. For over 30 years he has elaborated on that theme, about the diverse ways people think themselves into trouble, and various methods he has developed first to help himself, and then to help others, change their muddled attitudes and get on with satisfying their desires and goals.

Even before he became famous for Rational Therapy (later changed to Rational-Emotive Therapy), Ellis had become renowned as the preeminent contemporary sexologist and sex therapist. Most of his TV and newspaper appearances and notoriety have probably stemmed from that specialty: on the shows of Dick Cavett, Phil Donahue, Merv Griffin, Mike Wallace, and David Susskind, among others, and in feature stories in almost all of the major newspapers and magazines, plus a column he wrote for *Penthouse* magazine. Recent newspaper publicity concerns a follower and ex-student of his who started a women's group focused on extramarital affairs.

In childhood and youth, Ellis was a loner who avidly explored his world, and began writing about it in his teens. Briefly he was a paid political radical who broke with conventional revolutionaries on the issue of personal freedom. As he acquired sexual experience and knowledge in his early twenties, he became a sexual radical, writing and speaking for any sexual practices that did not harm oneself or others. He wanted to educate people in the variety of pleasures they could derive if willing to explore the possibilities, uninhibited by ignorance, guilt, or shame.

It was from this position that, in his late twenties and thirties, and as he gained experience as a therapist, Ellis devoted his main efforts to enlightening people on how to gain freedom to enjoy their entire lives, beyond his special interest in sex. Now he states that he has said most of what he wants to say about sex. Human troubles more generally, however, and how to think and act in ways that can make human lives more pleasing, consume almost all of his thinking and energies.

Although his material needs were always met, Ellis endured parental neglect and serious illness throughout childhood. What he learned to think and do to overcome his difficulties, and to generalize to humanity, constitutes most of the content of his unpublished and incomplete autobiography, and much of the early material of my interviews with him.

For an objective biography, his behavior and thinking must be subjected to more critical scrutiny than Ellis gives them — so as to encompass the environmental factors that shape us all. He may overlook or minimize them to focus on his self-control and direction — and distorted personal interpretations. Even his thinking, which is more objective than that of most others, is not independent of his human faults, at least not to the extent he wants to believe. Genetics, too, are important for the individual. That aspect he increasingly acknowledges as he gets older, and he tends to see the good and the controllable in his inherited characteristics, as well as the ways they may limit and control him.

It is well and good to believe that you have been born with high intelligence and the need to think and deal with your life rationally. It is another matter to believe, or at least to act, as if most others are similarly endowed, and will choose or want to depend on their intellect as much as you do, or to think that others will gain their greatest pleasure from exercising such powers.

There is significant evidence, for example, that there are different forms of inherited intelligence that include a body-kinesthetic type, whose major pleasure comes from physical activity, and a musical type, which derives greatest pleasure from the exercise of a musical sense (Gardner 1983). Ellis's dependence on verbal intelligence to shape his theories may be distorted by his particular kind of intelligence, or even by his physical body type, which in Sheldon's (1940) somatotyping language would be considered "ectomorphic," or mind-dominated.

Ellis also displays some singular behavior for a notable psychologist — for instance, his penchant for using songs, writing his own humorous lyrics to popular tunes, to propagandize RET beliefs. He likes and values them, leads group singing whenever possible, even at national meetings — and clings to the hope from his youth that he will write a light musical work of some sort. His interest in and knowledge of light opera and show tunes is extensive; he was an expert in his late teens especially, and he has capitalized on this background.

He lives both a hermetic life and a hermitic one. He has generally sealed himself off from outside influences even though he reads and debates widely in his field. Major critics claim, sometimes in sorrow, sometimes in competition, that he ignores original contributions to therapy that do not credit him and RET as their roots. And he prefers to lead an ascetic life in his Institute. Although he does talk with Institute clients and staff almost constantly during his waking hours, it is almost entirely for professional purposes, with himself as the dominant figure, and not for social pleasure.

His major idiosyncrasy, however, is to startle his audiences with vulgar language, then accustom them to it, for which he has become both famous and infamous. "F . . ." and "s . . ." are staples. Apparently no one who is close to him completely agrees with him that their use enhances his effectiveness within the profession or with clients, as he firmly believes. He wraps himself in self-justification about it, against the winds of criticism even from good friends, claiming that everyone thinks in such language, even if not talking that way, and that it liberates audiences and clients to have him release these suppressed words that they presumably often use at least silently, in their heads.

Ellis has, on rare occasions, bridled himself — at church schools, on TV and radio — but when asked publicly to relent and be more discreet in his language, he has been known to ridicule the request and the requester. It would be a foolhardy soul who would dare challenge him on the issue, knowing of his faith in the efficacy of his language and the power of his acerbic tongue unleashed.

He also invents words to suit his convenience, then uses them repeatedly to enhance his dramatic effectiveness. While he has begun to write and talk of introducing elegance into his theories, he garbs them in such words as "musturbatory," "awfulizing," and "catastrophizing," invented to fit his concepts. Some of his outrageous combinations sound more like musical comedy than scientific psychology. Yet they do what he wants them to — they vivify his meaning and color him uniquely.

How and why did this notable therapist and theorist blossom like a tightly compressed paper landscape unfolding in a glass of water? There was that skinny, sickly little boy, then the increasingly assured youth, poking into the crevices of life in the Bronx, eager to create something worthwhile, pressing life constantly, trying to write literature, compose music, propagandize for political revolution, liberate the sexually distressed. Finally, after two decades of trying, he found a medium where he could exercise his full powers of invention and persuasion for his most powerful concept — how to live well.

2
Early Childhood

Seventy-three-year-old Albert Ellis today describes himself as a child who was highly explorative, independent, inventive; a self-directed loner; a small replica of himself today, like one of those cherubs in a Renaissance painting with a mature, worldly face.*

The rough draft of his unpublished, unfinished autobiography is a treasure trove of facts about his life beginning at age four and extending to age eight. But his continuously intermixed account of how he was always, even then, developing his system of rational-emotive psychotherapy overshadows the nitty-gritty history of the child and youth. In actuality, there must have been a hit-and-miss genesis to his views, as with almost all the notions of the young, developed and held perhaps more intensely in stressful big city living. What he portrays as his thinking and conclusions in childhood that led to his present theory are not likely to have occurred as consistently and as early as he describes them.

Ellis was once a baby, a little boy, and an adolescent, looking, acting, and thinking like each one at the proper stage, though he overlooks those primitive steps in his own account. In some respects he was unique, as every human being is, but the course of his life is also likely to have been determined by his developmental age, genetics, and environment, as well as by his mind, to which he gives such exceptional precedence.

What was most special about him? By other accounts, Ellis must at least have been an unusually brainy, verbal,

---

*Albert Ellis 1984: personal interview.

problem-solving child who seldom got into mischief or antag-
onized others.* The elements of what has made him so equable
and settled an adult were visible at least in the way he rode the
waves he both encountered and caused as a lively, inquisitive
spirit. He does seem to have been born with that disposition.

Ellis emerged into the world in Pittsburgh on September 27,
1913. His mother, whose maiden name was Hettie Hanigbaum,
had been born in Philadelphia. She was a blue-eyed blond,
handsome, long-necked, and slender, who dressed too plainly to
be stunning. Her father, born German but reared in Krakow,
Poland, and her mother, also from Germany, were Jewish.

Hettie acted in several amateur productions in Philadelphia
and led a happy-go-lucky life, easygoing with friends and at
games and parties. She spent a minimum of time and concern on
her sons, daughter, and husband. The males seemed content to be
left alone, to relish their freedom, and to make the most of it. She
lived to be 93 years old, independent and affable to the end.

Ellis's father was originally surnamed Groots, which he
changed in 1915 to Ellis, probably to ease his way in business. He
was born near Vineland, New Jersey, to parents who came from
Russia, probably Moscow. His great-grandfather may have been
chief rabbi of Russia.† Albert's father was tall and thin until about
age 40, when he began to put on weight.

With his commanding presence and delivery, Albert's father
could readily influence business prospects. He was in and out of
many businesses during his life, far better at starting and
promoting the sales of all kinds of products than in managing and
sustaining them, which he seems rarely to have done successfully
for long. He proclaimed his generally conservative opinions
vigorously and authoritatively, and may have sounded something
like Albert does today with his more radical views.

Such a heritage suggests urban adaptability, a socializing
nature, and a flair for performing, promoting, and propagandizing. Strong streaks of energy, self-centered pleasure-seeking, and
autonomy also are evident. Both Albert and his brother have
always evidenced this legacy. Their sister's propensities were less
obvious, perhaps obscured by lessened opportunity for the female
in that era, and by more susceptibility to domination by her
mother and brothers.

---

*Paul Ellis 1984; Manny Birnbaum 1984: personal interviews.

†Albert Ellis 1984: personal interview.

The parents were apparently easygoing, sociable, chatty, independent of others and even of each other.* Each established a pattern of living that was individualistic and free of the other, which eventually led to the dissolution of the marriage without much pain. Yet they showed interest in and concern for each other until death, and their sons can recall little discernible antagonism.

The father was gone most of the time except on weekends, selling and promoting, on a small scale, such items as toys, liquor, and a beer cooler cleaner. He created no lasting business nor inheritance until finally, in his sixties, he established a prospering insurance agency.

He made good money at times, and the family would live affluently, even briefly possessing a limousine, chauffeur, and maid. At other times he did poorly, and the family lived meagerly on the mother's careful savings. Mainly, the children were left to raise themselves except for the material necessities, which were provided without much strain until the Depression.

As soon as the boys could earn money, in their teens, they did so. By then their father had left home, and they provided their mother with survival income. The only daughter was a very different sort from the two strongly independent boys. Her brothers say that she whined and cried a lot, and tried to be emotionally dependent on the mother. While she may have been damaged by being left alone by the mother — she certainly acted as if she were, until middle age, when she took to Albert's RET — her brothers appear to have thrived on a similar regimen.

Albert's mother told him he'd started out physically weak and colicky, and that he had cried a lot as an infant. He remembers no pain, however. He probably recovered from such early physical problems, and suffered no special difficulties until pneumonia and kidney trouble around age five.

His brother Paul, however, remembered him as a somewhat delicate child — he called Albert "sickly" up to early adolescence — needing to be safeguarded against physical stress. Paul recalled their mother warning him not to fight with Al, to be careful of him. He himself tended to be more sociable than Albert, and constantly in trouble. Otherwise they resembled each other strongly all their lives. Both were tallish and thin, they talked almost exactly alike, they agreed on most major political, social,

---

*Albert Ellis 1984: personal interview.

economic, and ethical issues. Paul agreed with Albert's views on
RET and sex, and almost from birth they showed the same fierce
desire to be independent.

Paul, however, led a much more conventional life. He was
married to the same woman until his death, reared one child in a
stable home, and held an accounting executive job in the same
business from early maturity until his retirement. In a sense he
was Albert's alter ego, maintaining similar beliefs, personality,
and general social attitudes and values, but without the need to
carve an important place for himself in the world or to preach a
message of salvation. He may have moderated his personal
habits, settling down in maturity after causing more trouble when
he was young, while Albert's course of life has been in an opposite
sequence. Albert was a relatively conforming child and youth,
becoming less conventional in adulthood.

They both read prolifically, and while Paul was more attracted
to athletic activity, their major interests were intellectual. Paul,
like his father, became a first-rate chess player, while Albert tried
but never took to games. Both boys lived at home sharing its
expenses until marriage in their mid-twenties.

Until Albert first married, he and Paul shared a bedroom, and
their mother and sister shared another; and they lived in relative
harmony. Except for Paul and Albert, none of them was close with
the others. They never fought hard with each other about
anything. Their disagreements always were relatively mild, and
about issues that did not rouse their emotions. They went their
independent ways, seldom confided in each other, and rarely
visited after they left home. Albert never went to see Paul in his
Lakewood, New Jersey, home. Both were virgins until they
married.

Their major difference lay in Paul's tendency to get into trouble
when young, while Albert's efforts were directed to staying out of
trouble. Paul was often a pest because of his rebelliousness. His
mischief annoyed others, and earned him minor punishments
that Albert carefully avoided.

Albert cultivated a "good boy" appearance and gained rewards
from adults. He was respected and consulted. He kept his
independent behavior within acceptable limits, particularly since
he was much less concerned with the approval of peers than of
adults. He could think anything — and did. But his outward
behavior was designed to save him trouble and pain, and he tried
to excuse Paul's derelictions to others.

Differences appeared later, too, as Paul pursued business and money interests, which Al has eschewed throughout his life, as soon as he could. After Albert obtained some graduate training in psychology, he worked at that profession for the rest of his life. Until then, however, he could earn the money he needed most easily by working at various business ventures, beginning with selling newspapers and ending by more or less running a small business for its owner. But he has had nothing more to do with business and money than was necessary for economic survival.

Until his death in 1986, Paul managed Albert's money and made his investments. Albert's lifelong accountant friend, Manny Birnbaum, still keeps his eye on the Institute's business and books. More than mere disinterest in finances, however, Albert maintains his lifelong frugality. The Institute shows it. Some furniture was getting shabby, the office reuses paper printed on only one side. There are no obvious touches of luxury — or waste. But in 1987, major refurnishing and brightening was done.

While Paul settled down after he married and never got into trouble, or even serious controversies, Al never has settled down conventionally, but continues to carve out an unconventional life for himself. He has seldom offended others personally. Rather, in deed, talk, and writing he has expressed his freethinking notions in ways that usually have not directly attacked others. He has, however, ever since he was 18, aroused considerable opposition and created many adversaries.

Ellis prefers to believe that, except for his illness over several years in childhood, he was hardy and spared himself no physical activity except where there was danger of injury. He was, however, diverted from vigorous games both by a faltering constitution in childhood and by an inclination toward more intellectual activity that prevailed increasingly from the time he began school. His denial of fragility or of any protective attitudes toward him, even by brother, mother, or best friend, is a bit of bravado that also shows itself in his disputing almost any kind of personal weakness.

His mother told Ellis that he had hummed and sung tunes when he was under two, as he was wheeled in his carriage. She called him "a little human scientist" and "quite a thinker" when he wasn't much older. He was thinking about the world, how to make his mark in it, and how to change it when he could. His musical interests blossomed later and remained lifelong pursuits in various forms. He is grateful for his inheritance of "emotional stability, high energy, and good intelligence."*

His earliest recollections begin at age four, while he was still living in Pittsburgh. Albert was apparently tall for his age and skinny, as he has been almost all of his life. Pictures show a good-looking little boy without the sharp features that he developed as an adult.

Albert remembers only a happy early life except for his years of sickness, and that is also the way his brother remembers it. No special problems nor troublemaking. His brother Paul was a year and a half younger; his sister, four years younger. As the oldest, Albert developed something of a parental attitude and helpful hand with the younger ones. At school he was called on to curb his brother's mischievousness, and at home he tried to abort the frequent fights between his brother and sister.

Upon beginning school at age four, either because it was all right then, or because his mother wanted him in school and lied about his age, Albert found that everyone except him seemed to know what to do. This view may have been true, or merely have reflected his desire to excel without knowing how. At home he had mastered the circumstances of living, and enjoyed his life and its freedom. He resented being sent to that foreign place, school, where the routines were regimented and he was ordered about. He thought he should at least have been consulted about the matter. His mother apparently did not think of discussing his attending school with him. Consistently she ordered her kids to do this or that, and kept after them until they did. He thinks this may have reflected an authoritarian attitude of their culture. She seemed to suffer no doubts nor remorse once she decided what her kids should be doing. Her assurance — and her husband's, the little he was around — opened little opportunity for debate with their children. The boys seldom thought to remonstrate, but when they did, it had little effect (though their sister's tantrums may have).

"The first sensible thing I can remember doing to help myself enjoy life and ward off potential misery," he opens his autobiographical manuscript, "was in regard to my going to school."† With no effective opening for protest, and no expectation

---

*Albert Ellis 1986: personal interview.

†Albert Ellis 1984: unpublished autobiographical manuscript.

of success from it, Albert apparently adapted quickly to school. Soon he was enjoying it more than being at home. "I always had this knack of using my head to save trouble, an innate bent for philosophizing."*

Very early he displayed insatiable curiosity about life immediately around him, and at some walking distance further. He crossed dangerous streets to school on his own by the time he was five, aware of risking his life. He also seems to have developed the capacity to see the best side of adversity, to adapt to new circumstances, to tolerate frustration, and even to reason about fearsome situations and to talk himself out of worrying about them.

At least he thinks now that he thought that way then. It seems quite likely that he did, according to his brother. There is no dramatic turning point in his life when he seems suddenly to have developed these characteristics. It is probable that he did have some innate tendencies in these directions that were clarified, strengthened, and verbalized as he got older.

Albert regretted that school was not open on weekends. He quickly found it exciting and challenging, both for the content of classes, in which he excelled, and for the competition of his classmates. He was very bright, almost always the quickest in his class with answers. His IQ shows every evidence of being very high now. Then, it would probably have measured somewhere between 135 and 160, a very rough estimate inferred from his excellence in the classroom, his easily achieved outstanding record, and, later, his score at the top of the Army Alpha test of general intelligence. He did not, however, display the extreme precocity of geniuses approaching the maximum IQ in an art, mathematics, or language.

He had new territory to explore while going to and from school, and dangerous streets to cross by himself. The scariness of crossing the streets, for which at first he accepted passersby's help, and anxiety about trying to make new friends challenged him even as he recognized his timidity in new situations and with people. He did not overcome it completely until his twenties, after he began to formulate some of the rules of philosophy and conduct that thereafter governed his life, and that became the foundation of his new therapy.

---

*Albert Ellis 1985: personal interview.

His anxiety did not stop Albert, however. He continually forced himself to advance on conditions that initially intimidated him. He insisted on creating ways to try to overcome his discomfort, to reach the goals he wanted. Eventually, though not for years, he finally did succeed in acting as boldly as he wanted to, particularly about speaking up in public and approaching girls.

Initially it may have been only relative to his family that Albert felt shy, and so considered himself through adolescence. Certainly from the way he handled school, neighbors, and generally expressing himself, it is hard to discern timidity. Or he may have felt inadequate only relative to his high expectations of himself, having much he wanted to say in class, for example, but not being as skilled as he wanted to be in talking or holding attention. And the same with girls; the desire to be a lothario made the necessarily halting first steps seem intolerably awkward to him.

He claims that around age four he began formulating and drilling into his head these rules:

a. Life is full of hassles you can't control or eliminate.
b. Hassles are never terrible unless you make them so.
c. What does happen could always be worse.
d. Making a fuss about problems makes them worse.
e. Wait before you panic.
f. It's interesting to seek solutions.
g. Fight to overcome troubles, but accept failure when necessary.
h. Use your head in reactions as well as your heart.*

It is this kind of analysis, appearing almost continuously throughout the autobiographical manuscript of his childhood, that is so suspect in describing his thinking when he was very young. While his thinking probably tended in such a direction, his present single-minded intensity in conveying his message likely limits his capacity to project into and portray his childhood thinking accurately. Yet no one can definitively contradict his interpretation. To his brother and his best friend, he appeared to operate rather as he describes it.

Compared to his parents and uncles, Albert may well have been socially stiff. His brother considered him to have few friends, though an ordinary number of acquaintances. He still has no wish to be gregarious except to further his views of therapy. All his life he has kept a distance from people and gotten quickly

---

*Albert Ellis 1985: personal interview.

bored with them. His brother was far more sociable.* Albert has learned how to handle people well but not to enjoy more than a handful of them, as fairly intimate friends, outside of his professional activities.

His mother, a compulsive talker, claimed to have been expelled from school in the sixth grade for talking too much. She, his father, and six uncles and aunts on the mother's side, plus three on the father's, all seem to have been gregarious people who may have overwhelmed Albert with their extravertive natures. He did not overcome his anxiety about approaching girls, speaking out in the classroom, or talking up in social groups in a way that he considered satisfactory until he was around twenty. It took a massive, calculated effort finally to conquer the problem.

In any case, Albert as a child seems to have thought and acted like a little man. He used his freedom well, which benefited his mother, since she also wanted to enjoy her independence. She never seemed to express disappointment in his behavior, perhaps because she didn't much notice it. She was preoccupied with her own relatively simple pleasures: errands, visiting friends, playing games.

When Albert was four, and thoroughly enjoying friends and school, the family suddenly moved to New York City, upsetting Albert especially because he was not consulted. He was uprooted from a very comfortable setting and placed in a foreign territory, probably because his father had better sales opportunities there. He remembers feeling disappointed rather than angry or fearful.

The family traveled on the mother's skimpy savings, she and the three children sleeping in one railroad berth. They always did manage remarkably well in close quarters. Albert went sleepless during the trying trip. Throughout his life he never did sleep well; perhaps the long years of living in close proximity to family members upset his sleeping habits. When young he probably did not consider his insomnia a problem, but only as meaning unhappily long nights. But though he would wake up frequently during the night, he nevertheless rose quickly and energetically in the morning. He didn't seem to need to sleep much.

In their new apartment on the Upper West Side of Manhattan, Albert's sister was immediately sick, his brother ran around getting into minor scrapes, his mother was busy in her typically disorganized way, and his father was gone even more than usual,

_____

*Albert Ellis & Paul Ellis 1985: personal interviews.

presumably on business matters. Very early Albert decided his mother was a "screwball," and he determined to "handle her" and never to take her seriously thereafter. She was so sloppy in her housekeeping, shopping, and child care that he increasingly intervened in managing the household. He believes that he was about as instrumental in raising her as she was in raising him.*

Albert was, as usual, left to his own devices. He explored the world largely on his own, in addition to doing household tasks and helping care for his siblings. At first he was anxious and miserable about it, he says, then consciously decided to quit moping, to accept the situation as it was, and to make the best of it.

In short order the family moved to an apartment in the East Bronx where they stayed for two years. Then, when Albert was seven, they moved to a two-story house, also in the West Bronx. Many kids lived in the neighborhood, there was an empty lot for play, a candy store for savory pleasures, and a special eight-year-old friend who took Albert on adventures and told him about sex.

In New York, Albert couldn't go to school until he was six, and he had to wait a year, probably having just missed the cutoff date. Angry at first, he put on his optimist hat (or, retrospectively, developed a proper RET principle) and decided to make the best of his surprisingly free time. His older friend taught him how to read.

When Albert finally did get into school, he enjoyed it as thoroughly as before. He excelled at all the work except oral recitation, where his heart pounded with anxiety whenever he was called on. He was a good student, mastering assignments readily, turning in outstanding written work, and trying to please his teachers.

So we have Albert, just before the most traumatic event of his childhood occurred, growing like a weed, with a logical mind that was gradually being revealed. His lively intelligence was leading him to a rich mix of new experiences, expectations, and desires, and to seek ways to extract what he liked and wanted from life.

He found himself moving inchoately toward acting on principles that were evolving in his mind: to take life as it came, to enjoy it as much as possible, to learn all he could, and never to allow himself to be upset or angry for long, because that would make him miserable when he could be having a good time.

---

*Albert Ellis 1985: personal interview.

Then two major events occurred that gave form and direction to his life in ways that were to persist until the present. One was falling madly in love with a "beautiful blonde" named Ruthie. Like many other notables seemingly blessed with energy that often became particularly intense with sex, he remembers lusting, after that, for every attractive woman he saw except his mother. Usually they were older than he. Except for Ruthie.

Just shy of age six, he and she would have long talks in his bedroom when both pairs of parents and his brother, who shared the room, were gone. The Ellis maid — for these were affluent days that also brought a Cadillac and uniformed chauffeur — left them alone.

Knowing nothing about sex, but curious as could be, they took off their clothes, hugged and kissed, felt each other's bodies, and confessed their love for each other. He had begun to explore her vagina when both sets of parents burst into the room and gave them hell. The fathers are recalled by Ellis as being relatively tolerant, the mothers as hysterical. Albert remembers being rather pleased with his boldness, as he thought his father also might have been. Ruthie's mother cried that her daughter would end up a streetwalker.

Albert was not physically punished, and he tried, as usual, to turn away anger by deciding he was foolish to get caught, vowing to try again more discreetly — and contritely apologizing. He still believes that both his parents covertly admired his audacity. But he never managed to gain Ruthie's company again; she moved away soon after.

He remembers having only the vaguest notions about specific sex with Ruthie, but wanting to hold her and talk. It was one of the most exciting experiences of his childhood. He thought about her for years, considered the event one of the most dramatic of his life, and felt a deep loss even when he had other loves. He maintains that he thus learned that what we believe and what we imagine — rather than what really happens — controls our emotional destiny. Long after she disappeared, he would imagine scenes with Ruthie that were far better than the real one.

The second major event was the onset of illness, a sequence of events that began with tonsillitis at age five, developed into a serious strep infection that required emergency surgery to save his life, and culminated in nephritis. Then he was hospitalized for pneumonia and recurrences of nephritis. His family seldom visited him for most of the year he was in the institution. This experience made him particularly protective of his health for the rest of his life.

Albert remembers little about the nephritis. In fact, because of a huge, bleeding wound from a brick that his brother dropped on his finger at about the same time, he associated the hospital more with the finger than with his kidneys. Also, he had been told that he was going to the hospital to have his tonsils removed.

He was not, however, told what surgery would be like: having an anesthetic forced on him, hurting when awakening, being unable to eat. The perfidy of all the meaningless reassurance he received ahead of time overwhelmed him at first. He hated everyone for lying to him and plotted revenge. Then he got a painkiller, ice cream, and attention, and decided to let bygones be bygones. But he was not home long when he had to return to the hospital because of acute nephritis.

He had no pain except for dreadful headaches every few days, so excruciating that he thought of killing himself. Then, he recollects, he considered that being dead might be terribly monotonous, and decided not to try it. He attempted to get rid of the headaches by various physical and medical means, and eventually they did diminish.

Meanwhile, Albert had a brush with religion. His parents never went to religious services, and his mother attended a Reform temple (the most liberal branch of Judaism) only for social and cultural reasons. But when his headaches were agonizing, among the devices he could think of, he tried praying for relief. Even then, he claims, he recognized his hypocrisy, at first attributing his relief to God, but then, when he recovered, quickly dismissing the Lord as his source of salvation.

Between the ages of five and seven, Ellis estimates he went to the hospital seven or eight times, all but twice for nephritis, staying once for nine months and the other times for a week to a month or so. There he got his fill of views of the female body when the youngest children in his ward, including himself, were bathed two at a time, regardless of sex, and he studied them assiduously. He enjoyed being bathed, especially by the prettiest nurses.

Days and occasionally weeks passed in the hospital without his family visiting him. Albert acclimated, and now claims that he developed a growing indifference to that dereliction. He talks as if he quickly made the best of an unhappy situation that, repeated so consistently through his childhood and youth, he came to see as an advantage. It is an interesting concept: Do we have to suffer for the rest of our lives from early emotional neglect? Or can we rise above it and suffer no handicap that later impairs our capacity for generosity, for emotional relationships, or for interdependency with others?

Ellis can be portrayed as either growing or suffering from the situation. My choice here is for economy of interpretation. One would have to stretch the few available facts to interpret that he has been crippled by the neglect. True, he might well be a different kind of person now, perhaps warmer, more sociable, less vehemently independent, more family- and child-oriented — in short, more like a conventional human being. But that package might also produce a less forceful and dedicated creator of a major system of help for troubled people. In addition, it would not be easy to find a more satisfied or happy — or whatever criterion one might use to designate the overriding personal goal of life — person than he, except by determining that he is not what he seems to be — a contented person.

The children's ward of the hospital became Albert's major social arena for much of his fifth and seventh years, intriguing for the inchoate sex, with the baths, the intimacy among the little patients — and the games. Around 20 boys and girls shared them. He invented one of the games that helped to pass the long nights. The children got relatives to bring flashlights, and would take turns standing on their beds in the dark with raised nightgowns while the others flashed on their lights for just a moment — before the nurses banned the flashlights.

In any case, his shyness disappeared in this group that he could lead. His boldness was rewarded with attention. And he fell in love again, with Gloria in an adjacent bed. They vowed to see each other when they left the hospital but never did, since both sets of parents vetoed it. He imagined her, and making love to her, for years. She never has been totally forgotten.

Albert never did feel much guilt, which, years later, astonished his psychoanalyst. He recalls deciding very early that some acts were worth paying a penalty for. In his eyes, his rebelliousness was always for a good cause, but he handled it tactfully and was able to turn aside most potential anger and punishment.

Apparently the only troubles that did not respond to his philosophical ministrations were headaches and insomnia. While the former did diminish substantially in time, the sleeping problem persisted and still remains the most intractable of his unwanted behavior. It was most acute in the hospital, where at times it seemed that he was up all night. Later he learned to maneuver around it successfully, getting on with his work regardless of it, accepting and living with whatever sleep he got, and even using the interruptions in his sleep productively. Presently, for example, when he awakes in the middle of the night, he eats a sandwich and brushes his teeth. He also decided that in this respect he was superior to heavy sleepers, having more time to explore and enjoy his life.

From childhood on, a rich mixture of reasoning, bravado, and denial has marked Ellis's confrontations with his difficulties. He solved his problems, he was not bothered to have his problems, and he had no major problems. He has even expressed modesty about them: "I merely want to note here my allegiance to the human condition . . . of being prone . . . to conquer one of my disabilities by fairly rational thinking, and then to fall . . . on my blasted face again and revert to my previous irrationality."*

One final time in his early childhood he was taken to the hospital. Just shy of seven, and with the nephritis recurring from time to time, he continued to swell in his ankles, legs, and belly. Once his abdomen bloated so immensely, as in late pregnancy, that the doctors decided to operate. They reassured him that his stomach would be just slightly punctured and the fluid drained, all so painlessly that he could stay up and watch. Again he thought of objecting, but decided not to.

So he squelched his fear, saw the large needle with tube attached stuck into his belly, and observed a huge amount of milky fluid drain into a basin on the floor. He remembers consciously deciding to ignore his fears and compel himself to become interested in the strange procedure. He forced curiosity to be his primary emotion. He actually enjoyed the experience: the attention, the relief, the exoticism, deciding once more that he did not have to suffer from anxiety if he did not choose to.

Can a child be so much master of himself? It is hard to challenge anything in Ellis's account except the extreme clarity and consistency of his thinking. The recollections of his brother and best friend from those times do not impugn it. And the remarkable congruence of this thinking with his behavior then, and for the rest of his life since, supports it.

But surely this extended period of serious illness and hospitalization at least prepared the way for and reinforced the

---

*Albert Ellis 1985: personal interview.

life of the intellect for Ellis. Even earlier, however, his life had been more controlled and determined by his use of his mind than is true of most children, even more than for his brother, who was so alike in most important respects. It remains unproved what role this most serious trauma in his life played in shaping him. From his viewpoint, it merely accelerated his development of RET.

3

Rational-Emotive Therapy Today

Preeminently the importance of Albert Ellis to psychology and the public today lies in his creation of Rational-Emotive Therapy (RET). This is his contribution to the eternal human effort to help people solve their problems, to live at peace with themselves, to find pleasure in their existence, to avoid pain, discomfort, and misery. He and most of his professional colleagues now consider this 33-year-old endeavor of his to be more important than his simultaneous influential attempts to enlighten our society about sex.

There is nothing unique about his current enterprise. Through the ages, notable philosophers and religionists first, then later and more specifically, professional helpers in medicine, sociology, psychology, and related fields have taken on the effort to aid human beings in handling their lives. Ellis is one of the latest of these laborers, more inventive and persuasive than most — and more contemporary with the progressing science of psychology.

His distinction is acknowledged in his profession and increasingly in the developed world at large. He has training centers in West Germany, Italy, Holland, Australia, Mexico, and England and affiliated organizations throughout the United States and in other countries. He has published over four dozen widely distributed books, along with hundreds of articles, demonstration tapes, and films; he has lectured and conducted workshops throughout the world.

He remains relatively unknown, however, to many intelligent and well-educated people. He is not as renowned as, say, Pavlov, Freud, or his great contemporary Skinner, nor does he seem to be as widely respected or admired as they. He may never achieve their stature, perhaps because of his more abrasive personality and more limited interest in changing the fabric and institutions of society, as well as the individual. Nor is the uniqueness of his contribution as clearly modern scientifically, since he so directly attributes its roots to ancient philosophy. Also there is an especially earthy practicality to his theories that reduces their appeal to sophisticated people despite their value.

Ellis is not inferior to them, however, in the forcefulness of his teachings, in his impact on those he reaches, and in his effectiveness at changing people's lives. He is a powerful propagandist, though he does lack a conveyed sense of profundity, adoring (as contrasted with appreciative) followers, and perhaps as many influential academicians willing to acknowledge his preeminence as a theoretician.

He would probably claim that restrained impact as a strength rather than a weakness. He wants to appeal to minds rather than to emotions, and to be evaluated scientifically for his effectiveness in helping people to enjoy life and reach their goals, rather than for inciting passionate followers to a mystical enthusiasm.

But has Rational-Emotive Therapy generated or applied powerful, unique truths? How has it extended beyond the philosophical principles of the first-century Greek Stoic philosopher Epictetus, to whom Ellis acknowledges his largest debt, down through Watson, father of behaviorism, and Adler, with his problem-solving orientation, whom Ellis also frequently cites? Has he revolutionized human thinking as have the two most influential psychological geniuses of this century, Freud and Skinner?

Freud was not the first to describe and analyze the unconscious, to delineate concealed reasons for human behavior that could be ascertained through scrutiny, and to apply his findings to human problems. The hidden meaning of dreams, for example, had been analyzed in the Bible, and bits of behavior had been interpreted as having major though hidden significance by many great philosophers and writers. Wise men always knew that humans were "unconscious" of some events and processes influential in their lives, but Freud spelled out a number of "defense mechanisms," dream operations, and such that advanced understanding.

Freud (1954) acknowledged others who had ideas similar to his, Breuer and Charcot among them, but he distinguished between people who had similar concepts and himself, who made them his focus and developed them. He described the difference as the same as that between an affair and a marriage.

He became the most powerful writer about, interpreter of, and propagandist for the existence and influence of unconscious forces that determine human behavior. He made his indelible mark in the world by the way he handled his ideas and by the manner in which he applied his beliefs to many social processes besides therapy, which he considered a secondary product of his theories.

Likewise, Skinner had predecessors who maintained that human behavior was shaped by rewards and punishments, conditioned by the environment, and determinable through external study alone, without regard for internally sensed mental processes. He did research specifically on how reinforcement molds animal behavior, and when and why it fails; and he generalized his findings to society, and how entire communities could be organized to take advantage of his behavioral research to achieve desired social goals (Skinner 1972). He spelled out the details of reinforcement schedules.

Has Ellis made a comparable contribution to the theory and methods of solving human problems? He freely acknowledges that his antecedents lie in Greek Stoic philosophy and Epictetus who provided Ellis's primary dictum: "Men are disturbed not by things, but by the views which they take of things" (1897, p. 218). Thus, one of our most modern theorists about therapy explicitly concedes his debt to one of the oldest of counselors on how to live well.

Ellis has not, however, adopted some other, crucial aspects of Epictetus's Stoic philosophy, such as that humans should calmly accept all events as the unavoidable result of divine will. He has adopted only what he likes. He does not believe that we should not try to exercise control in our lives, he does not believe in emphasizing unavoidable results, and he does not believe in divine will.

He does believe in, and uses, other Stoic principles: to work with the hard facts of reality; to avoid railing against what cannot be changed; to work (only) on what can be altered; and to depend upon ourselves rather than others to do what is needed. As Epictetus wrote: "When, therefore, we are hindered, or disturbed ... let us never impute it to others, but to ourselves; that is, to our own views" (1897, p. 218).

So three of the most vital tenets of RET are drawn from Epictetus: (1) What bothers us is not what happens to us, but how we view it; (2) Avoid concern with what cannot be changed; (3) Concentrate on our own responsibility for what disturbs us, and how it can be changed.

The fourth major tenet comes from what is usually considered to be a source totally divergent from Stoicism, namely hedonism. Ellis considers himself primarily a hedonist, believing that, above all, humans had best seek pleasure and try to avoid pain, with the reservation that such pursuit should be for long-term pleasure rather than short-term.

He demurs about using the word "should," since he inveighs against the "shoulds" that lead us astray. Nonetheless, when he changes "should" here to "is to be sought," he does not seem to alter its meaning significantly. In any case he does not approve of "mere" pleasure seeking that is trivial: stuffing candy into our mouths whenever we see it, or having sex to satisfy the least itch without regard to consequences. So tenet (4) is Work for long-term pleasure, learn how to avoid pain.

Ellis also believes in and applies behavioral therapy, as extended by Skinner, with its major emphasis on goal setting, specific tasks to achieve goals, and reinforcement (which, however, in Ellis's concepts comes more from reaching one's goals than from artificial rewards en route).

There is nothing particularly grand or theoretically coherent about joining these principles for problem solving and happiness taken from Stoicism, hedonism, and behaviorism. But Ellis does not limit himself even to these theories in devising his methods. He does not hesitate to adopt or create techniques, from whatever source that will help realize his goal of rational human behavior.

He does not demand or give priority to philosophical consistency. He draws from separate if not divergent philosophies if their stance helps with the problem-solving process. His major constant is a commitment to the scientific method to assess what works, with the intellect as its major tool, and with reasoning and rational argument as the main therapeutic process.

Ellis has always relied upon his intellect and logic to solve his problems, gain pleasure, avoid pain. Such faith and methods developed before his theories. He seems almost to have been born that way. Throughout childhood and youth he was evolving his notions about Stoicism and hedonism from experience, analyzing objectively and unemotionally what was going on around him, trying to devise solutions to his troubles and to have fun. Even as a little boy he rejected other ways kids try to get what they want, such as fighting, crying, complaining, pleading, sulking, withdrawing.

These attitudes are certainly not unique. They have been discovered and used by many successful people. Others claim to have originated the emphasis on intellect and reason as the best approach to solving problems and gaining happiness. Anyone could have, and many did, articulate similar views through the centuries.

What distinguishes Ellis, for one matter, is his overriding stress on how we may misread our experiences and derive irrational conclusions from them that obstruct our profiting from them. Ellis would have us develop a guiding philosophy that can correct for the nonsense we may tell ourselves. He wants us to evolve the attitudes and habits necessary to learn from and cope with whatever we may experience, to deal with events rationally so that we will face and handle reality, and move along toward our desired ends.

In Ellis's view, what gets us into trouble is a tendency to make such emotion-ridden, unrealistic statements to ourselves as It's terrible if this or that happens to us (and therefore we should be pitied, comforted, or incapacitated). Or that it is unfair that we should be subjected to this or that (and that therefore others or conditions should have to change, to accommodate us). Or that we must have this or that (or we are worthless or even detestable).

Such self-generated assertions and their implications are untrue or irrelevant, and tend to render us passive, helpless, or floundering, and thus unable to solve the problems confronting us. Instead, we need to face and work at resolving them, to substitute positive, useful behavior for inaction and self-pity, so that we can achieve reasonable goals.

Besides its ancient philosophical antecedents, Rational-Emotive Therapy has more contemporary precursors. Ellis considers the early form of behaviorism set forth by Watson as a foundation of his thinking, despite the fact that the behaviorism of Watson (1913), like that of Skinner, tends to depreciate the process of subjective thinking and to emphasize nonverbal behavior. It assumes, unlike Ellis's view, that what we call thinking will manifest itself in other, externally observable forms of conduct that can more readily be studied and changed scientifically than can thinking itself.

We can be conditioned by our experiences to think and act in unreasonable ways, so that instead of working to solve problems intelligently and rationally, we bog down in false statements about our fate and get diverted from objective analysis and solutions by emotional jags. The sense of reality and personal responsibility, especially, Ellis appreciated and adapted from Adler's views.

While Ellis was developing his ideas about RET, Skinner's work on learning and behavior change was gaining a fast-growing audience and an explosion of applications in education, therapy, and many other fields of human activity: chickens were taught to play baseball, and pigeons to aim bombs; mental patients gained social skills by earning coupons to buy privileges; communities were organized in ways that rewarded socially desirable activity; schoolchildren learned their lessons from machines that moved along according to the kids' speed and capacities.

Skinner (1972) would shape human habits by setting up conditions in the environment that reward desired behavior. In addition, he is interested in the larger scene, in how the world can be improved through reinforcement schedules for socially minded behavior. Ellis, while he is interested in mass methods of therapy, and committed to humanitarian and egalitarian values, chooses to operate more through the individual. He concerns himself only secondarily with institutions, when they serve as a more efficient way to teach his methods to individuals.

Ellis did not preempt the field of rational therapy for long. Soon after he started to expound his views in the mid- and late 1950s, at professional meetings, in professional journals and lectures, and in magazine articles and interviews, others began to express similar views. He certainly did not shoot across the sky before the multitudes as a brilliant new star. More accurately, he had broken from a constellation that was moving sluggishly in the direction of rationality in the practice of psychotherapy, as a kind of corrective to the intellect-ignoring procedures of behaviorism and psychoanalysis.

Others tried to establish claims to the territory. Bruner (1983) stated that the "cognitive revolution" began with Chomsky, and that he himself was original in writing about rational thinking strategies. Glasser (1964) named and described "Reality Therapy," a term Ellis says he initially considered for his views. Beck (1976) devised his version of "cognitive therapy." Others developed variants, with more limited applications than Ellis's, using the terms "rational," "cognitive," or "cognitive behavioral."

Neither Ellis nor any other contemporary totally originated the intellectually controlled, reality-centered theory of solving human problems. Its roots date back 2,400 years or more. Ellis found the crucial ideas in Epictetus (and Buddha), but he tracked down detailed ways to catch irrational transitions and transform attitudes to greater rationality.*

He was the first among contemporary psychologists to focus on, elaborate, and develop specific applications for it, to refine and ripen the use of reason, and to specify ways to eliminate irrationality in solving problems and gaining pleasure. He has developed and propagandized mightily for his views and the widest variety of specific measures that can be used to implement them.

Ellis's claim to priority in advancing rational methods of treatment began in 1955, when he started to discuss publicly what he originally called "Rational Therapy." He developed it informally with a group that began to meet regularly in his office in the early 1950s, presented it formally at the annual meeting of the American Psychological Association in 1956, and published an article on it the following year (Ellis 1957b). He thus gave it a specific cast as a therapeutic theory and method, and detailed, as no one else had, how it could be applied in sessions with clients. Others, however, had begun to emphasize the crucial importance of thinking as the strongest way humans have of getting themselves both into and out of trouble.

Ellis had to battle mainstream competing theories of therapy in the mid-1950s, and in the process became the toughest of competitors, adversaries, and propagandists. His main opposition came from psychoanalysis, nondirective therapy, and the Gestalt and existential movement.

Psychoanalysis was, and probably still is, the most powerful therapeutic influence in New York City, and provided the tradition from which Ellis's views emerged. Emphasizing the unconscious and uncovering past trauma, psychoanalysis implied that once the past was scrutinized, resistance to the relationship with the analyst was "worked through," and current existence was reconsidered in light of new insights, life would more or less automatically proceed with sense and satisfaction. The therapist acted as a detective into the past and as a relatively passive vehicle of interpretation. Analysts were not trained to attack current problems directly and vigorously, and to devise and implement practical solutions, even though many, including

---

*Albert Ellis 1985: personal interview.

Freud, did that. Many have now adapted their work to contemporary theories and research.

"Nondirective" theory, formulated by Rogers (1951) in the late 1940s, emphasized the expression of feelings, with the therapist providing encouragement and empathy in a relatively passive role, like the analysts in that respect. The implication was that life would be satisfactorily reshaped once feelings had been acknowledged and examined. The potential for change was considered to lie within the person, and, like a heat-seeking missile, mainly needed only to be stimulated and released to attack and solve current problems.

Then there was the Gestalt and existential movement, which was bathed in a mystical glow that suggested we should sensitize ourselves to our place in the world, with interpretive guidance from the therapist (Perls 1969). Eventually, then, we could intuitively somehow get in touch with an inner core, and do what was needed to live in harmony with the world and become personally happy.

Behavior therapy was not much developed when Rational Therapy began, and was not then, and is not now, clearly differentiated from Ellis's practices, though it is from his theory. In fact, the two forces can, and usually do, complement each other to the point that RET is now often included under the rubric of "Cognitive Behavioral Therapy."

In addition, there always has been, and certainly still is, that majority of therapists who call themselves eclectic or empirical, who choose not to commit themselves to any one theory but who draw on any of them as they find it convenient or useful. They are not especially interested in pinpointing exactly where the cutting edge of each theory may lie, in what it is that works or why, just so it does work for them at particular times, in particular ways.

Not only is there competition in the marketplace among those who claim to be first or best, but there is also resistance to acknowledging the importance or value of anything new. Barber (1961) wrote an article entitled "Resistance by Scientists to Scientific Discovery" that analyzed specific cases of reluctance among scientists to accept crucial breakthroughs. He concluded that while there is "the powerful norm of open-mindedness in science . . . in which objectivity is greater than it is in other social areas," nevertheless, there are always strong forces opposing new findings (p. 6). He quoted Huxley's reported comment that "'authorities,' 'disciples,' and 'schools' are the curse of science;

and do more to interfere with the work of the scientific spirit than all its enemies" (p. 6).

Ellis burst out with his highly activist, intellective problem-solving views, probably the more rhetorical for his having spent more than two years in the relatively passive stance of a client in psychoanalysis, and then four more, often frustrating, years as a psychoanalyst.

From childhood on, he was by nature antagonistic to passivity. While as an analyst he did active "detectiving," trying to discover areas of disturbance in clients' histories, he could not fully unleash his natural tendencies to argue, assign tasks, set concrete goals, persuade.

With Adler (1955) as his main contemporary philosophical spirit, Ellis began to promote the active, reasoning techniques he had noted in the literature of therapy as promising, talking and writing about them as rational methods, and eventually calling them Rational Therapy. He was heavily criticized for ignoring emotions when he had not intended to. At first he simply did not emphasize emotions as a major vehicle for change, as did Freud and Rogers, and depended upon the mind and reason instead. He did, however, use methods to evoke and then treat with them. In 1961 he and his then major collaborator, Robert Harper, decided to change the name of his theory to Rational-Emotive Therapy in order to indicate that they did recognize the importance of emotions in upsetting, changing, and enriching human behavior.

This change of name did not make any difference to Ellis's theory or practices. In fact, whatever other effects it might have had, the modification of name probably weakened his clear and continuing emphasis on intellectual functions as the major medium for altering behavior. Of course emotions enter into human behavior, but his is a view of the most effective means for changing conduct, and is not meant as a primarily research or exploratory method (as Freud intended for psychoanalysis).

Ellis (1983c) recognizes that

Cognitive therapies are many centuries old and in Western civilization notably go back to the philosophic writings of Epictetus and Marcus Aurelius. . . . Try to invent an entirely new form of psychological treatment and, if you do enough historical research, you will soon find its prototype in ancient history. . . . What, then, was exceptionally new about RET when I began to use it . . . in 1955? Not very much really. . . . If I have achieved anything remarkably new and different, I think I have done so by making RET into a somewhat unique therapeutic blend . . . a profoundly interactional theory of human (dysfunctional) cognition, emotion, and behavior.... More uniquely, it is the main — perhaps really the only — form of psychotherapy that clearly hypothesizes that if people only and purely think scientifically ... if they virtually never are dogmatic, absolutistic, pious, and sacramental in their attitudes toward themselves, toward other humans, and toward the world, practically all their "emotional" disturbance ... would disappear or be minimized. (p. 29)

The specific techniques of RET are discussed in another chapter. Here, only its place in the universe of people-helping methods is assessed. It has long and honorable antecedents beginning in ancient philosophy and extending early into this century without much controversy. Then Freud revolutionized the content of psychology by his focus on the unconscious and emotions.

Subsequently, clinical interest shifted to hidden notions and forces, feelings, and relatively passive methods designed to encourage clients to talk and emote freely in therapy about traumatic past events, sometimes true, sometimes not; it was hard to distinguish between them. Various applications of different analytic views became the fashion in psychotherapy.

The wonder is not that Ellis developed RET in the mid-1950s. The wonder is that it was ever necessary to reinvent the wheel, in the sense of returning to an emphasis on using the intellect and logical, scientific methods to avoid psychological distress, to solve problems, to achieve goals. It attests to the potency and impact of Freud's views that rational or cognitive theories about humans directing their own behavior needed to be reemphasized at all.

Ellis has, like most innovators in any human enterprise, met with resistance, competitiveness, and hostility — like Freud, who was attacked as a dirty-minded, weirdly antisocial hedonist, and Skinner, as a coldly calculating manipulator, and Rogers, as a good-hearted but simpleminded theorist. Ellis was, after all, presenting his views abrasively, in that den of psychoanalysts, New York City, where a large part of the most educated population seems to have been through analysis or to view it as the most sophisticated of therapies.

No form of psychotherapy is invulnerable to attack. No profession is spared even when it is relatively unified and based upon fairly continuous scientific progress. In contrast, the current universe of psychotherapy is composed of various adversarial "schools," each with passionate followers whose attitudes usually come more from the heart than from science.

All research on the relative effectiveness of different therapies has been grossly inadequate so far. There are so many variables that must be controlled — clients, therapists, procedures, and environments — that no one has even tried to do a full-scale rigorous simultaneous comparison of the major methods using adequate sampling and control procedures.

"Meta-analyses" have been done, evaluating studies rather than cases, but that process does not improve the quality of the original research. A good analysis of practically all controlled research studies is M. Smith's "What Research Says About the Effectiveness of Psychotherapy" (1982). She concludes that although "research shows psychotherapy to be effective in enhancing psychological well-being . . . [w]e have no advice about improving clinical technique or prescribing the most efficacious type of therapy for a particular set of symptoms" (pp. 460–61).

Typical of analyses made of any particular form of therapy was Miller and Berman's "The Efficacy of Cognitive Behavior Therapies: A Quantitative Review of the Research Evidence" (1983). They conclude that "these therapies do indeed bring relief to a broad range of patients. Yet . . . there is little evidence that they are more effective than other widely practiced psychotherapies" (p. 53).

In these reviews there is nothing particularly damaging to RET, which is now generally included as a cognitive behavioral therapy. It is simply that RET, along with all other forms of therapy, has not been conclusively validated by thorough, comparative scientific studies. It probably has generated, and is creating, as much research as any other form of therapy, however.

While many therapists promote their various versions of treatment, and most methods seem to help clients more than "no treatment" does, no one is thoroughly studying results except on a very limited scale of problems, methods, or clients. It is puzzling that no tough-minded, adept researcher has yet conceived and fought for a comprehensive cooperative research program on psychotherapy. It seems probable that, for a well-designed study proposed by competent professionals, large grants could be obtained.

Meanwhile, the competition is intense in the marketplace of therapeutic theory and practice. Ellis's RET is probably the most comprehensive blend of behavioral and cognitive methods now being practiced in a variety of cultures, with most human psychological problems, and utilizing many different methods of education and behavior change. Ellis has almost single-handedly developed its great diversity of techniques and written on almost all problems generated, including an analysis of its failures (see Ellis 1983a).

No one has made a larger contribution to the contemporary practice of psychotherapy.

4

Late Childhood and Adolescence

Between the ages of six and seven, life began to settle for Albert after his extended periods of hospitalization for kidney disease ended and treatment tapered off. Although he resumed normal living with a minimum of cautions, his frail and sickly appearance continued to condition his life in subtle ways that reinforced his intellectual tendencies.

His intellectual bent showed itself early, as he talked, then read and wrote precociously, and he avoided physical contact with others. Also, there was a certain attitude of protectiveness toward him. He wasn't allowed to play at school recess for a year or more after his illness, and he acceded to that pressure, though he probably could have ignored it if he had wanted to.

A best friend, besides his brother, came into his life around age six, one Manny Birnbaum, who lived across the street. Al, Paul, and Manny became inseparable friends. Manny remembers being tongue-lashed by Al's mother for "bullying" Al, followed by her demand that Manny's mother spank her son for it. Manny was always heavy and robust, and capable of hurting Al inadvertently, but they never engaged in more than horseplay. Al never came close to harm.

Mostly they did not engage in physical interaction, and Al didn't even try the tougher physical sports, such as football and wrestling, though he liked baseball and touch football — but not enough to play them much. Their main activities were long conversational walks, ambles around the Bronx Botanical Gardens, and, even at age six, long hikes to the public library on Saturdays, and to Van Cortlandt Park on Sundays, followed sometimes by the movies. Their main games were chess and cards, and a street sport called Chinese handball, in which the ball had to hit the ground before striking a wall.

Meanwhile, the middle-class kids around them, Irish, German, and other northern Europeans mainly, sturdy and more physical-minded, were playing baseball and football almost all of their spare time, and being taken to games by their fathers. These neighbor boys, fairly well controlled and behaved, did not disturb the close threesome. The three friends envied them their close-knit families, but not their robust athletic interests.

The one cultural event Al remembers from his family life was the acquisition, when he was eight or nine, of the *Book of Knowledge,* which he promptly read through.* Who bought it or why remains a mystery. It was a strange occurrence for his nonintellectual home.

Al had no relatives living closer than Philadelphia, and they rarely saw each other. The three friends considered themselves unique in the neighborhood in their intellectual pursuits. Al especially considered himself "disadvantaged," no good at what counted with the other kids — rough athletics and scorn for school. But he did attend to sports. He followed the teams, had heroes, and memorized batting averages. Later, in high school, he got an award for best attendance at school football games.

Manny's and Al's homes were similar in the absence of their fathers, who for years stayed away most of the time, neglected their wives, and did not see their sons for months at a time, and in the freedom their mothers allowed their children. They never talked about their family relationships or commiserated with each other about what they might have missed. They enjoyed their independence, and their mutual support probably made it even more rewarding.

Manny and Al took to each other immediately, at the start visiting from stoop to stoop, as was customary in the area. While they had periods of disengagement during and after adolescence, particularly when at college, they have remained close friends. Manny serves on the board of directors of the Institute for Rational-Emotive Therapy, and is Albert's personal as well as the Institute's accountant.

Ellis mentions his close friendship with Manny almost in passing. He refers to others equally when asked about intimates,

---

*Albert Ellis 1986: personal interview.

even though no one, objectively, came near to the closeness that existed almost all his life among himself, Paul, and Manny. All others he cites are clearly peripheral and relatively recent comers into his life, but he does not seem to differentiate emotionally among them.

He probably feels truly close to no one now except for Janet, his woman companion of over two decades. At least he shows no closeness in his behavior toward any others. Although from middle age on, he has had many friends, male and female, and shared congenial conversations and activities with them, it is almost always in relation to professional activity. Few of the friendships have lasted past periods of physical proximity or tasks at hand. Even Robert Harper, his longtime close collaborator and friend, seldom sees or talks with him any more except at professional meetings.

This illustrates what Manny has called an "aloofness" and "coldness" in Al, with his family and friends in the early years, and extending to others later. "It was a cold bunch, the whole family," says Manny, "showing very little feeling."*

The Ellis family certainly interacted that way. The father was gone from home almost constantly during the years of his marriage. Manny never did meet Al's father. The mother was a "bustling chatterbox who never listened." She expressed strong opinions about everything, but without explanation or substance. She'd simply expound, then go on to something else.

Ellis's mother seldom cooked, and when she did, it was done poorly. She shopped for food only erratically. She was usually in bed until after Al left for school in the morning from at least the time he was eight, and was rarely home when he returned. She did a little acting, singing, and comedy within her social circle. Her friends tended to be younger, of lower socioeconomic status, and they played a lot of bridge and mah-jongg.

He thinks his mother was neglectful of her family "because she could get away with it." But the situation was symbiotic. She could get away with it because her sons and husband apparently preferred to take care of themselves. Her husband was seldom present, and there were no other relatives or friends around the home who might have triggered her guilt — if indeed she would have responded to them.

---

*Manny Birnbaum 1985: personal interview.

But her daughter surely did not encourage such neglect. She apparently reacted against her mother's dereliction, but succeeded only in remaining miserable most of her life. It seems more likely that the sons resembled the mother more than did the daughter, and thus got on better in the free environment of their home.

Al bought and used his own alarm clock, made his own breakfast, prepared the lunch that he took to school. He says he loved the sense of self-sufficiency, of doing things his own way, of solving problem situations as they arose. "I invented RET naturally, beginning even back then, because it was my tendency," he says. He also believes that he played a major part in raising his two siblings. His brother only partly agreed, convinced of his own independence, even from Albert, even when they were little children.

Her sons treated their mother with nearly total disrespect. They either ignored her or dismissed her with a wave of their hands when she talked in their presence. Sometimes they simply locked her out of their room. Yet Al still thinks that he was the "apple of my mother's eye because I knew how to humor her."

Albert and Paul treated their sister in the same way, ignoring her, dismissing her, locking her out of their room, even though she was rather shy when others were present and didn't earn the same treatment the mother received. Paul hit her frequently, and didn't understand why, but still felt some residual hostility toward her long after her death. Both brothers best remembered her for her whininess.

Manny, too, excluded her, but only because her brothers did. He rather liked her, found her gentle, felt protective toward her, wanted to be kind to her. She could easily have been his friend, or the sister he never had, if her brothers had treated her better. He never saw the whiny side of her that so bothered them. Clearly, however, all three of them excluded all females, including her, from their most personal lives — until adolescence.

Even though Al recalls frequently being in love, and talking with girls individually, they did not enter his life in any important or continuing way, except in his fantasies, until his early teens. Despite numerous brief, dramatic episodes of falling in love — with a neighbor girl, a patient in his hospital ward, a schoolmate — usually only he, it seems, ever knew that they were part of his inner life. The threesome never talked about them, nor did anything with them, nor engaged in any social or recreational activities with them until puberty.

Emotion did not appear in any obvious way in the Ellis household. His brother and his best friend never visited Albert when he was hospitalized, nor did they show any worry about his physical condition except for taking precautions about roughhousing with him after his illness. No anger, no tears, no anguish, no depression, no exhilaration in the family can be recalled by his closest companions. Albert, however, does recall observing his mother's flashes of anger, his sister's spells of depression, and violent fights between Paul and their sister.

Much later Ellis would be accused of ignoring emotion, even though he added the word *emotive* to his method of rational therapy. He would be accused of being a rationalist, and then, to correct what he regarded as a misapprehension, would explain that he was, rather, a "long-term hedonist" and that he was committed to empiricism. Yet his critics may well have reacted to what they sensed in his personality, if not to his theory. To those who know him best, he was as child and youth, and still is, a stimulating, congenial, reasonable companion. He is not, however, an emotional, devoted, or empathetic one in a very personal, intense, or expressive way.

His early friends remained friends, though they were few through his late childhood and youth. He preferred to cultivate his personal education through reading, and to relate to others mainly through conversation about sports, school, and books. He was not (and is not now) critical of others except as they impinged on his territory or disagreed with his opinions. Otherwise he usually ignored their activities and values. They had little importance for him.

The three friends never fought with each other or with others. This lifetime objectivity in human relations kept Albert from common kinds of aggressive hostility throughout childhood. Arguments, yes, even occasional shoving or wrestling. But never angry fighting with fists, sticks, or other weapons, never bruising blows or bleeding, never vituperation or revenge. Such behavior never seemed worthwhile to him.

In the early years, the three boys' reading was not profound. Eventually, however, Albert supplemented his list beyond the Frank Merriwell and Horatio Alger novels that they traded among themselves. He was sensitive to light and wore an eyeshade when reading a lot, but never stopped.

Albert early extended his reading to political and philosophical books. He also played a little softball and baseball, as second baseman, as well as table tennis, a little tennis, and some touch football.

Paul and Manny grew closer in late childhood, while Albert began often to walk alone. He would not take teasing, was sensitive to personal criticism, and would simply walk away when offended. Summers the two brothers were usually off with their mother to Wildwood, New Jersey, where they hawked papers on the boardwalk, saving enough money to last them through the school year.

While Albert's recollection of those early years is that he helped rear his brother and sister, in the usual absence of their parents, his two companions remember differently. Paul believed he himself was the more practical one, good at finding solutions to problems, planning meals, taking care of the necessities of their lives, always logical and down-to-earth, while Al kept more to himself, planned ahead, and was less concerned with day-to-day matters.

Whatever their relationship on household affairs, the brothers got on well together and took care of themselves. Generally Albert seemed to go along with reasonable suggestions, as if he didn't much care who was ascendant. Even now he does not intervene in how the apartment he shares with Janet Wolfe is furnished or managed, even when he disagrees, as long as it does not disrupt what he wants to do.

So the years passed, until the boys were around thirteen. Then the threesome began to visit nearby St. James Park, Paul and Manny mainly to play tennis, and Albert mainly to talk. Boys and girls mingled there in some inchoate desire to relate to each other, without singling each other out for any obvious attention. There was lots of conversation, and Al found his place on a grassy slope where he would sit, spouting choice morsels of his recent reading and thinking, entertaining small groups that gathered around him.

When Albert was 12, what might have been a traumatic event in the Ellis household, and in his personal life, seems to have been turned into merely an interesting episode to the independent young boy. An acquaintance of his mother's told her that she had seen his father sharing a sleeper on the Twentieth Century Limited with his mother's best friend.

If this dramatic event shook his mother, Albert never knew it. He believes that, left to her own initiative, she probably would not have divorced her husband as a result of the revelation. He thinks she did so more because her friends expected her to than because she was keenly hurt or angered by his infidelity.* For years they had been more apart than together, and it seemed to make little difference in their lives whether they stayed married or not. Perhaps his father would not have divorced her (and then married the other woman) on his own initiative.

Albert's father spent little time at home, supposedly being gone on business, but also playing a lot of chess and cards, and maybe chasing women. Infidelity, however, apparently was never confirmed until the train episode. While both parents apparently valued and took advantage of their freedom within the marriage, his mother finally did divorce his father some time after she learned of the affair. He then married the woman he had been seen with, and stayed married to her for the rest of his life — happily, it seemed. Albert's father and mother remained friends.

Neither brother, and presumably no one else still alive, apparently knows any more than these basic facts about the episode. For a long time Albert did not even know of the divorce, since his father's absence was about the same, and neither his father nor his mother acted any differently. Only six months afterward did he learn of the divorce, when he overheard a conversation between his mother and her sister. While his father did not make regular child support or alimony payments, as he was supposed to, he did send money intermittently, presumably when he had it, and his mother made no complaints about the irregularity. Actually Albert began to see his father more after the divorce, perhaps coincidentally with his approaching manhood and a growing mutuality of interests. Eventually they went into business together.

Other than the antagonism between brother Paul and sister Janet, there was rarely any resentment or bitterness apparent in the reaction of anyone in the family to any other family member. The closest reaction resembling chronic ill will that can now be detected is perhaps the least deserved: the brothers' attitude toward their sister for not displaying the fortitude and independence that otherwise prevailed in the family.

Albert excelled throughout school, almost always at the top of his class in reciting, writing, and tests. Until his late teens he was usually anxious in formal presentations, but informally he talked fluently and a lot. He later forced himself to make speeches whenever he could, and it required two or three months of special

---

*Albert Ellis 1985: personal interview.

effort before he was satisfied with them. Only once does he remember a classmate tying him in grades.

Most of Albert's education came from his reading outside of classes. He remembers reading in physical geography at age 12, and immediately considering himself an atheist, feeling duped by religion and its notions about creation. Again there rather abruptly appears both a lifelong opinion to be preached to others and a stance on an issue that he felt was terribly important both for him and for the world — even at his young age. Yet, consistent with his acceptance of others as long as they don't directly challenge or compete with him, he has never held religion against anyone, he has worked effectively with religionists, and he has not been contentious about religion except in a philosophic way. One of the staff directors at his institute, however, broke with him because Ellis did not subscribe to religious values.

Only briefly, at about age 11, had Albert ever felt keenly religious, despite his mother's interest in and attendance at the temple. He went through a bar mitzvah to please his mother: as a ritual, not because he felt anything for it. He remains an atheist, and in early adulthood, he wrote assertively on the subject.

Around age 13 he developed an interest in light opera and musicals, and became expertly informed about such works and their composers. Once again, what attracted him became a concentrated preoccupation, never to be abandoned. He listened to everything written by Friml, Herbert, Strauss, and their ilk, and became their advocate as against such others as Gershwin and Kern.

Albert intended to write a book on this interest — and still intends to, when he has the time. When he was in his late teens, he used his knowledge to correct an author who wrote a book on light opera, and received an acknowledgment of his emendations in a subsequent edition. He now writes humorous rhyming lyrics for popular tunes, in order to advance principles of RET. Besides all their other similarities, his brother shared this specialized musical interest with him.

In their early adolescence, the threesome added to their intellectual and game activities some socializing at the park with other boys and girls. They became close friends with none of them, but Albert did develop skill and satisfaction in influencing others to his rapidly developing views about politics and philosophy. He entertained with comic verse as well. Albert must have excelled at, and attracted attention for, his intellectual and light conversational abilities. While he learned to be fairly easygoing, he was not popular. Rather, he was helpful, interesting, and entertaining.

Beginning in his teens, Albert found it necessary to curb a tendency to be easily irritated. He rarely got openly angry, but noticed that he "couldn't stand stupidity and dogma" in others, even though he himself "was more intense and at times more dogmatic than it was rational to be."* When he visited his father, he found a very similar kind of irritability in him that he considers an inherited tendency.

He was already trying to improve himself, to avoid anger, to seek solutions, to investigate what drew his interest, to savor pleasures and avoid pain and discomfort. By 12, he quit smoking. By 15, he quit eating candy because he read that it wasn't good for you. He tried various methods to sleep better. Having read that worrying about not sleeping is what keeps you awake, he tried to overcome his insomnia by reading, listening to monotonous sounds, working hard, and undersleeping. Although he no longer frets about not sleeping well, he does not yet control to his satisfaction his tendency to lie awake thinking. It still concerns him.

At about 13, Albert discovered H. G. Wells and Upton Sinclair, and at 16, Epictetus, Spinoza, Kant, and Bertrand Russell. He continued to read in philosophies, particularly practical ones that gave him specific guidelines for his own life. But the strongest appeal to his desire to influence others came from the political domain and the atmosphere of the country undergoing the trauma of the Great Depression. His mother's savings were wiped out, and his father didn't pay alimony, perhaps had no money to do so. The boys had to find odd jobs to help support the household. Albert thought ahead about how to acquire wealth, and decided to earn it in business, then retire at 30 to write full time.

All three boys decided to go to the New York High School of Commerce in Manhattan, where they could gain practical business skills that would earn them solid jobs in business upon graduation. They also planned to go on to college, but knew they would have to be able to support themselves through it.

They became members of Young America when Al was 18. It was a local organization of a dozen or so youths their age, started by a music teacher in the Bronx and dedicated to improving the economic condition of the country. It eschewed foreign

---

*Albert Ellis 1986: personal interview.

movements, particularly the Communist Party. It was committed to grow from native soil, with more practical, and less theoretical, ways of saving the world than pure Marxism, which it severely criticized.

It is fuzzy now just how they were to achieve their goals, but they savored the excitement of trying to save the world through their own efforts. Although the movement lasted only a few years, and never grew, it attracted Albert long enough for him to become a paid organizer for one of its more revolutionary offshoots. Young America represented his first major attempt to influence people to improve themselves.

And then there were girls. Even at 16 and 17, Al remained shy with them. He and his companions talked to girls in the park, and they listened while neighbor boys discussed having sex with a promiscuous girl nearby. But among themselves they never talked about sex, and they never had it, and they never even approached it, except for some mild petting, until they were married. All three maintain that this was typical of Jewish boys in that locale, and that they felt great physical frustration, but no serious misery, on this account. For them, intellectual activities were more attractive, perhaps because they found barriers to sex insurmountable.

Albert considers that he was always "sexier" than most others, by which he means "interested in and active around the edges of sex." He made many excuses for not trying to have sex with girls, despite his strong urges and frequent masturbation. He tried to curb this latter activity, though he claims to have overcome his guilt in his early teens by reading an enlightening book.* He admired those who were not as shy with girls as he was. His high school, however, was entirely male, and his temptations and opportunities rare.

When Albert finally did cut loose on sex, in his mid-twenties, it was with a power and intensity that swept most other activities, except earning a livelihood and writing, out of his life for years. He had been contenting himself with masturbation, but then heterosexual sex became a consuming interest. It was as much a political cause as a personal passion. He would try to free American society from its hang-ups as he had, finally, been able to free himself.

---

*Albert Ellis 1985: personal interview.

Albert was a good boy in high school, never in any kind of trouble for intellectual rebelliousness, as he was to be in college and thereafter. Skipping two years, he graduated from high school at age 16. After a slow start when he cared little about grades, he graduated seventh in a class of about 150. The English teacher who was his adviser encouraged him to do his work well and become a writer, and he did both. Also, he gained glory for the school, earning it points by winning weekly citywide competitions, sponsored by the *New York World,* for the best essays on outstanding news events.

Meanwhile, there were other fish to fry. Despite an excellent record, Albert faced a hard life as he finished high school, even though he did not particularly view it that way. Life always required his best effort; he was determined to succeed at whatever attracted his interest. At this point it was to earn a living, complete a business degree at college, gain a well-paid job, pursue his interests in politics and philosophy, and learn how to win and enjoy women — and become a writer. He had begun to write fiction, lots of it, and had the shining goal of becoming a famous author — which he also thought would help attract girls.

Despite his two close friends, Albert remained essentially a loner. He was developing other interests and a few friends he did not necessarily share with Paul and Manny, and he grew somewhat apart from them as he intensified his efforts to gain importance. He sought influence, power, expertise, and usefulness with others, via the written and spoken word. He had found his verbal skills had an impact on others. But he still needed to find more enduring subjects to propagandize.

Albert had already experimented with writing fiction, but he could not sell it. He had written lyrics, but could not write the music to go with them, and so could not sell them. He had experimented with politics, and while he had found his first professional job with a new little organization, that obviously had no future. Yet he craved an audience, influence, creative opportunity. He knew he could hold the attention of groups for whatever he chose to communicate about.

But above all, Albert needed to earn his living. There was no one else to pay for anything, except for the board and room his increasingly impoverished mother provided. He didn't need to earn much for himself and his family, but he wanted to accumulate enough money to live on while doing what he wanted to.

So he set off for City College's Baruch School of Business and Civic Administration, where tuition was free to residents of New York City. He would become an accountant, not because he thought he'd especially like the work but because it was a good, sure livelihood. He didn't want money for material goods; he never did want or need much. But he did want his freedom, to be able to write or do whatever he desired, regardless of the money he could earn at it.

All three of the friends decided to become accountants through City College, and to make a living from business. To them, college was for vocational education. It was a major step toward adulthood, for which earning a livelihood was the most important step. Not politics, not sex, not adventure had so important a role in their lives at that point.

After graduation, Albert's brother and Manny would continue in separate businesses, in which they prospered. Albert, however, with his eye on a different game — to influence and preach to the world — stayed in business just long enough to put himself through graduate training in psychology. Then he made a new, entirely different life for himself.

5

Reaching Maturity

Immediately upon finishing high school at age 16, Albert — and a little later his brother Paul — and friend Manny enrolled at the Baruch College of the City University of New York (CCNY then). Preparing to earn a living must come first, whatever else they might want to do when they had survival income.

Albert had no serious problems with self-doubt or anxiety that would impede him. His vitality and drive made any reasonable goal readily reachable. But he did have trouble sleeping; he could not will himself to sleep as soundly and as long as he wanted to. He experimented with various methods and eventually found that listening to his own monotonous breathing until he fell asleep was his best method of coping with insomnia.

His fantasies at that time were commonplace: about doing very well, about becoming famous, about having sex with girls — but above all, becoming famous as a writer after he had made money in business, and having girls coming after him as a result. At college he was practical, had little trouble with any courses, and proceeded to complete his work on schedule.

Albert's dreams lay elsewhere. He continued to write prolifically, his major works being novels. Before he entered graduate school, he had completed over 20 manuscripts, most nonfiction works on politics, philosophy, and sex, as well as novels, plays, and poetry. None was ever accepted for publication, although a few came close. He still thinks of trying to resurrect some of them and submitting them again. He does not like to give up. He thinks he is merely laying the works aside for a more propitious time.

Albert's lyrics gained some publishers' compliments, but he couldn't write the music for them. He thinks they may have been considered too sophisticated for the time. In any case, they were never published. Lately he has written new lyrics to popular songs to teach his therapy methods. During the earlier period he also wrote his first book on self-help therapy, an unpublished manuscript entitled "The Art of Never Being Unhappy," now lost.

He acted out his rebelliousness at college more than ever before. He formed a "No Tie" organization, with himself as the only officer and member, to protest the college policy requiring conventional dress. He never wore a tie. He wrote a column for the college paper that gained him a brief suspension for political radicalism and erotic verse. He kept writing as his major extracurricular activity. He graduated in four years, with a B.B.A. degree in accounting.

For a year, Albert was a paid propagandist for a radical little organization of Manhattan youth that embraced the notion of a classless society. After a couple of years, however, he abandoned the group as too alienated from the reality of effective action, and returned to writing fiction.

Meanwhile, however, he had written a socialist primer, never published, presenting Marx's theories of communism for the public.* It was his first serious effort to educate the public for its own good, the kind of enterprise that thereafter marked his life. It was a simple question-and-answer book presenting the essence of Marx's three-volume *Das Kapital*. His intent was to expose the flaws in communism's theory of surplus value, to quit discussing it, and to get on with the revolution. He believes he could have gotten it published with the backing of either the Socialist or the Communist Party, but chose instead to oppose them both for their dogmatic positions.

By then Albert had pretty well abandoned his efforts to write songs and operettas. He had been unable to teach himself how to play the piano or to write music, presumably because of his weak eyes. His eyes may have been affected by a pre-diabetic condition, though he apparently did not have diabetes at that time. In any case, he has always protected his eyes, perhaps since his early bout with kidney trouble. While that has not diverted him from reading, he did and does avoid bright light and efforts that seem to strain his eyes, often keeping his eyes closed when sitting. For a

---

*Albert Ellis 1985: personal interview.

while when he was young, he wore an eyeshade when reading or writing.

Soon after he finished college, Albert and his brother started a pants matching business that he left after a couple of years for his job as a paid organizer. They found extra pants, or had them made, for a suit when the original pair wore out. Later, for a short time, the two sold pants directly from a manufacturer. They did poorly, so they returned to the matching business.

Albert's major activity outside of work remained political; he read and wrote extensively in the field. His brother left the pants business about 1938, when he got a job with an oil shipping company by saying he wasn't Jewish. He stayed with the company with considerable success until his retirement, rising to an executive position.

Albert went into a couple of his father's abortive businesses. His father frequently raised money for new enterprises; he was very good at it. But the businesses almost always failed after a short period. Near the end of his life, the father tried unsuccessfully to get Paul to take over his finally successful business, an insurance agency.

With his father, Albert helped promote a bridge game board you could play by yourself, following the Four Aces approach instead of the Culbertson system, on which an existing board was based. He became an expert bridge player. He also helped his father promote a beer cooler cleaner. In apparent imitation of his father, Albert would experiment with any reasonable business prospect.

Once, through an acquaintance of his father's, Albert almost got a job writing for the *New York Times Magazine*. He had written his application in verse. But at the decisive job interview, he was told that he was too thin and would lack the necessary stamina. He listed on his application form that he was a free-lance writer. Never since has his thinness or stamina for a job been deemed a handicap.

Albert graduated from college at age 20 but did not enter graduate school until he was 28. He continued to live at home with his mother, brother, and sister until his sibs married and left, and when, briefly, he did, too. He and his brother continued to be the main support of their mother and sister until the latter married. Then they contributed to their mother's support for the rest of her life.

Albert was called up by the draft when he finished college, but was rejected for a number of reasons: He had sugar in his urine, a chronically dislocatable shoulder, and a history of kidney trouble as a child. For a sickly youth, he has lived a remarkably long and healthy life — and worked hard, without a sense of handicap, on more conventional problems of youth.

He had worked hard to overcome his anxiety about public speaking and approaching girls. He forced himself to talk to groups in his political and social activities. But his task with girls was tougher. In his twenties, one June he decided to open a conversation with all the women sitting alone on the stone benches in the Bronx Botanical Gardens. He did, systematically, until he had talked to 100 — and for his efforts got one kiss and one date, which the girl did not keep. He felt it was a turning point in his sexual life, that he would be able thereafter to ask women for dates and sex without anxiety. And he has been able to ever since.

At 24 adult love struck Albert, this time diverting his life, like a break in a dam, for years before he got it under full control. It ignited with a beautiful, vivacious girl named Karyl, a WPA actress and writer, who lived with her parents. Initially he was drawn to her because of her troubles with a boyfriend who was abusing her, in Albert's opinion, and he wanted to save her from being victimized.

Until then Albert's sexual experience had consisted of frequent masturbation and occasional light petting. He and his two close companions claimed this was common among their Jewish classmates in the Bronx, but it surely was not typical of spirited young men in their early twenties elsewhere. Their inhibitions seem to have been sustained by their limited range of friendships and also, perhaps, by a kind of snobbishness that youthful intellectuals sometimes assert toward associating with women "merely" for sex.

In any case, Albert's pent-up desire for women was unleashed, and all the fervor of his desire to preach to humankind was directed both to save and to win Karyl. He wrote love letters 20 to 30 pages long. He advised her to quit going with bums, to protect herself. He saw her as much as he could. From his growing experience with her as well as his extensive library research, he reached out to advise his friends on their sexual problems, and learned more from their reactions. He sent Karyl a 99-page letter revealing his feelings in elaborate detail and analyzing all the advantages and disadvantages of marrying him.

Albert was still a virgin but tried to have sex. She said a physical problem made intercourse impossible, and she resisted him. He counseled her to have surgery; she told him to see a physician in order to put on weight, since she thought he was so thin that he looked "repellant." He did consult a physician about fattening up and, briefly, he succeeded somewhat. The relationship was off and on. She'd be warm and friendly, then turn cool and fearful. He would become ever more frantic to win her.

Finally Albert took a contemplative midnight walk in the Bronx Botanical Gardens, and concluded that he should abandon his desperate need for Karyl. And did. Desire, yes; necessity, no. Then she proposed that they get married instead of breaking up, and he decided it would be a worthy experiment.

Karyl insisted that they keep their marriage plans secret from her parents, since they objected to his appearance and financial prospects. So they kept the scheme secret — until she felt she had to tell them. They persuaded her not to marry. Albert accepted that. Then she proposed again that they do it secretly. Finally they did elope. But that same evening she told her family of the marriage, and Albert, in disgust with the continuing turmoil, sought an annulment.

In three months the annulment he sought became final on the trumped-up grounds that she had promised a religious ceremony, then refused to go through with it. It was a convention demanded by New York State law, which then had extremely limited grounds for divorce and annulment.

But that was far from the end of the relationship. Karyl had suffered a "nervous breakdown" when 15, and she called Albert, feeling on the verge of another one. Her new boyfriend had gone off to China, to his woman friend there. Albert came to her place to comfort her, and they slept together for the first time. Karyl's landlady evicted her for having men in her place. She had no money for a new apartment, so Albert took her home with him, to his mother's apartment, to sleep with him on a daybed in the living room.

Finally they moved out of his mother's apartment, continuing to live together at several different places in Greenwich Village while he was counseling her on how to straighten out her life. A year later, with Albert's encouragement, Karyl began to live with another man, who eventually became her husband. Albert then moved back to his mother's apartment. He continued to see Karyl occasionally, however, and they remained friends. Even now she attends his public therapy demonstrations off and on, considers him to be a "genius," and rather wishes she had stayed with him.

Following the annulment, Albert needed more remunerative work to pay the legal fees. He got a regular salaried job as assistant to the president of a small gift and novelty distributor. He did everything including get to work at 8:30 A.M., as everyone else did. Confident of his performance, he asked, instead of a raise, for the privilege of coming in late, at 10 or 10:30, and of leaving early if he finished his work. Invariably he was done early, often after three or four hours, which permitted him eventually to attend graduate school while holding a "full-time" job.

His boss was extremely conservative. He wore dark suits and ties, and talked and acted rather formally. He disapproved of Ellis's appearance — tieless and wearing blue denim shirts. But he was smart enough to appreciate the value of his bright, energetic assistant who could do all the necessary work efficiently and cheaply, so he put up with the garb. But though he treated his assistant well within the sharp limits of cost, mainly by leaving him alone, Albert expresses little feeling for the man.

This coolness is typical of Ellis's attitude toward his bosses, even those who treated him well, or at least left him alone. He speaks fairly and objectively about them, but there is no call on his emotions toward his first boss, his other bosses, his Ph.D. adviser, or his psychoanalyst. Admittedly, they all were important to his development. He gained their support and he speaks well of them, but he never acknowledges his need for them, any affection either way, any continuing relationship beyond the immediate situation.

Ellis's career as a sexologist flourished after his tumultuous first affair, which developed into marriage and annulment. He read voluminously in the literature of sex, and counseled with friends and acquaintances to pick up more knowledge, as well as to help them. For years, he specialized in sexual problems, became a leading expert in the field, and wrote and lectured prolifically on the subject.

In the sexual area itself he has made a notable place for himself in the profession and literature of psychology, as well as in the public eye (which will provide a separate chapter). It would probably have been sufficient to bring him an enduring place in social history even if he had not created his system of psychotherapy.

In 1941, at the age of 28, Ellis began graduate training at Columbia University, then a leading center for the training of clinical psychologists. He gained his master's degree in one year from the psychological services department, which later became that of clinical psychology. He then hung a sign in the window of his mother's apartment announcing that he was "Albert Ellis, M.A., Psychologist." There was a private entrance to his little office, and eventually he saw three or four clients a week.

At first he experimented with Rogers' relatively passive, nondirective approach, which had just been described in Rogers' book *Counseling and Psychotherapy* (1942), using it with adolescents at Columbia University. But it was a bad fit for a therapist who had been a lively activist all of his life. It went against all his inclinations, and as soon as he felt comfortable with clients, he pushed ahead with more active counseling. Not with certainty, however. He was still experimenting for a comfortable method, and it would be several years before he found it.

Most tyro psychologists with creative bents experiment with different approaches before they find one that matches their values and personality, and gives them personal and professional satisfaction. No one who knew Ellis would have thought that the empathetic, relatively inactive method of Rogers could possibly work for him — or the psychoanalytic approach, for that matter. Yet Ellis did not foresee the difficulties. Gaining professional skill was his overriding consideration, and he chose where and how he thought he could best acquire it, as most psychotherapists do. He had to learn more about himself through experience before settling on a satisfying form of practice.

Despite the university rules against taking a full-time program while working, Ellis held his job with its eventual 10 A.M. to 2 P.M. hours. He lived at home, did a little therapy there, and pursued women and sex. He characterizes it as his apartment "where he allowed his mother to live."

He still got quite tense when presenting a case to the graduate seminar; his heart beat wildly, though he told himself there was nothing to fear. He never considered trying to get out of presentations, but instead forced himself to speak up more than the other students. Without consciously analyzing his fear, he just pounded ahead, trying to make his mark as a propagandist for whatever attracted him most at the time. During this time the pounding heart quieted and he was on his way to dramatic fluency as a public speaker.

Just before Ellis began graduate school, his friend Manny introduced him to a cousin of his, Gertrude, and for four years she became the great love of Ellis's life. It was his most passionate relationship, and it lasted in dilute form for the rest of her life. She wanted to send him through medical school. She wanted to marry him. She also wanted a big, open house without doors between rooms, and several dinner parties a week, which he would not accept. They were at an impasse.

He didn't want to give her up, but she found a man she wanted to marry and who wanted to marry her on her terms, and they did marry. She was "the great love of my life," he says. But the intense intimacy did not last long enough to test their capacity to sustain it. They never lived together. So she, and their romanticized love, still sound fresh as he talks about her.

Ellis remembers well the rest of her history: the accidental early death of her first husband; the child she aborted after his death; her second marriage; her son's disappearance; and finally her death from cancer.

He says: "I'm a monogamist. . . . I've always been devoted to one woman at a time."* It's a strange definition of "monogamy," which generally means to be married to one person at a time or to be married for life. He means that he has only one serious affair at a time. His sense of the word is to love one woman, for whatever time the relationship lasts, intensely, devotedly, emotionally. But perhaps to have light affairs at the same time, and in between.

Ellis has had many women in superficial, almost purely sexual relationships, but only a few with whom he has lived or has seen often, and has considered himself committed to. The engagement is not, however, conventional. It does not mean no affairs or no other sex — on either side. It does mean no loyalty to someone else that might interfere with their close, primary relationship. It also means seriousness with and support of the most important companion, and honesty between them.

He has gone mainly with younger women, mostly ten or more years younger than he. They are more attractive and malleable to him than those his age or older. All have been bright. He liked to be able to influence them. Both his first lover, Karyl, and his long-term partner, Janet, admittedly were heavily influenced by his indomitable zeal and firm notions to become more thoughtful, rational, and life-enjoying human beings. They both call him "genius."

After five years Ellis completed his doctorate at Columbia University, technically in psychological research but actually in the program in clinical psychology just being established. He had no problems with the program until he chose to do his dissertation

---

*Albert Ellis 1985: personal interview.

on the love emotions of college women. After a year of encouraging him in collecting data, the department turned down the project, presumably because it feared repercussions from publicity on sex research at the university.

He didn't fight the decision because two senior professors were unalterably opposed. Instead, he chose an innocuous topic involving the use of conventional personality tests. But he never forgot his passionate interests and ideas. After he completed his degree, he plunged ahead in the sexual arena with research and writing that were sensational to the public, and that gained him notoriety as well as fame.

Ellis practically never abandoned his interests, values, or goals when thwarted, but merely adapted them as necessary to the circumstances and limits or temporarily laid them aside. He had plenty of courage when he was on his own, but when he was under the control of others, as at the university and, later, with the State of New Jersey, he was discreet and careful not to harm his status unless he thought he could gain his objective through forcefulness.

Shortly after completing his doctorate, he took a job as psychologist at the Northern New Jersey Mental Hygiene Clinic. He then rented an apartment in Manhattan, in order to live alone and to expand his private practice.

Ellis began a personal psychoanalysis and other training to become an accredited psychoanalyst and perhaps a training analyst. This was with the encouragement of his analyst, who was close to Karen Horney, whose institute supposedly did not accept nonphysicians. One must reconstruct the times and the milieu to understand this choice.

Regardless of one's orientation in psychology and psychotherapy — whether one was influenced during training by the psychoanalytic bent of one's department at Columbia University, by the cultural atmosphere of New York City, or by an adviser, or whether one was trained in a behavioral, empirical department, such as that at the University of Minnesota — most bright young psychologists at that time thought that psychoanalysis was the most profound, intellectually challenging therapy available, and chose it for their personal therapy. They also believed that, regardless of need, getting personal therapy was a desirable, if not an essential, experience for learning how to do treatment.

Ellis only partially chose his analyst. He called the Horney Institute in New York City, an unorthodox institute for the training of psychoanalysts, for a recommendation. Luckily, he was referred to the ideal person for him. Dr. Hulbeck was bright, well-read in several cultures, a professional writer in fiction and journalism, an unorthodox analyst, an aesthete, and a wise practitioner. He had contributed to the Dadaist movement in the arts, and his wife was an artist. All of this made Ellis admire him as cultured and sophisticated beyond anyone he had ever known.

His name in Germany had been Charles Hulsenbeck, shortened to Hulbeck in the United States, to which he immigrated after living in Switzerland. He fled from Nazi Germany, though he was not Jewish. He had been analyzed by Rorschach and, as part of his unorthodoxy, did not emphasize transference. He practiced out of his apartment on Central Park West in Manhattan.

After Ellis's first session, when he lay on the couch and free-associated for the full hour, his analyst noted mildly, "My, you certainly can talk, can't you!" He had hardly been able to get in a word. And then, before they went any further, "You're already half analyzed, you can associate so well." After two years, he offered to provide Ellis with training to be an analyst, which Albert accepted. For two years he did a "control analysis" with Hulbeck, also twice weekly as his therapy had been.

One's feelings seldom are neutral about one's analyst. Usually they are powerfully positive, as with a good parent, partly because the experience is so intense and preoccupying that it resembles brainwashing toward what becomes a lasting interpretation of one's life. Partly, also, one must justify to oneself the enormous expenditure of time, energy, preoccupation, and money that analysis requires. But Ellis's attitude, in retrospect at least, is typical of him: benign, friendly, appreciative, but low-key. This despite the fact that he talked freely to the man twice a week for two years, and would have doubled the number of sessions if he could have afforded it.

His analyst made referrals to him, and he to the analyst, one measure of mutual respect. Later, Ellis was eager to introduce his new girl friend to Hulbeck, and phoned to make a social call on Hulbeck and his wife. The interaction was awkward. Far from showing interest in Ellis's girl friend and making conversation, the Hulbecks got totally immersed in recounting their own experiences traveling, hardly giving Ellis, who was not shy, the opportunity to talk. The Hulbecks didn't even interact with each other. Ellis never again tried to call on them, and the friendship dwindled away.

The preponderance of Ellis's feeling for Hulbeck comes through as favorable. He respected and liked the man. But he ended up quite disappointed, all but concluding that Hulbeck must have been a bit crazy to behave the way he did on their one social occasion outside the therapeutic office.

He shows the same kind of ambivalence toward his father. Albert wanted to, and indeed does, express respect for the man's intelligence and skills — in the face of facts that were bound to disappoint him: his father's failures in business and his distance from his family. But while clearly critical of such important people in his life, Ellis seems incapable of bitterness, as if he wants to preserve a fragile tundra of positive emotion between them that might barely have existed originally, or perhaps not at all.

His unorthodox analyst didn't emphasize the transference relationship, and had existential views of one's place in the world. Albert disagreed with some of his interpretations, but generally thought they made sense and occasionally were useful in handling his life. He believes he "got over" some of his irritability and his compulsivity. It might be more accurate to say that they were reduced, and that he felt more relaxed, since most observers would probably think he still has a good deal of both. He currently characterizes himself in those ways, but as only "mildly" or "moderately" so.

What he did conclude about the results of his analysis, which he attributes only partly to the therapy, and the rest to his own independent efforts, was that his irritability was irrational. That is, people did what they did, and there was no good reason for him to get upset about it or them. So he tried to control it, and believes he diminished it substantially.

Also, though even now, and perhaps even more now, Ellis safeguards his time, hates to waste it, and wants above all to work at and complete his projects, he says that since his analysis he hasn't watched the clock as he used to; no longer gets upset about the fact that he cannot read, write, or propagandize as much as he wants to; accepts that he will never get everything done he wishes; and no longer keeps records of everything he does and reads.

He believes that he lost the frantic quality of his timekeeping and record keeping. He decided he might write 100 instead of 200 or 300 books. He no longer had to be the world's most prolific writer. He changed from needing, to wanting, to accomplish all his goals.

Thus, by age 35, Ellis had completed his formal education and most of his training as a clinical psychologist, had acquired experience as a therapist, had broken the ice on sex, had found a voice for himself by writing, talking, and publishing as a psychologist, and had become knowledgeable and critical about conventional views of psychoanalysis and sex.

He also had obtained his first professional job, had opened his first office, and had set a pattern for occasional, intense, sustained love affairs. He had even, in a fine, symbolic gesture of emancipation, "shipped" his mother off to California to live with his sister.

Thus Ellis had reached maturity in the sense of a mode of living that would mark the rest of his life. It would be elaborated and modified in some emphases, and lead eventually to his major contribution in the field of psychology, the invention of Rational-Emotive Therapy. Clearly his apprenticeship was over.

6

Emerging from Psychoanalysis

In 1948, with his brand new Ph.D. degree, Ellis began his first full-time job as a psychologist. It was at the Morristown-based Northern New Jersey Mental Hygiene Clinic, from which he could commute to New York to visit his psychoanalyst and conduct a small private practice. At first he continued to live at home, but soon he sent his mother to California to stay with his sister, while he found himself an apartment in mid-Manhattan where he could live and do private practice.

He gained rich clinical experience in the New Jersey program, beginning on the mental hygiene staff and advancing to chief psychologist of the central diagnostic center from which patients were assigned to various programs and institutions. He spent his last two years in New Jersey as chief psychologist for the entire state psychological program.

Ellis could not have stayed in so large and regimented a program for long. He had never tolerated well what he could not control, and, not being a physician, at that time he had no chance of gaining command of the state program so that he would have professional independence. It was not that he needed to dominate administratively. He has never insisted on that even at the institutes he has founded, even though he usually has prevailed.

It is clear, however, that Ellis requires freedom to do what he wants to do. And he has always enjoyed a leadership role, being looked to for counsel and ideas, lecturing to and training others. It is also clear that he leads mainly as a model and influencer rather than as a demander, that he does not enjoy manipulating and dominating others, that administrative power in itself holds little attraction for him. But being beholden to others administratively would inevitably prove intolerable, and serious trouble predictably would come fairly soon on some issue or another.

In New Jersey, Ellis interviewed, tested, and treated the widest range of clients: psychotics, neurotics, psychopaths, and delinquents; old and young; from all walks of life. Those four years were his major experience with clients other than the middle-class, neurotic, and at least fairly financially secure who have constituted the overwhelming majority of his clients ever since. Such was the case also with the clientele of Freud and most other leaders in psychotherapy. They invented systems that depended upon relatively normal thinking in their clients, or at least fairly rational behavior. More physical means — medicines, shock, surgery, confinement, rigorous behavior control and direction — are the more common modes of treatment of the psychotic and psychopathic, whose thinking is more deranged.

Since he returned to Manhattan in the early 1950s, Ellis has lived a relatively hermetic existence, sallying forth almost exclusively to give speeches, conduct workshops, and, rarely, to take out women and to go to parties. It is as hard now to conceive of him ever commuting regularly to New Jersey as a student, client, and lustful youth as to think of that peerless, fat, fictional detective Nero Wolfe gadding about New York. In maturity, neither hardly ever left home except under extreme provocation, and then increasingly for professional reasons only.

Ellis belongs to and stays in his office, receiving others, writing, propagandizing. In that sense, he seems almost always as an adult to have been old, settled, and staid, while his intellectual career has caromed brilliantly in professional circles.

The parallel to two great fictional detectives is striking. Like Nero Wolfe, Ellis practically always stays home, except when on missions of exceptional professional merit. And like Sherlock Holmes, he constantly, intellectually, and earnestly seeks truth in a scientific way, with utmost concentration on his work.

Unlike the two detectives, however, Ellis has made sex a serious part of his activity ever since he could succeed at it. But even it is secondary to his work, and it is not hard to imagine his having chosen to be ascetic sexually as well as socially (though he never has) because of his dedication to his profession. Regarding sex, he is most concerned to educate the public with accurate information about the satisfying practice of it. He doesn't look or act like a lusty, slick, spirited Don Juan even though he may write and talk like one.

He can be charming at will, but his life has been so dominated by self-direction and self-control in pursuit of professional interests that he doesn't seem likely to elicit warm feelings from women in general, though he has from a select few. He admits to having been prompted when adolescent, and somewhat throughout his life, to achieve fame as a way of attracting women. And there's little doubt that, since his maturity, he has been sexually successful at least partly for that reason.

Ellis would disagree. He sees himself as an all-around human being, especially in his youth, passion and intellect in good balance. Yet it is difficult to imagine or document his youth — I did not know him until his middle age — as radically different from now. Apparently he was always hardworking, serious-minded, and dedicated to intellectual pursuits, though their nature varied at different periods of his life.

Oh, he did at least a few colorful things: There was what he called a "sex party" at one psychological convention where he passed around pictures of nude and lingerie-clad women, to try to determine which were more alluring. Even that was supposed to be serious research, however. (Incidentally, nudes were judged the more appealing.)

There was the autographed napkin and breast imprint of a famous stripper who visited his table at a nightclub. There was fun with limericks, kidding old friends, making small talk at cocktail parties. But even at five, by his account, he was thinking and acting gravely, in the main, trying to puzzle out the meaning of life, to handle problems, to make the best of difficult situations for himself and for the rest of humankind. His diversions from that path have been few and brief, except for an occasional, sometimes impassioned, love affair.

In his early professional years in New Jersey, Ellis's goal was to complete a control analysis, then to settle in Manhattan as a full-time psychoanalyst in private practice. But his tendency toward radicalism would not disappear just because he got a good job. It's doubtful whether he ever thought clearly of settling down and becoming content with the bare bones of independent professional practice on a part-time or full-time basis, following someone else's theories.

He had one major love affair during the New Jersey period, with a woman whose garish life she reported to him as full of all sorts of sex, assaults, even murder. He was smitten with her sexually, they talked of marriage, even announced their engagement, and he came close to marrying her.

Eventually Ellis decided that she lied much of the time, and that he could not distinguish her truth from her invention. He pulled away before it was too late. But the affair did become known — apparently she was coveted by others in the program — and Ellis may thereby have aggravated his imminent troubles in the New Jersey state program.

He began to write prolifically at that time about his professional ideas and research. Research subjects were easily available, he had an intense desire to write and to publish, and for the first time he found his manuscripts accepted. It was far easier then to get printed in psychological journals than it is now. Now there are 15 or 20 times more psychologists competing for publication (though with his current reputation, he has little trouble getting published).

Ellis published 10 or 12 research papers on problems and questions in the New Jersey state program that caught his attention: peculiar names, mongoloids, women's allure, among others. His first published article was "The Sexual Psychology of Human Hermaphrodites" (1945). His first book was *The Folklore of Sex* (1951), and his second book consisted of selected papers entitled *Sex, Society and the Individual* (Pillay & Ellis 1953).

But his administrative difficulties, mainly the minor hassles and annoyances that occur in almost all large organizations, culminated in an affair about credit for a book on sex. Eventually it was published as *The Psychology of Sex Offenders* (Ellis & Brancale 1956).

Besides a disagreement on whose name should appear first, accusations were made that Ellis should not have been conducting a private practice along with his state job, and that he should have lived in New Jersey while working there. There were also administrative objections to his outspoken interest in and public discussions of sex.

In a letter quite dramatic for its improbable, almost abject humility, Ellis wrote his coauthor at great length about how he, Ellis, had behaved with inexcusable arrogance, that he recognized his insensitivity to the feelings of others, that he acknowledged and would heed the wisdom of his collaborator's criticism.

Ellis makes no apologies for the humility that he now says had the sole purpose of winning over his coauthor so that *The Psychology of Sex Offenders* could be published. It is the only example of naked submissiveness and apology I have found in his correspondence or history. It had seemed an especially humble, moving document, yet apparently represented nothing more than the successful effort to remove a barrier to his goal of publication. He didn't really mean what he wrote; it was his way of solving the problem at hand.

His private practice began slowly. He got referrals from his analyst and others. He particularly enjoyed his sexual and marriage counseling, but it soon became obvious that neither group would provide a full-time load, so he took almost anyone who came to him for help — and still does, with rare exceptions. But he has almost never seen psychotic or psychopathic clients in his private practice.

By the time he quite the New Jersey job, Ellis was able to make a sparse but sufficient living from his private practice. He never has wanted much materially, always living very frugally. Except for his quarters, which have become rather luxurious since he moved into the Institute building and has lived with Janet, he probably spends about the same amount now, compensating for inflation, with an income of around a quarter million dollars a year, as he did when he had only a bare subsistence compensation.

Of course, during those early years he did pay for an expensive psychoanalysis two to three times a week for a couple of years. He always worked very hard, but accepted the fact that he could never turn out as much as he had planned to, and would have to be content with much less.

In 1942, the 28-year-old Ellis began a 20-year romance with the woman he loved most intensely and with whom he maintained a relationship almost as long as he has with Janet Wolfe. Even though he never married Gertrude, he considered it the most torrid affair of his life, particularly the first three years, which survived her two marriages, and lasted at least intermittently until she died of cancer. He is not any less involved with Janet, but the fires burned hotter in him at that younger age.

Yet he could not bring himself to marry Gertrude. Again he came close — he was not nearly as practical about marriage and his priority for his professional work and independence then as he became later. But he backed off when he realized that she wanted frequent dinner parties, people around constantly, and to go out often. At that time he was more ambivalent than now about a social life, and about wanting to please the woman he loved. He wanted the woman, but finally drew the line at having to oblige her to the extent he was afraid she would demand. So their affair continued, but on a subdued basis after she obtained from another man the kind of settled social and family life she wanted while continuing a warm relationship with Ellis.

In 1952 he resigned his job in New Jersey to live and work full-time in his apartment on Park Avenue in midtown Manhattan. He was practicing and known as a psychoanalyst, although he soon began to do an unusually active form of it. Always an activist, he continued to be one even in the commonly passive trade of the analyst.

He applied the approaches of Ferenczi (1955) and Adler (1955), pushing his interpretations, trying to set specific goals, suggesting ways his clients could move toward their objectives most directly. And he vigorously exploited the opportunity to search the patient's past for traumatic events and relationships.

In practice there is great variation in the application of psychoanalytic theory, from those who are extremely passive explainers of what a dream, deed, or feeling may mean, and then lapse into silence awaiting the client's reactions and projections on the purposely ambiguous figure of the analyst, to very active expounders of what a dream, feeling, or act means, and how that explains a multitude of current distraught feelings and unreasonable acts. But almost always the emphasis is on hidden meanings and unconscious deeds, and the analyst's role is kept purposely vague, to be seen by the patient in whatever distorted ways his or her unconscious and irrational feelings dictate.

Ellis soon was writing and talking critically about both the passivity of the traditional analytic posture and the unscientific ways that analysts interpreted their clients' responses. He wanted to practice analysis and be called an analyst, but he wanted to do it his way. He wanted to push to the limits of direct intervention, and counsel patients on how to take better hold of their lives and make them go more satisfactorily as soon as possible — as Ellis had learned to do with his own life.

He also wanted better confirmation and substantiation for the presumed discoveries he made about his clients' lives. He did what he called "detectiving" to uncover forgotten past experiences and feelings that caused his clients to distort and handle current situations irrationally. Above all, he wanted analysts to become more scientific in their pursuit of the truths about their clients' lives, how they had come to their unreasonable current conclusions, habits, and attitudes, and how to cure their pathologies. He wanted to validate scientifically the causes and cures of human problems.

Despite his belief that his own analysis had value, his liking for his analyst, and the privileged status his training as an analyst conferred on him in New York City, Ellis became increasingly critical of the field — from within it, at first. At first he was deferential in his criticism. In his early critical articles he complimented analytic authors while undermining their views.

In his first critical article, "Towards the Improvement of Psychoanalytic Research" (1949), after discussing examples of good and poor analytic research, Ellis concludes that "psychoanalysts, if they are consistently to uphold their own basic tenets, should be in the vanguard of those concerned with the problem of objectifying, experimentalizing, and bettering research procedures and presentations" (p. 142). He then lists four ways of improvement: training analysts in the scientific method; setting higher standards for publishing research; more critically reviewing each other's research; and striving "at all times to satisfy that portion of their superego which may be deemed the scientific conscience" (p. 142).

Six years later, in his "New Approaches to Psychotherapy Techniques" (1955), he summarized 431 articles on psychotherapy from the early 1950s as indicating, among ten major findings, that many different methods were being used after a breakout from the therapeutic mold of "expressive-emotive and insight interpretative techniques" centered in psychoanalytic and nondirective systems, toward "activity-directive and supportive therapy" (pp. 40–43). They included short-term techniques, fewer sessions a week, more equality between therapist and client, setting positive goals and values, the general philosophy to use "any technique that will help to get the client better, no matter what orthodox theory may or may not have to say" (p. 43).

In another five years, he was stating, in "An Impolite Interview with Albert Ellis" (1960b), "When I was practicing classical analysis, and later . . . psychoanalytic oriented psychotherapy . . . some of the major analytic assumptions simply do [did] not work . . . for example, you can give patients loads of insight and they still often do not get better. You can show them exactly how they got to be emotionally disturbed in the first place and again they don't significantly improve their feelings or their behavior" (n.p.). And they ". . . do not generalize their analytic transference teachings and sagely apply them to their outside relationships. . . ." He then ". . . gradually evolved the system of rational psychotherapy" (n.p.).

Ellis still does not publicly attack analysis and analysts with quite as much acerbity as he reserves for many others who disagree with his present views on therapy and sex. It is more with regret than with bitterness that he comments about his own analyst's insensitivity when Ellis visited him and his wife to introduce his girlfriend. It is the only time I can recall him expressing disappointment that he was not more welcome, better accepted.

He began to use his shockingly vulgar language around this time. He gives several different versions of how it started, and his closest friends can shed no light on how or when it developed. They do agree that it did not occur during his childhood and youth, that he was quite careful and precise about his speech then, and that he did not use even the ordinary coarse talk of the neighborhood streets when he was growing up.

Ellis provides several interpretations: Around 1950 he first used some of the disapproved words at American Psychological Association conventions as a way of being unconventional and gaining attention for the message he was presenting. When he began work with delinquents in New Jersey, he found it useful to adopt their language to get through to them. After he began to practice analysis, he was influenced by two papers by analysts who claimed that they engaged patients better by using street language. It was part of becoming his own man, discarding his jacket and tie at the same time, and even abandoning an English accent that had replaced his Bronx accent for a brief period.

In any case, probably in his late thirties, the calculated, vulgar language developed that has become one of his trademarks. It did not appear naturally, as with most people using it, who adopt it early and learn to curb it under the more respectable conditions of adult living. Rather, he has purposely cultivated it, pushing earthiness, commonality with other humans, and spectacle as a way of gaining attention and influence for his views.

Ellis claims that he is merely talking the way his clients and other listeners think, which in turn frees them to think and talk less inhibitedly. He believes that they are relieved and pleased to hear him use such familiar language. I favor his attention-getting interpretation. It does grab attention. He is a great actor in the practice of his profession and in his public appearances. This behavior contributes to his effectiveness, not so much through rapport or because it makes him seem like one of them to his clients, but because it startles them and gives him more power by gaining their awareness and then influencing them.

This period also was the beginning of his most productive years as a sexologist. He began turning out articles and books by the dozens, mounting into the hundreds over the next 25 years. Beginning with his own frustrating ignorance, Ellis started learning about the sexual field through voracious reading, and eventually through liberated living. He then passed on the information he was acquiring to friends, and finally to clients and public audiences.

He did as much sexual and marriage counseling as came his way, and had a field day in this area, which was riddled with mythology, antiquated ideas, prudishness, censorship, secrecy, and inhibition. It was ready-made for his scrutiny, acerbity, propagandizing, sermonizing, verbal power, and fluency.

Three themes predominate in Ellis's relationships with the women in his life: They remained his friends and admirers after their affairs had dwindled; he would not adapt to their desire for more socialization than he wanted; he enjoyed sex and their company, but not at the expense of his work. He systematized the characteristics of the women he had loved, with or without sex, on a seven-page list beginning when one of them (and he) was 5, and ranging to one who was 40 at the beginning of their relationship.

Before 1952 was over, Ellis finally decided to quit struggling to reform psychoanalysis and to strike out on his own. He told his clients to quit calling him a psychoanalyst, and while he continued to get calls from prospective clients who thought he still practiced analysis, he would try to talk them out of asking for it.

He had had enough of analysis himself — four years of analysis and training and three years of independent practice — and tried to persuade prospective clients to choose another form of therapy for the same reasons that had convinced him. He wanted to practice more efficiently to solve their problems through more direct action, arguing with them about their false (irrational) beliefs, and with less preoccupation about their past and how they might have developed their troubles.

Furthermore, he wanted to be more scientific. That does not mean, as it implies, that he would be doing more tough research, using quantitative measures, statistics, rigorous controls. Despite his belief in strong scientific research, he has done few such studies. He does not have adequate reason not to have if he had become as intense about it as he has about other causes. He blames lack of money and time. But his primary interests and skills always have lain elsewhere.

Ellis's forte as an adult has been as a propagandist, teacher, and demonstrator, and he exercises his most powerful influence in those areas. He has read widely and retentively in the scientific literature of psychology and psychotherapy, and he puts together what he reads critically and well, so that his views almost always incorporate the latest scientific findings in the field. But he does not choose to do basic work himself.

By seeking to be more scientific, he means being as objective, rational, and knowledgeable as possible in interpreting the facts that others have discovered, and applying them to the solution of human problems. He has done that with great power and effectiveness.

The ground was thus cleared for Ellis to develop his own theory of psychotherapy, as well as interpretations and applications of the growing body of scientific data about sex that would stamp him as a revolutionary. Thus he would enlighten humans about the most effective ways they could change their attitudes and habits so that they, in emulation of Ellis, could derive the greatest long-term pleasure from their lives.

He was also tackling head-on two of the most powerful social beliefs in the New York City culture of the time: the influence of psychoanalysis that had almost preempted the field of psychotherapy there, involving the most sophisticated and established people of the city, and the more obvious force of prudery about sex that dominated American life, despite a few sexology pioneers and literary outlaws.

Ellis was well-tempered for such opposition. He had forged himself to strike out on his own with unimpeded independence. He had no interests more compelling or seductive than his work. He had learned how to bend people to his views, with tact, acerbity, reason, and debate. He had honed his sharp mind to handle his increasingly comprehensive views and arguments. He was ready to cut loose.

7

Developing Rational-Emotive Therapy

In 1953, at age 39, practicing as a psychoanalyst in that mecca of psychoanalysis New York City, Ellis decided to give it up and to strike out with his own brand of therapy. By his account, it was a remarkably easy decision, and one about which he had no doubts nor regrets despite the fact that he had spent years establishing himself as an analyst and would have to break new ground in his views, his methods, and his private practice.

In "The Origins of Rational-Emotive Therapy (RET)" (1983c) he said of his analytic clients, "Almost all of them felt better, but alas, did not, in any realistic sense of the term, get better" (p. 29). If they did express dissatisfaction, he answered like any good analyst: "We just haven't gone deep enough yet into your repressed feelings." There never is any lack of reasons for why analysis must go on longer and deeper to achieve results even if it has already extended for years with several sessions each week.

He then noted that when he sometimes "dropped my passive, torturous mirroring of my clients' past traumas and present feelings and gave them clear-cut reassurances or encouragement," or "engaged them in involved philosophic discussions about the legitimacy of their feelings of guilt and shame," or "directly showed them and vigorously attacked their unrealistic beliefs," or "insisted that they do something outside the sessions to change themselves and gave them activity homework assignments," they might "make rapid and remarkable changes and did begin to think, feel, and act much more sensibly and happily."*

---

*Albert Ellis 1985: personal interview.

He observed further that he had used such activist methods on himself to solve his own problems from an early age, and not analytic techniques, which deal with more obscure material. Also, he had been interested primarily in philosophy, not psychology, since age 16, and enjoyed philosophical discussions with his clients. In addition, he had "always had a profound interest in efficiency," believed that "wasting time (and effort) is . . . one of the cardinal sins," and thought "that psychoanalysis was in many ways philosophically superficial and extraordinarily wasteful."*

Furthermore, "psychoanalysis was . . . in its orthodox manifestations, incredibly unscientific, dogmatic, and devout. . . . I published several papers trying to reform these antiscientific aspects" with "virtually no impact on the orthodox analytic movement."†

There was another important event that led Ellis away from psychoanalysis, and to the creation of RET. He wrote a work, begun in 1953 and published two years later, entitled "New Approaches to Psychotherapy Techniques" (1955), which emphasized that there was a wide variety of effective therapy methods that he should try to integrate into a consistent, comprehensive process.

In 1954, at the Conference on Psychoanalysis and Philosophy of Science at the Center for the Philosophy of Science at the University of Minnesota, he gave a paper entitled "An Operational Reformulation of Some of the Basic Principles of Psychoanalysis" (Ellis 1954b). In his critique of the orthodoxy and unscientific methods of psychoanalysis, he made a profound impression on his sophisticated audience with his keen mind and intellectual approach to therapy.

At first glance it may be mystifying that Ellis could get deeply involved in so esoteric a method of counseling as psychoanalysis despite his practical habits of thinking and living. He had used a very different approach throughout his childhood and youth to solve his own problems. Furthermore, most therapists then (and now) considered themselves "eclectic" and used a wide variety of methods that seemed to work, regardless of theory and without any kind of orthodoxy.

---

*Albert Ellis 1985: personal interview.

†Albert Ellis 1985: personal interview.

In any case, Ellis soon found a philosophic home in Minnesota clinical psychology, because its leader, Starke Hathaway, taught and practiced hard-headed, pragmatic methods of doing therapy that had become a tradition in the area. In fact, Hathaway (1958) had published his views in the same journal about the time of Ellis's review of psychotherapeutic techniques.

The critical insights about psychoanalysis that seemed to come so slowly to Ellis might be attributable in part to the cultural environment of New York, where psychoanalysis reigned. For several decades it was the leading edge of hope for a universal power of psychotherapy to solve human personal problems and even major social difficulties.

Over the years the main body of psychoanalysis had changed little, and critics had gradually expanded from those originally threatened by its implicit revolutionary power to include those faulting its arrest in the ideas of Freud. Some, like Jung, simply wanted to explicate subjectively based theories of their own, while others objected that psychoanalysis did not readily accept growth in knowledge about psychotherapy and incorporate scientific progress in knowledge of human behavior.

Ellis seems to have been caught up in the web of psychoanalysis that invaded and then dominated intellectual and psychological thought in New York, and he took years to extricate himself from it. Others never got so involved, and either did not so wholly embrace analysis, accepted it as only one among many ways of doing therapy, or soon abandoned the perception of it as the preeminently profound way to practice therapy. Freud himself had concluded, in his classic article on "Psychoanalysis" for the *Encyclopaedia Britannica* (14th ed.), that psychoanalysis was a scientific tool for the study of human behavior rather than a therapeutic method to produce behavior change.

In any case, Ellis created a problem for himself by embracing and schooling himself in psychoanalysis, then having to solve the problems that could have been predicted from the previously practical-minded tenor of his life. Many others were struggling with a similar problem, though it was not stated or acted upon in the same way. Phillips, for example, was writing his book *Psychotherapy: A Modern Theory and Practice* (1956) during the same years. In it he also concluded that therapy should be more active and directed to current problems and thinking, rather than an analysis of past causes.

Phillips's stance, which was more common than Ellis's, though also fueled by the parochialism of his psychoanalytic training, was dominated by his sense of "the discrepancy between the clinic and its methodological and theoretical unsophistication . . . and the world of science" (p. viii). As Paul Meehl wrote in his foreword to Phillips's book, "Dr. Phillips . . . has to unsettle us . . . before he can develop his own constructive position. . . . The tradition [of psychoanalysis] is so powerful that I suspect nothing short of such sledge-hammer blows will do the job on us" (p. vi).

Ellis began to discuss his views about "rational therapy" with a small group of professionals that started to meet with him in his apartment in 1955. Its members included Penelope Russianoff, who is still a devoted friend and follower. Although she was immediately attracted to his theory and has practiced it ever since, she differs considerably from Ellis in projecting warmth and empathy, which make her portrayal of a therapist in the movie *An Unmarried Woman* (1978) seem unlike an RETer even though she wrote her own lines. Others, too, have remained committed to RET since those earliest meetings in Ellis's apartment-office.

He first addressed a public forum about Rational Therapy at the annual convention of the American Psychological Association (APA) in 1956 and published his first article about it in 1957 (Ellis 1957b). Another basic paper, "Rational Psychotherapy" (1958a), appeared shortly after and was based on his APA talk. *How to Live with a Neurotic* (1957a) amplified his views. Since then, the outpouring of articles and books has been unceasing — the books in the dozens; the articles, lectures, and seminars in the hundreds.

Ellis began by emphasizing the logical and disputational aspects of his therapy. He argued with his clients and tried to get them to adopt more enlightened, logical, scientific views of their problems and how to solve them. He wanted them to quit blaming themselves and others, and stop burdening themselves with guilt and depression instead of trying to solve their problems directly. Ellis wanted them to adopt his view that seeking and achieving long-term satisfaction by reaching basic goals is usually the best way to gain happiness in life.

He tried to mobilize the full mental capabilities of his clients to solve their problems. Being an intellectual, he must have conveyed the notion that, in this process, the intellect had primacy over feelings. He was roundly attacked for his view. He denied that he ever intended to ignore emotion, but his own personality and speech were such that, even if he did not mean to make his theory sound so rooted in intellectual argument, he almost inevitably came through that way — and still does.

Ellis points out, however, that he is quite emotional in making his arguments, in fact has been criticized by colleagues for coming on so strongly on behalf of his views. He also believes that irritability is an emotion that he often displays, especially with people who make trivial or stupid arguments or interrupt him with phone calls. Janet Wolfe has called this to his attention.

Academicians particularly often want fewer passionate speeches and debates, and more data. So although there is little doubt that Ellis's basic method and arguments are founded largely on the value of rationality and scientific method, he does come on as "passionate and firm" (his words), even "aggressive or hostile" and "incensed" when speaking on behalf of his theories and techniques and against others.

Responding to professional criticism, Ellis soon claimed that it was not his intention to ignore emotions, that he did recognize their importance and work with them. He tried to defang his critics adding the word "emotive" to the name of his theory in 1961.

But Ellis himself is above all else an intellect-dominated person. Sheldon (1940) would have body-typed him as an Ectomorph (brain-dominated), as opposed to the Endomorph (gut-dominated) and Mesomorph (muscle-dominated). While in this theory most people are a blend of these three in various strengths, Ellis is clearly the prototypical Ectomorph with some Mesomorph thrown in. Argument is an intellectual activity; he quickly adopted it as a primary technique of his therapy. Many of his colleagues are committed to the primacy of emotions instead, and encourage their clients to identify and express feelings, to be guided by them, to live for them, to devote therapy largely to them.

Ellis does not deny the importance of emotions. Along with many others, however, he believes that emotions follow and give color to thoughts, attitudes, and actions; that they are a consequence and can be assumed to change when the mind directs changes in attitudes and deeds. It may not matter which changes first, or how, between thoughts and feelings. It does, however, seem easier and more direct to try to change ways of thinking than to change feelings, and that fact gives support to Ellis's preference.

In any case, Ellis insists that from the beginning "I have always made RET a cognitive behavioral mode of therapy and not the purely cognitive therapy that some critics erroneously keep insisting that it is."*

He writes in *Reason and Emotion in Psychotherapy* (1962): "The theoretical foundations of RET are based on the assumption that human thinking and emotion are not two ... different processes, but ... for all practical purposes, essentially the same thing. Like the other two basic life processes, sensing and moving, they are integrally interrelated and never can be seen wholly apart from each other" (p. 52).

Ellis does not claim originality except in the way he put together a consistent method of psychotherapy, drawing its strength from cognitive and behavioral theory. RET is powered by techniques of all kinds that are integrated with goals and perspectives of theory to produce change as efficiently as possible.

Ellis finds the roots of therapeutic theory mainly in ancient Greek and Roman philosophy. They are bridged to our time by various agents from a wide variety of professions, beginning with philosophers, physicians, and ministers, and more lately by psychologists, social scientists, and psychiatrists, who have applied scientific methods to the study of theories and techniques. Above all, he puts his trust in the scientific method and would put RET to that test as he would any other theory of therapy.

"More uniquely," he writes in "The Origins of Rational-Emotive Therapy (RET)" (1983c), "it is the main — perhaps really the only — form of psychotherapy that clearly hypothesizes that if people only and purely think scientifically, if they virtually never are dogmatic, absolutistic, pious, and sacramental in their attitudes toward themselves, toward other humans, and toward the world, practically all their 'emotional' disturbance ... would disappear or be minimized" (p. 3). If his views were not to hold up under the scrutiny of scientific method, "I hope that significant changes ... and important modifications ... will continually take place" (p. 3).

The founding tenet of RET, from Epictetus, is that men are disturbed by the views they take of things. Further, "When, therefore, we are hindered, or disturbed, or grieved, let us never impute it to others, but to ourselves; that is, to our own views" (Epictetus, *Enchiridion*, 1897, p. 218), and "Demand not that

---

*Albert Ellis 1985: personal interview.

events should happen as you wish; but wish them to happen as they do happen, and you will go on well" (p. 219).

The first injunction is the most crucial one underpinning Ellis's theory. The latter ones give force to his disputational methods placing responsibility on the client to change after accepting life as it truly is rather than distorted to what one wants it to be.

Despite the fact that he does not cite the other relevant injunctions of Epictetus, Ellis has pursued the other instructions given above as his own, as much as the one he so invariably quotes. It is fundamental to his philosophy that you accept responsibility for your fate — whether you have been victimized or not — so that you will make every effort to change and control it. Further, you had best accept the world as it is, not as you want it to be, so that you can cope with it realistically.

What he has named the "ABCs of RET" are as follows: A stands for "Activating" events or experiences that affects us. B stands for "Beliefs," the ways we see and interpret the As. C stands for the "Consequences" that follow the Bs, after whatever distortions we introduce into our perceptions of As. Our beliefs about our experiences may be rational, in which case we adapt well to the events, or they may be irrational, in which case we don't handle them effectively because we see them in a distorted or unrealistic way, and thus cannot react successfully to them (Ellis 1973, pp. 56-60).

What gets us into trouble is that instead of seeing our environment and events objectively, as they truly exist, we distort them in our minds. This produces our irrational reactions and behavior that are not well adapted to the world as it really is; thus we cannot solve our problems. We create justifications for our unhappy feelings and behavior (defenses); we feel sorry for ourselves, depressed or guilty; we may strike back, retreat, and otherwise twist ourselves to avoid, flee, or ignore the true problems and their solutions that would give us satisfaction.

Ellis believes that we are born with the capacity to see matters wrongly and to reach false conclusions about them. Furthermore, we can be reared in ways that nurture these wrong-minded attitudes and habits. It then becomes the task of the therapist to help change these maladaptive attitudes and habits to more objective, accepting, and problem-solving ones.

The wrong-minded cognitions can range from "cold" to "hot," the cold ones being the most objective and requiring little therapeutic attention; the warm ones sometimes leading to medium upset that can be accepted and let be; the hot cognitions tending to lead to more serious feelings of disturbance that need to be changed in therapy by the substitution of reasonable reactions for such unsatisfactory results as rebuff, failure, conflict, rejection.

Extreme and rigid rules for living are the troublemakers: One must always be liked, by everyone; one must always succeed; one must always be happy; and so forth. The world will rarely provide such invariable satisfactions, the absolutist beliefs will seldom be fulfilled, and therefore, for longer-term satisfaction, one had better be convinced of and adopt different, more realistic perceptions of the world and the consequences of disappointment.

Thus the focus of attack in RET becomes such beliefs as "If I don't do well, it's awful, and I'm terrible"; "If I don't get what I want, I can't stand it, I'll be utterly miserable"; "If I fail at something, it's because I'm a worthless person who deserves nothing better." The sense of disaster has to be countered. "Musts," "awfuls," and "shoulds" are anathema to Ellis, and need to be replaced by "desires, wishes, and preferences" (Ellis 1973, pp. 164–165).

Ellis has documented prodigiously the ways in which humans distort their world and their roles in it. He will argue in any way at hand in order to clear the air for more rational, coping views of what is causing trouble for clients. Following that, he prescribes tasks stemming from the improved perceptions that will move them efficiently toward their goals. What clients need to learn and apply are the methods of science: seeing situations objectively, devising ways to solve the problems, applying and experimenting with such methods, modifying or replacing them until solutions are found.

Ellis's focus is mainly "on human survival and happiness rather than on any absolutistic or authoritarian world order," with emphasis on "will and choice rather than rigid determinism or fate.* He has been called a rationalist, but he rejects that notion because he does not consider the rational life as an end in itself, but only as a means. His goal is pleasure, satisfying one's desires. That is leavened by the ideas of not hurting others in the process, of choosing among various pleasures when they conflict, and of

---

*Albert Ellis 1986: personal interview.

giving priority to those which will bring the longest-term and most profound satisfactions.

Ellis may expect too much fine adjusting from clients in this process, and too much similarity to himself. He is so rational, so intellectual in his ways of handling his own life, so clearly a model of thoughtful and social-minded living and goal orientation, that he may overestimate the capacities and intentions of others in these regards. There is little doubt that he does achieve many remarkably good results. The literature of RET is replete with results reported by others. But his personal model is nevertheless beyond the reach, or even the wish, of many.

He adopts all kinds of therapeutic techniques from almost any source, even when they may have no special relationship to the basic theory of RET. They could as well belong to any other form of therapy. The stress Rogers put on the therapist's unconditional positive regard for his clients, for example, Ellis from the beginning adopted as his own. He has stated that he and Rogers are the only major therapy theorists who take this stance.*

Ellis criticizes therapists who indulge their own needs during therapy sessions. He encourages the appreciation of, but not love for, the therapist, and totally rejects any sexual relationship with clients. He emphasizes the role of the therapist in helping clients to become successfully independent of, rather than dependent upon, the therapist. He encourages clients to accept and endure temporary pain in order to gain their goals. Therapy is hard work.

He will use lectures, publications, diaries, schedules, groups, homework, seminars, demonstrations, group sessions to advance therapy. Anything Ellis reads, hears, or thinks might possibly be useful, he is apt to try out to decide on its value. He rejected some methods after trial — for example, long, unrelieved, locked-in days and weekends of intense propaganda. He shortened his rational encounter marathons to 14 hours instead of 48 hours because he decided he could accomplish the same results in the shorter time.

Ellis demonstrated the practicality and value of conducting the first to eighth years of grade school for children at the Institute, then abandoned it because it didn't work out the way he wanted: to be able to study its results over time. Despite apparently good

---

*Albert Ellis 1986: personal interview.

outcomes, parents would take their children out after only a year or two because they moved, got divorced, wanted more extensive facilities, or a wide range of other reasons, so good follow-up research became impossible.

Like many other therapists, Ellis has rejected the value of pretherapy assessment and clinical team meetings to try to diagnose and plan the treatment of new clients. His Institute uses neither routinely. Some of his staff do diagnostic testing, and senior staff do supervise and consult about therapy.

Phillips (1985) has published extensive research indicating that early termination rates for new clients are similar in a wide range of settings. He concludes that therapists should adapt to the fact that clients often terminate therapy before their therapists think they should, because they have gained what they wanted from treatment. The therapist is not prepared for such early results, and calls these patients "dropouts." Even team meeting time is wasteful, often taking more time than the eventual therapy (Wiener & Raths 1959). Ellis wastes no such time extending treatment or using teams. He works as fast as he can.

Clients make demands on themselves and others that get them into trouble.* They often insist upon absolutes: "I must have this or that"; "Others must act this way or that"; "I can't stand it if this or that happens"; "I'm a rotten person if I can't do this or that." The therapist then proceeds to confront the client with the fact that events do not cause the troubled reactions; rather, the way the client sees or interprets the events causes the trouble. He instructs them in how perceptions or cognitions can be changed so that the client sees them differently, as problems to be solved by flexible positions and means rather than inflexible attitudes and methods.

D and E have been added to the original ABCs of RET. D stands for Disputation, in which the therapist disputes clients' irrational beliefs until the clients learn, by example, how to argue with themselves. They then come to E, a new Effect, the habit of considering problems and events that occur in their lives in more rational, problem-solving ways. Therapy may still be needed in case problems cannot (yet) be surmounted, but only so long as it takes for clients to be able to practice on their own the philosophy that the RET therapist seeks to imbue (Ellis 1973, pp. 59–60).

---

*Albert Ellis 1985: personal interview.

Much else could be written here about RET. But it is described elsewhere in this book and surveyed extensively in the literature. Mostly the literature restates and extends these principles and techniques of effective practices. Ellis has in general adopted any that appear to change behavior effectively, from whatever source. He is impatient with passivity and endless analysis. He favors active methods because they are more efficient.

He is fixed on solving problems, so he tends to ignore methods that simply elicit feelings but do not try directly to resolve difficulties in handling life's predicaments. He does not consider approaches that minimize use of intellectual powers, although he and his staff will sometimes refer clients to physicians for psychotropic drugs when they might facilitate accessibility to RET. They also recommend good health measures and giving up alcohol and drugs when they interfere with the thinking process.

Ellis speaks powerfully to his patients, in a firm, clear, strong voice that may at times overwhelm them with its forceful arguments and confidence. He has laid himself on the line in public far more than any other therapist, putting on countless demonstrations before thousands of people, with members of the audience presenting their problems to him in front of the group.

Almost invariably he comes off very well, impressive for his consistency in practicing his beliefs, his sharpness in delineating problems, and his ability to suggest intelligent lines of solutions on the spot. His commitment to RET and his steadiness in practicing it in such situations overshadow the possibility that he will come through like a newspaper or TV counselor, improvising answers without an underlying theory.

The elements of RET shine clearly through everything Ellis says, writes, and lives. He has held essentially the same attitudes from childhood. When he did begin to organize, write, and speak them in the 1950s, when he was in his late thirties, he immediately attracted followers, a small group that has grown into the thousands, perhaps hundreds of thousands, in all walks of life, from street people in New York to bankers in Kuwait.

Dozens, perhaps hundreds, of methods of relatively practical actions to solve human problems have been described and even given names during this century. The newer developments are in a line of direct-action theories that rose from the ferment of the 1950s, as an expression of dissatisfaction with the dominant passive-emotional-analytic therapies.

Theories have proliferated since then, centering on cognitive or cognitive-behavioral views, based upon research findings about how thoughts and attitudes can both generate and solve problems, and also on how behavioral conditions can both create and resolve problems. Sometimes they are combined, so that methods of changing thoughts are combined with methods of changing behavior by direct action through rewards and withholding rewards (sometimes called punishment). Kendall and Bemis (1983) have comprehensively described some of these approaches.

Ellis created the first of the theories Kendall and Bemis describe, but did not substantiate it with quality research. Others did good but very limited research on specific problems. Ellis's early deficiency in spelling out his specific methods was later corrected, but he shares with all theorists the problem of rhetoric and claims that outrun their scientific underpinnings.

Even Skinner, whose theory had experimental laboratory study as its foundation, has been far more widely applied than his research justifies. Freud's data were almost entirely subjective. Rogers did some of the best scientific research on therapy, but his method faded because of its limited power.

Some new theories rose as much in opposition to Ellis's demanding didactic habits as from disagreement with his basic grounding in Epictetus. Most scientists conclude that research has not yet carried us to a unified theory. So Ellis with his RET competes in a crowded marketplace. Its most novel notion was to change self-defeating irrational attitudes and thoughts by a variety of methods that he specifies, mainly through intellectual arguments. Then the troublesome behavior will be modified because it will be interpreted differently, and new behavior will be practiced.

His views have not changed fundamentally since his early years. His own life is his message; the two are integral. Resuming his life history at this point will indicate how he has given force to his movement, amplified it, propagandized for it — and enlarged his own life in various professional directions while restricting it ever further in the ordinary wasteful, sporadic ways of human beings.

8

Settling In

In 1953, having quit struggling to reform psychoanalysis into a more scientific, active, and pragmatic method, and telling his patients to stop calling him a psychoanalyst, Ellis struck out boldly to practice and preach his own form of therapy. He was living and working in a one-bedroom apartment at 56 Park Avenue, in mid-town Manhattan.

For a couple of years more, however, he continued to criticize psychoanalysis, meanwhile experimenting with other approaches and developing and expressing his own rapidly formulating ideas. He utilized Ferenczi's notions about active techniques, tried Carl Rogers's idea of empathizing with patients' feelings, and applied Adler's concepts about setting goals and assigning concrete tasks to help clients to achieve them. But he had become "highly disillusioned with practicing psychoanalysis . . . and used some Adlerian approaches . . . [even before] I became a psychoanalyst."*

Within a few years Ellis had developed his own views sufficiently to invite a small group of colleagues to join a seminar in his apartment to discuss his ideas. One of the earliest members of his little discussion group was Penelope Russianoff, mentioned earlier, a psychologist still practicing in New York City who has since become best friends with Ellis's present companion, Janet Wolfe.

---

*Albert Ellis 1984: personal interview.

It is difficult to detect that Dr. Russianoff thought she was portraying herself as a follower of RET in her movie role previously mentioned. It may well be that way with others of Ellis's followers whose style may differ greatly from his, though the content of therapy may be the same or similar.

Sitting in on his seminar with his staff, I found it difficult at times to recognize that the others were attempting to do the same therapy as he. True, they did use the same concepts and the same phrases, but their power, compared with his, was substantially attentuated by their lesser forcefulness, their lack of self-confidence, their weaker zest for contesting with clients and trying to override their objections. Probably no one sounds as much like Albert as his brother did, even though Paul was an accountant and had never practiced therapy. But his brother's manner of talking and giving advice was nonetheless much more similar to Albert's than is that of most of those who try to imitate him in conducting therapy.*

Ellis can be quite rigorous about presentations of RET. Despite his professional generosity, open-mindedness, and acceptance of argumentation, he refused to endorse and write an introduction to a demonstration recording by his good friend and loyal follower Penelope Russianoff and her collaborator. He thought she did not present RET accurately enough, and included some psychoanalytic interpretations objectionable to him. They remain good friends, though she was disappointed by his rebuff.

Russianoff recalls very well those early years when RET was developing. Many colleagues dismissed Ellis as "ridiculous," derided him because he had rejected psychoanalysis, and belittled his aggressive presentations of his own beliefs. But he also had his admirers even in those early days. They grew in numbers year by year as he extended his influence through his forceful personality and unceasing flow of oratory, demonstrations, and writing.

In the exchange of clients between Russianoff and Ellis, she has referred to him her toughest, most recalcitrant ones who needed shaking up, while she warms those he refers to her who find him too aggressive and grating. Some have told her that they believe he's a brilliant therapist, but "prefer her womanliness and warmth."

---

*Paul Ellis 1986: personal interview.

Russianoff believes that Ellis has become even less sociable with age because he has a sense of time running out, and "he really wants to leave a legacy."* He maintains, however, that he prefers work to any social distractions because that is what gives him maximum enjoyment.

Russianoff has tried very hard over the years to get him to her and her husband's place in Connecticut. But he hates the country, and will not go there any more. He also finds most social conversation "pretty much a waste of time after 15 minutes," even though he likes most people.† His present companion, Janet, goes to the Russianoffs' most weekends.

Ellis was quite abrasive in his earlier years and remains so, sporadically, even today though he has moderated greatly. It takes considerably more provocation to set him off now. When quite young, he became fairly impervious to criticism, argument, and sarcasm from adversaries, and in fact seemed to enjoy doing battle with them.

To those who would, under similar circumstances, be troubled with guilt, obsessive anger, depression, insomnia, or other emotional reactions, Ellis (1982) writes: "I think that I can honestly say that I have not had a single day — hell, even an hour! — of anxiety, depression, self-downing, or self-pity in about forty-five years. Nor do I intend to have one in the future."

On can reasonably doubt the validity of such a statement from any human being. Even though Ellis is far superior to most in putting his philosophy to work successfully, there is reason to be dubious even about him. Several friends and acquaintances have observed apparent discrepancies in such bravado.

There was the time, for example, in the late 1960s when a colleague observed the deputy mayor of Edmonton, Canada, serve as moderator of Ellis's keynote address on sexual problems at a national counselors' meeting. Appalled by both his language and his notions, she gently but firmly vented her feelings in language something like this: "Dr. Ellis, I really don't know whether our people up here have the kind of problems you so ably discussed, but if I hear of anyone who has, I'll refer them to you."**

---

*Penelope Russianoff 1986: personal interview.

†Albert Ellis 1984: personal interview.

**Dr. Henry Borow 1986: personal communication.

At an open house afterward, Ellis seemed mystified and hurt — "wounded" was the word the observer used — as if chastised by one's mother. This story is not unique. Others who know him well refer to his disappointment about not being elected to certain offices, not being sufficiently honored as a leader in his main fields of sex and therapy, or having ex-followers or friends criticize him.

One cannot know whether such people are projecting on him how they would feel about such slights, but I, too, would interpret some events I've observed as indicating hurt. He would call his reactions minor, however, being "a few moments of silence" that "don't include self-pity and self-downing."

In any case, Ellis has engaged in lively conflict all of his life, has developed a highly skilled public speaker's and debater's ability to persuade and overwhelm his adversaries, and almost always keeps his attacks and reactions impersonal. He does manage pretty well to practice his trust in attacking attitudes and beliefs, but not the person expressing them.

In the early 1950s when he was just beginning to make his mark as an independent in the field of psychotherapy, criticizing psychoanalysts in their den of New York City and asserting his own notions of an aggressive, direct, relatively new formulation of therapy, he was subject to much vituperation.

While Ellis almost always tried to depersonalize and to welcome debate and criticism, he likely did experience some down moments. Particularly he seemed to react when he felt let down by friends, personally attacked, or a failure at persuasion by what he considered to be outstanding arguments and scientific data.

Meanwhile, he did not neglect his other major interest, sex, in either his professional or his personal life. In the early to mid-1950s, he laid the groundwork for his reputation as perhaps the world's leading sexologist since Havelock Ellis, to whom, incidentally, he was not related (despite the FBI report linking them). Kinsey probably assumed that role when his research became widely known, and later, it was taken by Masters and Johnson, but Ellis remained the outstanding popularizer of their scientific data, which he almost immediately incorporated into his own writing.

At that time he began a prolific outpouring of books and articles about sex that only recently has almost ceased. Lately he has concluded that "I have said just about all I have to say about the subject."* One of his last major works about sex was to correct what he considered to be a growing body of egregious nonsense about how to succeed at sex, *The Sensuous Person* (1972). Later books on sex updated earlier publications and included *Sex and the Liberated Man* (1976), and *The Intelligent Woman's Guide to Dating and Mating* (1979).

In 1953, Ellis published *Sex, Society and the Individual* (Pillay & Ellis 1953); in 1954, *The American Sexual Tragedy* (1954a) and *Sex Life of the American Woman and the Kinsey Report* (1954c); in 1956, *The Psychology of Sex Offenders* (Ellis & Brancale 1956); in 1958, *Sex without Guilt* (1958b); and in 1960, *The Art and Science of Love* (1960a), which became the most popular guide to sexual practices for many years.

Besides his numerous books and professional and public articles on sex, he lectured both to his profession and to the public, and for a couple of years wrote a column in *Penthouse* magazine.

Ellis's sexual ideas were original, forceful, rebellious against conventional thinking, assertive of human freedom and independence, and philosophically consistent with his views on psychotherapy. (His sexual views will be the subject of a separate chapter.) He was able to handle both of his favorite fields of interest with force and influence, with consistency, and without disadvantage. To sex he brought his rational goal and methods of achieving harmless, long-term pleasure in whatever ways were preferred, without guilt.

His adversaries remained the conservatives, in both areas, who were sensitive to his attacks and to his freshly emphasized, though not necessarily new, notions of seeking long-term pleasure that did not harm anyone.

Despite the fact that Ellis has always managed to get his professional books and articles published, in the 1950s it was not easy. While he has been accepted by some of the larger and best established publishers, such as Prentice-Hall and McGraw-Hill, the overwhelming majority of his books have been published by less known and more adventuresome presses, mainly Lyle Stuart.

Until 1959, he could not get his books on sex advertised, much less reviewed, in the *New York Times,* despite his sharp letter to that paper, which he was as willing to tackle as he would any street critic. Because of his particular difficulties with some of his writings about sex, in 1965 he published a paperback

---

*Albert Ellis 1985: personal interview.

entitled *Suppressed: Seven Key Essays Publishers Dared not Print* (1965b).

Ellis's most studied criticism of psychoanalysis, though he was not quite ready with his substitute, came in a paper delivered in 1954 at the University of Minnesota Center for the Philosophy of Science, "An Operational Reformulation of Some of the Basic Principles of Psychoanalysis" (1954b). In it he discussed the scientific status of psychoanalysis and his objections to it, mainly its unscientific foundations, its disinterest in rigorous research and critical scrutiny, and its weakness in translating its theories into practical methods of changing human behavior.

He had been invited to present his views formally to this sophisticated and critical audience of philosophers and scientists by Herbert Feigl, cofounder of the Center, a notable "Logical Positivist" philosopher who had so named his school of philosophy (later calling himself a "Logical Empiricist" to emphasize his scientific commitment). Feigl had been analyzed in Vienna by Jokl, a student of Freud's, in a culture where enlightenment included being steeped in psychoanalysis.

Ellis received a warm reception from Starke Hathway and Paul Meehl (a cofounder of the Center), the leading clinical psychologists in Minnesota. They valued Ellis's outspoken criticism of what they viewed as the fuzzy-mindedness of most therapy theorists at that time, and the need for a vigorous spokesman for smart problem-solving methods applied to human difficulties. Above all, they appreciated his intelligence, his application of it to try to clean up vagueness and mysticism in the field, and his emphasis on intellectual activity to accomplish behavior change.

Meehl, who has called himself a "sixty percent RETer," has continued to be drawn to psychoanalysis, torn between his "Dust Bowl empiricism" and the intellectual stimulation he found in analytic theory.* He takes a reconciling stance between RET practice and analytic theory with which Ellis is not comfortable.

In 1956, Ellis presented his theory of therapy to a public professional audience for the first time, at the annual meeting of the American Psychological Association in Chicago, and published his first paper, based on the oral presentation, in 1958 (1958a). The same views were amplified in his first book on rational therapy *How to Live with a Neurotic* (1957a).

---

*Paul Meehl 1984: personal interview.

While science generally proceeds through both revolution and evolution, it is almost always possible to find in contemporary psychology and the other sciences concerned with human behavior, prime elements dating back to early philosophers, particularly Greeks and Romans. Other ancient cultures may contain equally related philosophies, but they are not as well known in the United States and Europe.

In any case, Ellis's theories sparkled clearly while similar views were still struggling unfocussed, and he early attracted devoted professional followers and clients. He rose more cleanly than all but a handful of other psychologists from the widespread ferment about psychotherapy in the 1950s, as it was struggling to become more specifically problem-oriented and intellectually powered.

In the 1950s and 1960s, many psychologists were impressed with Ellis's keen mind, his demonstrated clinical skills, his forensic ability, and the practicality of his views in his speeches. There were other psychologists with very bright, creative minds who also were speaking and writing provocatively about therapy: Rogers, Skinner, Mowrer, Sullivan, Phillips, and George Kelly, among others.

Many colleagues did not acknowledge Ellis as first among the new theorists who were developing useful cognitive systems, while some sympathizers, particularly intellectuals and academics, were put off by the vulgarity of his language and the simplistic nature of his design and presentation. At times, he sounded to them like a midwesterner's view of a populist New York street politician: crude, tense, posed for attack, argumentative, judgmental about good and bad in his field.

As they have become better acquainted with Ellis's work, and he has endured and enlarged his skills, they have acknowledged his solid and original contributions. At times he still presents himself somewhat abrasively, on occasion vulgarly, and very aggressively. He hides and denies his sensitivity, moments of doubt, softer feelings that would have made him more endearing.

In the mid-1950s Ellis offended many conservatives in his profession and the public, as well as those who had their own axes to grind, who were set to resist his claims and powers of persuasion. He was most attractive to people who liked strongly assertive behavior and objective criticism, who had respect for the intellect, who were not provoked to defend their habitual views.

In addition to those his personality offended, there were and still are those in psychology who do not want to admit that he was foremost among contemporary psychologists to define the irrational attitudes that generate self-defeating behavior and the use of intellectual powers by human beings to change their lives.

Several of the psychologists previously cited claim to have initiated the notion that rational thinking strategies needed taking apart for study just as much as the Freudian irrational ones. In many reviews of the cognitive therapy literature, Ellis's publications of the mid-1950s were ignored, and he was equated with psychologists of the 1960s and 1970s in developing ideas about the intellectual control and direction of behavior.

Does it matter who came first, except for the egos of those directly involved? Certainly not to the march of science. What is validated over time may be associated with one person or another, often through chance publication or timing or because of the superior verbal fluency of the one who best put fragmented views together for the profession and public — as Freud did so eloquently. There is little doubt, however, that Ellis most forcefully first put into the context of modern psychology and psychotherapy the view that it was not events, but how we view them, that determines our problems, and also how we can use our rational powers to solve them.

In writing of William James, Kazin (1983) commented: "William was to credit his recovery from depression to his belief that he could prove the freedom of the will by exercising his freedom . . . his way of thinking is that of a man arguing himself out of one difficulty after another" (p. 4). Does anyone come closer to defining Ellis's way of life and therapy?

Ellis was not only powerfully developing and promoting his views of psychotherapy and sex; he was taking an active part in many other professional activities as well. He has been a professional joiner, founding, belonging to, and taking leadership in many psychological organizations working to advance psychotherapy, family and marriage counseling, sexual enlightenment, humanitarian goals generally, scientific rigor, anthropology, joint activity in the social sciences, hypnosis, private practice, and anti-nuclear concerns. His latest Who's Who (Marquis Who's Who in America, 1986–1987) biography lists membership in over a dozen organizations.

Ellis was also involved with women. Since his maturity, they have almost always been his best friends as he reveled in sex, and sometimes even lived with them. He has never lived with males outside his family residence, and seldom with females except for his later years with his second wife, Rhoda, and with his present companion, Janet. He did, however, live with his first wife for a year despite their annulment, and with another woman for a summer, both when he was in his twenties.

He has not lived well with anyone except for his family, with whom he stayed in close quarters, in fair harmony, into his twenties. For the women he has lived with, there has almost always been a problem with his disinterest in socializing. They expected some recreation with him, as his family never did. But they never succeeded in diverting him much from his devotion to his work.

Ellis's second wife was Rhoda Winter, a dancer, to whom he was introduced in 1955 by a psychoanalyst friend who had known her when she was studying and working at the University of Wisconsin. After three months of spending much time with each other, they decided to live together. Not being able to find a larger apartment to live in where he could keep his work somewhat separate from their living quarters, she took an apartment in a building across the street from his. They kept this arrangement for four months, got married in 1956, and then were able to rent a second apartment in the same complex where he had his office. They lived in the two apartments at the Parc Vendome on West 56th Street until she moved to California, where she continued to dance. He remained at the Parc Vendome until he moved into his Institute building in 1965.

Rhoda was bright, attractive, well educated, and dedicated to her work much as he was, so he was not afraid of having his time preempted by her demands for companionship. They delighted in each other's sexual responsiveness and openness. They were due to be filmed by Kinsey; Albert was, but Kinsey died before recording Rhoda.

Rhoda was almost young enough to be his daughter. When they married, she was 24 and he was 42 but that never seemed to be a problem. Her second marriage was also to a man 17 years her senior. The marriage to Albert lasted two and a half years. He thinks it was good for about a year and a half. They disagree on the reason for the divorce; she says its came from her desire to live in California, while he claims that she became dependent after an injury.

They had perhaps his most socially companionable longer-term relationship. Ellis was willing to go out with her to dance performances and parties that were important to her. They even considered having a child. They seldom saw each other except after 11 P.M., when he would return to their apartment for dinner, and on weekends. Now, almost 30 years later, that is still the pattern of his life with Janet. Both he and Rhoda were very busy at other times with their professions so this arrangement suited them both well.

Rhoda visited California and found its lifestyle a "revelation," relatively free of the intellectualism and regimentation in New York. She wanted to stay there to practice as a movement therapist and to continue dancing. She then filed for divorce with Albert's willing consent.

Albert's acerbity when discussing RET had bothered Rhoda. She couldn't understand why at social gatherings he came on so strong with his theories that he offended people, and why he insisted on living so regimented a life. She also believed that some of his asociability came from wanting to avoid germs. He does protect his health rigorously, and it seems to pay off.

She remembers being annoyed, too, by the way he treated her cat and commented on her dog after their divorce, acting as if the animals were totally bothersome impediments. He has this manner about children also. He inquired some years ago about my "brats," and asked Meehl's little daughter once about her sex life. He's not likely to ingratiate himself over creatures that do not enter his life directly.

He and Rhoda remain friendly, retain respect for each other, and make no bitter or critical comments about each other or their breakup. It was a calm and rational event. It was so amicable, in fact, that Rhoda says some of her friends were encouraged to seek divorces if they didn't need to be adversarial. She, like his first wife, and his present companion, considers him to be a genius, and never argued much with him. In fact, she taught movement therapy at the Institute after their divorce, in the late 1960s and 1970s. He has since visited her, and she has visited him and Janet.

Rhoda says that "Albert underneath that discipline is a very, very sensitive person," that he can, in a narrow area, "experience joy and be deeply hurt — but not be very troubled." "I think," she remarks, "he's just as human as anyone else. . . . He doesn't take time to show it."*

Sometime before marrying Rhoda, Ellis had a physical exam for life insurance to protect her. It was then, at age 42, that he was formally diagnosed as having diabetes. When he was 19, he had been determined to have renal glycosuria, which is often a precursor of diabetes. It required no treatment. He had sugar in

*Rhoda Winter 1986: personal interview.

his urine but not in his blood. At 40, boils had suddenly appeared on his back, another precursor of diabetes, but they disappeared on the low-fat, high-protein diet he instituted. His sister was diagnosed as having renal glycosuria several years after Albert, and she, too, later developed diabetes.

Ellis began a treatment routine that has remained essentially the same ever since. Almost immediately he began injecting insulin, eating eight to nine times daily, including one or two sandwiches when he awoke at night. Initially, on four meals, he had quickly lost several pounds. He eliminated almost all sugar, cream, and desserts, and limited fats. His small, frequent repasts, then and now, consist almost entirely of two hot meals a day, sandwiches of peanut butter or low-salt cheese, and raw fruit.

Ellis claims to have accepted immediately the diagnosis of diabetes and its consequences, and to have had no adjustment problems. There never has been any evidence otherwise (except as noted). He has practically always acted and appeared to be healthy, except for minor accidents. Even at 74 he is active, vital, and alert far above average.

He has had no important side effects from diabetes with one exception: Until he reduced his insulin dosage, he was having shock reactions two or three times a year. Observers have said they were quite funny; he sometimes acted, and was taken for, drunk, though he does not drink. He swore, made outrageous comments to whomever was around, was wild, bizarre, and loud. Janet and Harper were not amused. Janet was quite concerned that he easily could hurt himself or get into trouble when she was not around. One night he entered his elevator, naked, in his bathrobe while going into shock. Fortunately, she awoke, found him, and gave him a glass of sugared juice, which promptly restored him.

He's therefore had to make adjustments in his insulin dosage. From the time he began the shots, the insulin had built up slowly until his mid-sixties. Janet finally objected that he was too irritable and was having too many hypoglycemic episodes. She took him to a diabetes specialist, who cut his insulin dosage to 24 units. He has kept his blood sugar level under control through regular self-administered blood tests, and no further hypoglycemic reactions have occurred.

Ellis's writing poured on, including books and articles by the dozens. Most of his publications up to the 1960s were about sex. He had formed his views about it in a satisfying and stable way before he did about psychotherapy, and presented liberal attitudes and education in it before he developed his expertness in psychotherapy.

He did not, however, have any coherent new theory about sex or how to practice sexual therapy uniquely, nor did he ever develop one — nor has anyone else. Eventually, though, he would apply RET to sexual problems in the same way as to other human problems; they proved to be no different from any other human difficulties in their susceptibility to his form of therapy.

Masters and Johnson (1970) have perhaps come closest to a unique view and practice of sexual treatment. Even they, however, along with the Ellises (Havelock and Albert) and Kinsey, made their contributions primarily by encouraging the liberated and extended practice of sex more than with an original theory of treatment. Even they, who have concentrated on therapy, have been able to contribute only a few new techniques for overcoming impotence and frigidity.

In 1959 Ellis founded and incorporated the Institute for Rational Living, located in his Park Avenue apartment. Initially he was its first and only officer, executive director, which is still his title, although now there are many other directors and staff. It was dedicated to treating and educating the public in Rational Therapy. It did not have its own home and staff until he moved into its present building in 1965. To it was added a second institute founded for professional training, with eventually the sole name of the Institute for Rational-Emotive Therapy.

Ellis was by now well established in the structure and content of what would become his lifelong activities: educating the public and the profession in RET, practicing it, and training others in it; and conducting sex education. He did not waver significantly from those goals over the next three decades, which brings us to the present. He did, however, continually expand the scope of his activities in these areas.

Nor did his personal life develop much beyond this point. He managed, despite his early divorce and stance against remarriage, to continue to live his hermitic social life, though he remained active sexually. For most of the next quarter-century he had a companion, Janet Wolfe, with whom he lived congenially and fondly. He had found a stable maturity that permitted him maximum productivity in the areas he valued most: advancing his views of therapy and sex, and helping liberate humankind by teaching it how to live more rationally and pleasurably.

9

Ellis on Sex

Albert Ellis remembers savoring sexual pleasure from early childhood on. His earliest bliss came from an "affair" when he and Ruthie took to feeling each other. He had almost penetrated her manually before their parents burst into the room, the mothers shrieking their horror, the fathers letting the mothers go at it. At six, he led the other children in his hospital ward in nighttime peeking at each other's naked bodies with flashlights, and getting aroused.

He fell in love with the female children and nurses when he was hospitalized, and felt warmly about them and many of the other females he encountered throughout his childhood. But he didn't have intercourse until, in his twenties, after he had married — and even then not until the marriage was annulled.

At first Ellis had vague sexual stirrings that he could not even imagine in practice. He yearned for something nameless, inspired by the faces and bodies of the girls he fell in love with, until he was seven or eight. Then he concretely imagined intercourse and other forms of sex.

Since then, longing and love have dwindled in his thoughts and vocabulary; now he talks specifically about sex and companionship, and has little time for the passions and vagaries of romantic notions. Even before he was into his sixties, he had gotten quite practical about sexual relationships. They were friendly, congenial, mutual — but terminated when they became inconvenient, or he left town and returned home.

His passions are still aroused, however. In objecting to my reference to his ardor cooling with age, Ellis hastily compiled and sent me a list of all the women he could readily remember with whom "I have been enamored — and I mean enamored, not merely sexually attracted to or involved with."* It includes 84 first names, chronologically arranged and assessed physically, by age and religion, year of involvement, and nature of the relationship.

Most of the associations did not involve sex (especially on the first and last pages), and most of the women were in their twenties and thirties. The oldest one was 40 at the onset of the relationship. He begins his list with Ruthie, age five. Besides age, he covered a wide gamut of other attributes, though he summarized his tabulated preferences as "tall, big breasted, attractive, very bright, quite sexy females."† It's remarkable how sustained his lust apparently could be without inhibitions except for doing no harm, or forcing himself on the women. Perhaps more humans could similarly flourish into old age if they mentally freed themselves to do so.

There is a side of Ellis that is not seen by an outside observer, but that he asserts and is confirmed by women who have known him intimately: He has quickly and passionately fallen in love, and has intensely pursued the objects of his ardor. But he does not permit them to distract him from his work.

His most passionate and sustained love affair was with Gertrude, in his late twenties and early thirties. It remained strong for three or four years, then continued companionably for the rest of her life. He had apparently lost much of that sustained heat by the time he married for a second time at age 43. By then he was speaking of affection, companionship, sex, the woman's beauty, and two strong, independent careers that did not impinge upon each other. The passion kept erupting, but not the intensity nor the continuity.

In subsequent affairs, Ellis considered himself and the women involved to be equal and congenial comrades rather than fiery lovers whose passions dominated their lives. It is that kind of cool, deliberate competence, friendship, and sex that has ruled his subsequent liaisons — and shaped his writings on sexuality.

In his views of sex, as in those on psychotherapy, his life and writings are consistent with each other. He lives what he expounds. Thus the nature of his sex life until his mid-thirties,

---

*Albert Ellis 1986: personal correspondence.

†Albert Ellis 1986: personal correspondence.

when he began his outpouring of publications about sex, has crucial relevance for his writing. He did not write extensively on sex until he had settled into his present pattern of behavior, until he had burned off the youthful anxiety that frustrated him into his late twenties, until he had learned how to get what he wanted from it.

By then Ellis had damped the passion that might have inspired novels, but not the cool and often scientific treatises that he finally did produce to educate the public and his professional colleagues about sexual practices. If he once had produced such heat in his novels, he no longer wrote in romantic tone in his professional works. He still felt, but did not express, the passion.

His first book on *The Folklore of Sex* (1951), published when he was 38, was written when he was still working for the State of New Jersey and was editor of two journals about marriage and sex. It was based upon his extensive reading of the popular and professional literature of the day, and cited thousands of references. Essentially, he chose a day at midcentury, January 1, 1950, to document what the media were saying about sex — and his rejoinders to them.

Ellis included an eclectic mix ranging from Nelson Algren to *Walt Disney Comics,* the *Catholic Digest* to *Vogue* to the *Psychoanalytic Review.* He considered the movie *Sands of Iwo Jima,* the musical *South Pacific*, newspapers, popular songs, and radio and television shows. He tried to sample comprehensively all publicly presented material of that date. He anticipated recent books of photography titled *A Day in the Life of . . . ,* when photographers took pictures to portray a cross section of the life of a country on a particular day.

He presented the common beliefs of the day about sex, and he tried to correct, as scientifically as possible, the almost universal misapprehensions they conveyed. He pointed out the dramatic discrepancies between what people actually confided about their sexual activity and what they professed to believe.

Jokes, novels, newspaper accounts, almost all the mass media reports and attitudes, and fiction depicted sexual relations as widespread, varied, and different as possible from what religious, political, and educational leaders affirmed and taught as proper. For example, he cited organizations dedicated to wiping out venereal disease that refused to demand mass exams for and treatment of it. They didn't act logically on what they publicly professed to believe.

The teasing examples of sex in ads and jokes that were appealingly provocative to a mass audience and simultaneously condemned by ubiquitous censors were subject to his scrutiny and derision. He concludes that " . . . if moralists did not fret and fume about directly expressed sex desire and participation, it is doubtful if the sexuality indirectly expressed in . . . pin-up photos, risqué stories, sex-tinged gadgets, et cetera, would be as popular as it obviously is today" (Ellis 1951, n.p. available).

There is heavier going in the book when Ellis confronts the wall of prudishness about sexual intercourse and its cultivation to gain the greatest pleasures. The case he makes is that ham-fisted censorship produces pathological behavior that diverts normal and harmless desires into lawbreaking and guilt-ridden secrecy. (And here we are, 35 years later, blaming our sexual troubles on permissiveness, even though the same troubles prevail as when censorship and rigidity were called the main villains.)

Ellis believes, however, that we remain basically puritanical, not truly permissive, as we still insist on combining sex with love, proscribe nudity, and decimate inhibitions only in pornography, "which is distorted in other ways."*

In his 1950 study (Ellis 1951), he tabulated all the references he found, according to the medium involved, into liberal and conservative attitudes, and found that conservative attitudes predominated except in plays, and in humor and men's magazines.

He concluded that

> . . .virtually every living American — is completely muddled-, mixed-, and messed-up in his sex views, feelings and acts. Much of the time he is quite consciously confused. . . . Or else he keeps changing his mind. . . . Or he engages in sex acts which he feels he should not perform but which he would feel even more uncomfortable about not performing. . . . Debarring certain modes of sex behavior often results in individual and social hypocrisy, evasion, and downright lying. (p. 272)

And finally:

> The ultimate choice, then, seems to be between our going forward to be as consistently liberal in our sex views and acts as the limitations of human nature will allow — or in our going back to consistent, ultra-conservative

---

*Albert Ellis 1985: personal interview.

sex attitudes and activities. Both these alternatives comprehend human risks and dangers, and involve the development of patterns of thinking, feelings, and living which are radically different from those most of us follow today. (p. 285)

Ellis's second publication on sex came as coeditor of *Sex, Society and the Individual* (Pillay & Ellis, 1953). It contained 45 articles, mainly by leading sexologists, covering the gamut of sexual problems and information. Ellis wrote three of the chapters: "Is the Vaginal Orgasm a Myth?" "A Study of 300 Sex Offenders," and "Recent Views on Sexual Deviation."

In the first article he concluded that various forms of vaginal and nonvaginal stimulation could be pleasurable, that coital and clitoral gratification need not be mutually exclusive but could both be cultivated, that many psychological factors affect sexual success, and that both men and women have a lot to learn about all kinds of sexual activity.

Regarding sex offenders other than rapists, he determined that rarely did they use serious force, that they usually showed other emotional disturbances, and that they were not unusually dangerous, impulsive criminals. His paper on sexual deviation does not develop as consistent a theme as his others. His views are more fragmented, citing others' beliefs about various deviations. He did not draw them together with principles related to therapy, as he did with his other notions, and as he does now for sex in all of its aspects.

The one exception to the fragmentation was homosexuality, about which Ellis had already published his opinions. He had more experience with homosexuals when they were sexually troubled than when they were not. He was impressed by how they expressed the same romantic irrationalities as heterosexuals about fidelity, love, and intimacy.

But his main contentions, which he still holds, were that homosexuality should not be illegal, that it should be treated when homosexuals are disturbed by it, and that it can be "cured," at least when it is an obsession, if the client wants it to be. It boils down "to the usual psychotherapeutic problem of helping individuals to overcome their phobias, fixations, obsessions, and/or compulsions" (p. 338). He applies the same view to heterosexuals.

He summarizes thus:

In the course of psychotherapy, the homosexual individual may also be helped to accept his homosexuality without the enormous amounts of guilt and anxiety that usually accompany inversion. But if an exclusive homosexual is only enabled, through psychotherapy, to accept his homosexuality, and if he is not in any way released from the neurotic fixations, phobias, obsessions, and/or compulsions which are forcing him to be exclusively homosexual, then very little real therapy has been accomplished, and he is still as basically neurotic as when he first came for treatment. . . . When people tell me that homosexuals are incurable and I think of the twenty years I have been curing them, . . . I answer "They're not." And have done with it. (p. 343)

These early views of Ellis's about homosexuality can be compared with the later ones expressed in his book *Homosexuality: Its Causes and Cure* (1965a). His basic orientation of liberality, nonpunitiveness, and optimism about treatment was unchanged. He did, however, become more specific in applying the tenets of RET. It is not homosexuals' mistreatment by society that causes their anger; it is that they tell themselves they "can't stand it; and it shouldn't be that way!" Much of the book is devoted to the treatment of homosexuals, detailing a number of case histories and transcripts of recorded sessions.

They can remain displeased by the realities of discrimination and try to change it, but

If they are truly interested in attacking their own deepseated anxieties and hostilities, they can, by using the rational-emotive approach . . . almost invariably   acquire   a   good   measure   of   heterosexual adjustment. . . . Many will want to rid themselves of the worst disadvantages of their ways of living, but . . . will not want to work hard or long enough to become heterosexually or ambisexually oriented. (p. 269)

"Exactly the same was [is] true of fixed, compulsive *heterosexuals*," he also says now. He will "only try to help change homosexuals who clearly *want* to change — as well as heterosexuals who clearly *want* to change. My contention is that *any* person, with enough effort, can change his or her heterosexuality, homosexuality, or bisexuality — even though they may still be born with some strong *tendencies* to be the way they now are."*

Incidentally, Ellis's relationship with homosexual groups has changed as the course of the homosexual movement has altered. Because of his outspoken advocacy of sexual freedom when it does not harm others, his nonpunitive stance, and his emphasis

---

*Albert Ellis 1986: personal interview.

upon problems that homosexuals share with heterosexuals, Ellis was originally a hero to homosexual groups, and often was invited to address them. One prominent homosexual spokesman, Donald Cory, endorsed Ellis's views publicly and in writing, as did others.

In recent years, however, as the homosexual movement has become more aggressive and outspoken, and has broken with many conservative heterosexual views centered in monogamy, puritanism, child rearing, romantic love, and such, Ellis has lost his unique role for the group. Perhaps the most vitriolic argument between him and some, though far from all, homosexual leaders concerns his view that homosexuality can be cured. His adversaries in the movement seem to believe that you are born that way, and that the notion of "cure" is a cop-out, not facing what you were born to be.

Some of his most extreme adversaries maintain that there never has been a cure of a homosexual. Ellis maintains that cures are commonplace, not only in his practice but in the experience of many other therapists, whom he cites, who have written of their results. But he does not hold a fixed position that all homosexuals should seek to be changed. And he sees many gays with the same behavior problems seeking the same kind of "cures" as heterosexuals.

He would encourage them, the same as everyone else, to be whatever they want to be sexually as long as it harms no one. He would, however, seek to change anyone who holds to an obsessive, irrational viewpoint that he or she must be this way or that, and has no choice in the matter, as he would with all who believe that there is only one form or act of sex that they can possibly enjoy.

This is perhaps the most significant difference Ellis and Janet have about RET theory and sex. She believes that sexuality is more genetically determined and does not believe in trying to change its orientation unless clients insist on (not merely want to consider) it. This disparity causes no apparent trouble between them. Ellis does not consider it a major heresy about RET. Besides, he believes "that humans are exclusively homosexual or heterosexual for two biological reasons: innate predispositions for sexual preferences; and innate predispositions for rigidity and emotional disturbance."

The American Sexual Tragedy (1954a) is a study of then current American attitudes about human relationships that are beyond sex but are affected by it. It is also the second volume of the study, begun with *The Folklore of Sex* (1951), that tabulated one day in the life of the American mass media, January 1, 1950, through Ellis's voracious reading. This volume extends his summary of American attitudes on specific sex topics to love, marriage, and family relations.

After reviewing all of the data and extending them to these other areas of sexually affected activity, Ellis concludes:

> The American sexual tragedy is not . . . merely the fact that our sexual attitudes, and especially our attitudes toward non-marital and non-coital sex relations, sabotage and negate a considerable amount of both male and female sex satisfaction. . . . Its much greater measure is found in the fact that, in addition to causing widespread sex deprivation and ruination, our puritanical sex views create untold havoc in our love, marriage, and family relations as well. (1954a, p. 289)

He adds further:

> At bottom, the sabotaging of human sex-love relations is a problem which is socially rather than individually created, and which therefore cannot be solved on a broad scale without widespread societal changes in sex attitudes. . . . The Kinsey findings unmistakeably point the direction in which we should change our sex attitudes. Dare we take the clearly indicated road to sexual sanity? (p. 291)

Ellis grew more specific as he continued to write on the subject, though his basic attitudes changed little. His next book on sex, *Sex without Guilt* (1958b), implemented his findings and views in concrete ways. He applied them to such specific sexual problems as masturbation, petting, premarital relations, adultery, censorship, female frigidity, and male inadequacy, ending with a chapter titled "The Right to Sex Enjoyment." The book still sells well.

He concluded in this book:

> If a sufficient number of Americans believe, as I do, that truly harmful and antisocial sex behavior should be curbed, but that other sex participations should be if anything, encouraged; and if enough of these sexual democrats openly say . . . what they believe, our antiquated, anti-human, antisexual codes will more quickly . . . wither away. . . . Everyone has a human right to sex-love involvement of his own taste, preference, and inclination. And the more he speaks and fights for that right, the more, in practice, he (or she!) is likely to realize and enjoy it. (pp. 185–86)

Incidentally, Ellis's use of the word "right" rears an ugly image for a theorist who tries hard to eliminate all such absolute terms as "ought," "should," and "must." Inadvertently he occasionally uses these latter words, though if he catches himself at it, he will modify them with qualifiers such as "preferably should," or go round about to eliminate them. Such slips do not change the nature of his view or the thrust of his practices, but they do indicate a difficulty about getting by without using such terms.

Ellis experienced vicissitudes one would not expect in the growing era of so-called permissiveness that began, presumably, about the time he started to publish his sex books. Kinsey's work (Kinsey, Pomeroy & Martin 1948) had recently been printed; the major censorship cases involving *Ulysses, Fanny Hill,* and Henry Miller had already been won. *Playboy* benefited when *Rogue* magazine got the postmaster general's efforts at censorship overruled, and nudist magazines carried their day in court. Ellis testified for the nudist magazines, as well as others, against sex censorship, against the prosecution of homosexuals, against rigid laws governing sexual practices.

Even the *Report of the Presidential Commission on Obscenity and Pornography* (1970) had a profoundly liberalizing effect on what could be freely published by finding that pornography was essentially harmless. It became a best seller in adult bookshops, with its samples of the pornography it scrutinized.

Still, publishing houses and newspapers maintained standards that forbade most advertising for even scholarly sexual books, retained censorship, and avoided certain coverage that the law was by then almost sure to permit. Most of these liberalizing decisions were rendered before Ellis began publishing his books. He could reasonably have expected even broader-minded court treatment because his works were mainly professional and scientific, and for a select audience, but he encountered trouble nevertheless.

For example, Doubleday & Company grew skittish about publishing *The Folklore of Sex* (1951) after signing the contract, because of some purple quotations Ellis had included from well-known authors and papers. Some he had deleted at the publisher's request. Finally, though Doubleday actually printed it, it took its name off as publisher and substituted Charles Boni's. Few papers or magazines reviewed the book and the *New York Times* and the *Chicago Tribune* refused to accept any ads for it.*

---

*Albert Ellis 1984: personal interview.

Doubleday had an option on the second volume but would not even look at it according to Ellis. A third book, *Sex Life of the American Woman and the Kinsey Report* was contracted to Popular Library for a paperback edition simultaneous with the hard-cover version. The company insisted that two of the chapters, on masturbation and on prostitution, be eliminated, then decided against publishing it. Greenberg, which did publish it, omitted the same two chapters.

Sex, Society and the Individual (1953) had no censorship problems because it was published by its coeditor, A. P. Pillary, in Bombay. Not until the late 1950s would the *New York Times* finally accept ads for an Ellis sex book: *Sex without Guilt* (1958b).

Ellis is not alone in his experience with the sexual prudishness and censorship that still exists in American society. As late as 1981, the *New York Times* did not review probably the most important book to date on homosexual politics, *Homosexuality and American Psychiatry* (1981), which detailed how homosexuals got the American Psychiatric Association to revise its classification of homosexuality as a mental illness. And as recently as 1984 the *Times* was just opening a dialogue with gay leaders that resulted in homosexual news stories in the *Times* (*Village Voice* July 2, 1985).

What appears to have happened in the United States as result of the sexual pioneering of Ellis, Kinsey, and Masters and Johnson is that educated, enlightened people have felt liberated to cultivate and practice a wider variety of sex without guilt. Meanwhile, a large body of ever more explicit pornography, in the form of books, movies, and videotapes, has sprung up to meet a growing market and take advantage of legal permissiveness.

But the main body of the American media remains conservative in what it will cover sexually. A dichotomy has resulted, a sharp split between what appears in the more respectable media and what is available in adult bookstores and even at ordinary newsstands. It is the scientific and educational press that appears to suffer most. Only with difficulty can it portray and distribute detailed sexual facts to the largest and youngest audience of educated Americans.

A full-page ad in many newspapers countrywide in December 1986 pointed out, "They did it 20,000 times on television last year" and "How come nobody got pregnant?" Television showed sex and nudity, and advertised vaginal sprays, tampons, and hemorrhoid medicine, but not contraceptives, the ad pointed out. It could have said the same for sex toys and explicit practices.

The boundaries of "good taste" keep getting pushed back, but limits persist. They are, however, nothing like what they were when Ellis began his crusade. He was one of the major pioneers in discussing sexual liberalism and the widest range of practices. He was laying out the information and advice that Dr. Ruth Westheimer would offer 30 years later on television and radio.

Aside from his information gathering and publishing, which was monumental, Ellis got earthy and practical in the advice he provided to sex-hungry but inhibited Americans. He told them exactly how to obtain sexual companions and partners without patronizing prostitutes, how to separate and enjoy sex regardless of love or marriage, how to satisfy partners whose pleasure as equals could enhance theirs.

That he was simple, direct, practical, and at times seemingly vulgar offended many, particularly academics and colleagues, who were used to a more obscure, euphemistic, and guarded style. But he was impervious to such fastidiousness.

Ellis still contends with conservatively oriented media that play along with moralists who do not even attempt to bridge the gap between what's said about sex and what's done, even by themselves. As long as such hypocrisy flourishes, Ellis remains in fighting trim, sure as ever that he is waging a necessary and useful crusade.

Since writing those early books, he has gone on to apply his knowledge and attitudes to a variety of audiences. He wrote his best-selling handbook for couples, *The Art and Science of Love* (1960a); his manual for marriage, *Creative Marriage* (Ellis & Harper 1961); help for women seeking men, *The Intelligent Woman's Guide to Man-Hunting* (1963a), and for men seeking women, *Sex and the Single Man* (1963b); and *Nymphomania* (Ellis & Sagarin 1964).

Although he had already issued his message challengingly and frequently, he continued to write books on the subject: *The Art of Erotic Seduction* (Ellis & Conway 1967), *Sex and the Liberated Man* (1976), and many, many articles in professional and mass publications. Perhaps his best overview of nonsensical sexual advice is contained in *The Sensuous Person* (1972).

In this book he is at his acerbic best in dissecting the how-to-do-it publications about sex, the debater par excellence.

If you ... want to try to be more sexual, sensual ... that is probably fine. ... But if you positively, absolutely have to be the Sensuous Woman, a Sensuous Man, the most Sensuous Couple ... you are inevitably doomed. . . . What have you actually let yourself in for but a continual comparison of your performances with those of . . . everybody else in the world who endeavors to be the Sensuous Person? . . . Stop the nonsense! You can't with such impossible goals, ever win. . . . Try to be saner and more realistic. . . . Sensuality can be, for some of the people some of the time, a fine goal to work for. But try to stay inimitably, indisputably human. For that's the only way you're ever likely to be! (p. 163)

Although he mentions his own experiences occasionally, and some are included in his books, Ellis does not describe in detail his personal ways of gaining sexual satisfaction and what pleases him most. He omits very little, however, about how a man and a woman can gratify each other, very specifically, in all ways.

You will find concrete examples of almost any sexual problem and solution in one or another of his books. For many years, he far transcended any other contemporary sexologist in the explicit instructions he provided, as well as in his expansive attitudes and in applying the principles of RET to sexual as well as all other human problems.

Ellis has been detected in no egregious errors of fact or concrete advice. Frank Harris (1963) lied about his own experiences, though he was well-intentioned and his attitudes were open, liberal, and instructive. Ellis (1972) lays out the deficiencies of recent sexual advisers like "M" (1971) and Dr. Reuben (1969) and documents their wrong-mindedness and misinformation. No one has outdone him in his concrete and scientifically based advice to people seeking to solve their sexual problems.

He found his personal answers relatively late in life, well past the time of usual adolescent experimentation, and used them to enhance his mastery of the scientific literature about sex. He then interacted with, and applied his knowledge to, thousands of clients and the public. He also found ways to gain personal satisfaction in a series of relationships that seem to have left no harm in their trail, only relatively friendly residuals, which seems as happy an outcome as is usually possible with sexual experiences.

What some may regretfully miss is a sense of passion, of overriding affection, of romantic love, which may leave the sex he speaks of seem relatively dry and lifeless. "Romance" and "romantic" have many definitions, and Ellis has a definite distaste for them. But if we take one appropriate definition of "romance" for this purpose, "a strong, usually short-lived attachment or enthusiasm," (American Heritage Dictionary, 1st ed.), or for "romantic," "imaginative but impractical," we at least begin to touch a powerful emotion that he has experienced.

Many erstwhile Don Juans make the most of it, base their lives upon capturing and recapturing it. With them it may become a compulsive pursuit that diverts them from serious and profound relationships, to satisfy momentary itches. But most people want to integrate romantic feelings, however short-lived, with sex.

Ellis had plenty of erotic feelings toward female children, girls, and young women as he was growing up. Even with his early petting, his notions seemed more romantic than specifically sexual. He sustained his vague longings, he thought frequently about these girls and women, and he frequently showed the symptoms of romantic love.

However, as soon as he got specific about sex, he tried to become as skillful as possible in its practice. Presumably he did become quite competent soon after he began, and he never turned back. In short order, satisfying sexual desires mutually became his sine qua non of affectional relationships with women. He took little interest in expressing romance and love thereafter.

Ellis considers himself to be permanently romantic — without believing in romance. He considers himself to have been romantically attached many dozens of times, with or without sex. He may have experienced the anguish of love countless times when young, yet he has not spoken or acted that way except, perhaps, to his paramours, though those I have interviewed have not spoken of it.

There is no basis to doubt what he states were his passions, his loves, his longings. Yet they cannot be seen or even inferred from his present relationships. He has the musical taste of a romantic, however, preferring Tchaikovsky, Verdi, Romberg, and Offenbach to Bach, Mozart, and Handel.

Ellis would fall "madly in love" quite easily, but he early learned to control it, might even not tell the objects of his fantasies about them, and learned to curb such emotions in order to work efficiently and to avoid commitment. He did not want to "need" anyone — or anything, even love. He learned that lesson when "madly in love" with Karyl, who became his first wife. He "contains" his love affairs.

How could one expect anything different from him? With a cold family, he did not seek the warmth of dependency or even interdependency in his life. He would not acknowledge the need that so many others feel for affection, love, romance after his childhood and youth, during which they did seem to show somewhat in indirect ways. They more profoundly affect warmer-blooded and more affectionally reared adults, who consider his sexual instruction too cool and calculated.

Nevertheless, Ellis can instruct well without being dependently in love, or showing and expressing passion. He says he feels passion, and showed it toward some of his lovers. He had at least one affair where his passion seemed sustained for years. Yet his cool manner and friendly, but almost always rational, attitudes seem to belie the passion he refers to.

The most any friend has said of his present long-term relationship with Janet is that there is "much genuine affection and respect" on both sides, and a growing sense of loyalty to each other. But passion, love, romance? Unlikely since early in the relationship, at least on his part, at least detectably. Even the greatest passion of his life did not carry into marriage, which Gertrude wanted. Their incompatibility about socializing made him reject the notion. Passion could not contend with that rational decision.

This is not to diminish in any way Ellis's huge contribution to the movement toward sexual liberalism and enlightenment. He stands forthrightly, predictably, and steadfastly for a congenial rationality in human relationships. It is surely a substantial personal goal for human beings to try to gain in the sexual area. Sexual problems are a major cause of much of the misery and obstructionist behavior that impairs the most intimate human relations: living together, rearing families, and seeking enduring companionship.

Perhaps it is best that Ellis not become involved in the more ambiguous and perhaps hopeless swamp of such emotions as romance, love, interdependency, longing. Perhaps, as he believes, such notions only obstruct what we can gain and sustain from our everyday relationships. He has much to teach us about how to enhance the quality and pleasures of our associations without obscuring what they are, how they function, and what we can do about them, with concepts we cannot yet define, much less contend with. He is passionate about his beliefs, he can be passionate about his loves; but like the other pleasures of his life, ultimately he weighs them against his other desires and decides as rationally as he can how to order his priorities.

10

Is RET the Ultimate Therapy?

Ellis and his followers, like any school of therapy, tenaciously and expansively talk and write as if they have found the ultimate therapy. They do not say that no other form of therapy will ever prove better than RET, but neither does that possibility interest or attract them. Ellis has repeatedly stated his open-mindedness to such a development, however.

Ellis has often maintained that he is dependent upon research to buttress his case, and that he will change whenever data justify it. No one can reasonably foreclose the future, and the likelihood is that RET, like every other system of psychotherapy before it, will prove to have serious flaws and limitations, and will be superseded by other forms that not only work better but also expand the applications of therapy.

One obvious limit of RET, admitted by Ellis, is that it is not very effective for those of limited intelligence, even though it can be simplified to some extent. It also has restricted usefulness with psychotics, who often are not accessible to its reasoning and argumentative methods. Nor is RET probably helpful with most psychopaths. They aren't likely to seek psychological help except, perhaps, when in legal trouble, or to accept arguments based on long-term considerations.

Another limit is that RET has not yet fully encompassed in its theory some powerful influences for changing behavior that have been described — though it does tend eventually to embrace such forces or techniques once they have established their merit for psychotherapy. It does not focus on them, however, or acknowledge their priority with special cases.

For example, behavior modification has a fairly well established value that depends primarily upon applying carefully assessed rewards and penalties to steps in a change process. It can most effectively be applied to clients over whom the therapist can exercise crucial control, which is true mostly for children, who can be directed by parents or parent surrogates, and for psychotics and psychopaths, who are in closely controlled institutions. It has also been used with some other clients, such as anorectics, who are hospitalized, may be bright and not psychotic, and are willing to subject themselves to strict regulation to get over their problem.

It could also be used with outpatients volunteering to accept formal daily rules designed to modify their behavior. They would choose the objectives, but the constraints would then be exercised over them without the kind of thought-changing effort of RET. This happens with people who go to "fat farms," where they voluntarily accept rigorous management of their diet.

Phillips has pointed out in his book *A Guide for Therapists and Patients to Short-term Psychotherapy* (1985) that since long-term therapy has generally proved to be inefficient, ineffective, or both with various kinds of clients, they should not be given psychotherapy at all, but instead be turned over to outpatient forms of care, such as groups that care for each other, public health instruction, and board-and-care homes.

Another criticism of RET is that its theory is not broad enough to include some potent methods that it nonetheless uses, but only because they work. For example, Ellis uses task setting as one of his many techniques for accomplishing change. It does not necessarily derive from the ABCs of RET, of changing ways of thinking that get clients into trouble. Task setting is a helpful tool for reaching goals of practical value that can just as well be used by other theorists. In fact, Freud recommended tasks to his analysands as commonsense advice, which he was not at all reluctant to provide.

Ellis points out, however, that task setting, as he uses it, is not merely or even primarily to help clients to master a problem. Rather, tasks are assigned "because they are often the best ways of convincing people to change their self-defeating thinking."* In other words, he sees them as part of RET's argumentative method utilized to prove a point — though they need not be used that way.

---

*Albert Ellis 1984: personal interview.

What we do get in the guidebooks by Ellis are excellent compendia of everything found to work well up to the point of his most recent publication. The best of the books by him on theory probably is *Theoretical and Empirical Foundations of Rational-Emotive Therapy* (Ellis & Whitely 1979), while the most popular one for clients is *A New Guide to Rational Living* (Ellis & Harper 1975). Also excellent for public use is *A Practitioner's Guide to Rational-Emotive Therapy* (Walen, DiGiuseppe, & Wessler 1980).

Additions are constantly being made to the armamentarium of practical, useful methods in RET. They do not necessarily derive from RET theory, although if they are not consonant with it, Ellis will reject them. For example, in a paper on the dangers of behavior therapy (Ellis 1981) he rejects the notion of rewarding (reinforcing) clients with the therapist's approval because that would increase their belief that they need such approbation — or love.

He wrote of other hazards of behavior change methods. Some of the techniques, such as desensitization, provide the kind of confrontation that he favors. Others, however, such as relaxation, meditation, and other ways of inducing calm, he rejects because they may distract you from your problems and make it less likely that you will face and overcome them (author's note: such as tranquilizers).

Briefly to repeat Ellis's original theory: It begins with Epictetus's dictum "Men are disturbed not by things, but by the views which they take of them" (1897, p. 218). It proceeds to postulate the ABCs of RET: Activating Events or Experiences filter through one's Belief System to produce Emotional or Behavioral Consequences. Ellis then goes on to describe Disputation as the major therapeutic technique to produce the New (rational) Effect (D and E). Active homework to counterattack one's irrational beliefs is also a major RET method, "so RET is invariably cognitive and behavioral." RET theory now also encompasses the initial formulation of goals.

Walen et al. (1980) have produced an excellent textbook really on psychotherapy generally more than on just RET, for they have listed and discussed almost all useful methods from various theories of therapy. For example, they include transference (from psychoanalysis), empathy (from Rogerian, nondirective therapy), self-disclosure (by the therapist, as taught by Mowrer), but only in their "good," that is, ancillary forms to supplement basic RET. They make Ellis's theory and methods primary, but they also

bring in anything else that might work and help people make
what Ellis calls "a profound philosophic change."*

The list of techniques used and taught by RET therapists
includes most of those which might be used by eclectic therapists
who are not devoted to any particular theory: diaries, homework
assignments, voice intonations and inflections, humor,
confrontation, self-disclosure (by the therapist), empathy,
transference, role playing, silence, maneuvering the client into
giving therapeutic answers, confrontation, marathons, lectures,
songs, almost anything within reason.

They may miss a few techniques, but perhaps not. Somewhere in the huge literature of RET, most of it written by or with
Ellis, these apparently overlooked techniques may be covered:
consumer control to forestall arrogance, incompetence, or rigidity
by the counselor; inhibition of "spontaneity" until new habits
become automatic and a more useful "spontaneity" is created;
basing frequency of interviews on the time span the client can
maintain progress without therapy sessions; having clients
phone in briefly when they need encouragement to tackle a
problem; conducting therapy by correspondence when distance
is a problem, and a written record of goals and methods is
desirable.

The core of RET is thought control and direction — by the
client, at the instigation of the therapist. It is learning how
to think objectively about what is in your best interest, what
most effectively moves you toward your chosen goals, and how
to make yourself do it. It gives intellectual functions priority
over the emotional, or at least puts reason at the service of
emotions. Presumably emotions fuel human behavior, and for
Ellis it is long-term pleasure that is his ultimate goal. You cannot
think rationally or control your behavior with your emotions, nor
can you define, react to, and profit from reality with your
emotions.

Ellis truly is intellect-dominated. He is in superb control of
himself and his life, and he comes through that way to others in
speech and writing, no matter that he does acknowledge other
forces within humans that affect their behavior and give pleasure.
Not ignoring emotions, he seeks to fulfill them with reason. He
believes in "forcing yourself to do what you fear and making

_____

*Albert Ellis 1986: personal interview.

yourself deliberately uncomfortable" when it is necessary in order to achieve long-term pleasures.*

It was no oversight that he originally named his method Rational Therapy (RT). That says where his main interest and focus lie, determining the vehicle for solving problems and gaining long-term pleasure. When he was under severe attack for not placing sufficient emphasis upon emotion, he added it to the name of his therapy, since he had taken its role for granted. It might have been clearer to leave it out.

Intellect truly is Ellis's chosen vehicle of change, and while emotions must affect how the intellect functions, contribute to goals, and define the vitality and passions of his life, he clearly leads with his mind. It dominates his own behavior, and it appears as primary in what he teaches his clients and staff. If ever there was an intellect-centered person, it is he. His emotions are given play, but clearly at the direction of his mind, even while he uses his mind to fulfill his emotions.

To understand Ellis, for he strenuously objects to the separation of reason and emotion, as does Meehl† for philosophical reasons, one must differentiate his personality from his theory. That is, in terms of body type or personality, the primacy of his mind stands out. He simply is not dominated by a search for intense feelings or by giving spontaneous vent to emotions.

Nonetheless, he does consider himself to be a passionate person, to be dominated by pleasure seeking, to put reason at the service of emotion, which ultimately determines his pleasures in life. Reason thus serves as the instrument for the achievement of goals and is the most effective device humans have for that purpose.

The ultimate control lies in the mind, as it picks and chooses, decides what to pursue and how best to pursue it, and what's unrealistic or distorted and is to be changed. His self-professed hedonism is controlled, directed, fulfilled by his mind and its capacity to gain his goals. His intellect is what determines, for example, that his pleasure seeking, which he says is the purpose of his life, is to be pursued only on a long-term basis, rather than being a short-term itch that is satisfied without further consideration.

---

*Albert Ellis 1985: personal interview.

†Paul Meehl 1986: personal interview.

Ellis expands the concept of pleasure seeking to include the gratification from using his mind to read, write, teach, do therapy. Pretty serious and thoughtful stuff to call hedonism. Most people would probably not consider him a hedonist except in the sense that everyone is a hedonist, seeking some kind of pleasure in living.

He may be sensual, he considers himself strongly to enjoy sensual satisfactions and to be passionate, but perhaps one must think of his relative priorities, how he would rank as sensual compared with more intellectual activities. He spends relatively little time on the physically sensual, or sensory, compared with the exercise of his mind.

He tries hard to live by, as well as to practice, the RET approach. He succeeds quite well. Other major psychologists have managed to appear to live by what they preached. Freud (1954) was forever analyzing the psychological forces around him, trying to understand their meaning and impact on humans — and getting into trouble with colleagues and the public for insisting on their acquiescence. Rogers' image (1942, 1951) was that of a sensitive and empathetic person trying hard to interact understandingly with others. Skinner (1972) usually seems to be trying to direct his own life through a system of reinforcements, reminders, and other influences he exerts on himself.

Ellis has done just that with the RET approach, living his life rationally and with relatively little irrational emotionality. He considers himself passionate, albeit in the interest of rationality, and rational in the interest of his pleasure seeking. Yet in his professional practices he often comes through as a preacher, propagandizing mightily for his beliefs, sometimes with intimidating zeal.

In my files I found unpublished correspondence of 25 years ago between Paul Meehl and Ellis on this very subject. Meehl was calling Ellis's attention to his (Ellis's) forceful presence and its likely effectiveness quite apart from RET. Ellis accepted the possibility in good grace, remarking only that he would eschew such a role, and considered it a weakness on his part that he would try to correct. Forcefulness is still an integral part of his personality, however, and shows itself even today, particularly in his lectures, demonstrations, and personal conversations.

Now he thinks he was wrong in that earlier opinion. He believes that zeal is an essential part of him. He believes also that it differentiates RET from cognitive behavior therapy, which is more cerebral, while RET is more involved with emotion, at least in the forcefulness of its practices.

Many therapists act in ways that belie their professed beliefs, a manner that may overshadow what they say. They can be charming (both Freud and Ellis turned on the charm when they wanted to), they can be forceful, they can be persuasive. They can exercise all these powers and more, and influence their clients to make sensible changes in their behavior because of personal potency for which their theories may be secondary or irrelevant. With Ellis and RET, however, powerful argumentation and other methods of influence are integral to the effectiveness of the theory and its practices. He claims that he "converted my personality, interests, and style into my theory of RET."*

Because of his personal power, however, there are probably few (if any) therapists who are as effective with RET as is Ellis. One can, if one wants to, choose a more passive, or mellower, or more empathetic posture within its framework. Penelope Russianoff has exchanged referrals with Ellis on this basis, she being a more laid-back, sympathetic kind of therapist. But if you want the whole dish thrown at you with as strong and direct an effect as possible, you would choose Ellis over anyone else. This despite the fact that RET is a relatively forceful method.

Ellis would probably be an effective therapist if he were a witch doctor providing commonsense advice for getting along well within a primitive culture that did not have "psychotherapy" in its vocabulary. However, RET is more than his personal style, and he has taught it to hundreds of other therapists, some of whom practice it quite differently from him even while applying its principles. There are many others who practice mostly like him but call their therapy by a different name. They tend to come together under the rubric of "cognitive (behavior) therapy."

It is difficult to imagine Ellis practicing any differently from the way he does, or arriving at any other theory of therapy. Still, one can imagine him practicing psychoanalysis in his own way, not very differently from the way he does therapy now, except that he might get more into clients' backgrounds from an analytic viewpoint before he directed them toward his RET views. Therapists tend to convert whatever theory they profess into a form suited to their personality, interests, style.

---

*Albert Ellis 1984: personal interview.

Ellis has invented certain steps for the process of doing therapy, utilizing a reasoning process to proceed in a systematic way that has proved very helpful for teaching other therapists and clients how to solve their problems. It is a noble venture. Historically, however, it will probably be viewed as one small part of a long, strenuous effort to make solving problems and changing behavior in humans into an ever more efficient process. Psychotherapy will probably go through many other theories before, if ever, it is stabilized. In a larger sense it represents humanity's effort to cope with the world, which is a never-ending effort, with the world changing while the effort goes on.

RET is surely not *the* ultimate therapy, nor is any other theory likely to prevail for long. But it is a very good theory for our time, as effective as any and perhaps more effective for most human problems. It seems likely to produce more satisfied customers than its competitors because it immediately and directly attacks the major problems in the forefront of clients' minds and provides clear measures for its success.

Phillips is currently writing extensively about universal "attrition" rates, basically saying that most clients drop out of therapy before therapists want them to.* These attrition rates appear to be similar in practically all forms of therapy in almost all settings and in different countries. Often such "dropouts" are called failures in therapy. But often the clients quit because they have gotten what they want in a way therapists don't recognize.

Early success in therapy, as well as closer consonance between what the therapist and client think about outcomes, seem most likely to happen in RET with its thrust toward the prompt results that most clients want. In this sense RET appears to meet the widest range of client needs and to provide a basis for closest correlation between therapist and client assessment of results.

---

*Phillips 1986: personal correspondence.

11
Running the Institute

By the end of the 1950s, Ellis had developed his views and advice about sex and his theories and practices for psychotherapy to the maturity that remains basically the same today. There have been elaborations and modifications (of his views on homosexuality, for example), major additions to the methods of RET, and specific criticisms of alternative techniques, but no serious changes in basic views, such as the ABCs of RET or his critique of psychoanalysis or sexual strictures.

By the early 1960s, he was in his late forties, had settled down to what became his permanent pattern of living, and would make no major changes in his habits or attitudes toward himself, living essentially alone, immersed in his work, and advancing his professional goals in every reasonable way. Nor did his health or his recreation change, although he restricted his physical and social activities even further.

In 1959 Ellis founded the Institute for Rational Therapy as a nonprofit educational organization. To it he could divert all of his professional earnings, and through it he could begin to train professionals to practice his theory; could advance his views to the public through individual and group therapy, lectures, books, and seminars; and could nurture additional institutes in other cities in the United States and other countries.

The Institute was located in his Parc Vendome apartment until 1965, when he bought a building to house it, slowly added staff, and was on his way to creating a fertile, busy, and expanding physical entity that looked like as well as functioned as an institute.

His personal life was relatively unsettled until he began living in the Institute's building. After his divorce from Rhoda, Ellis took a dim view of marrying again, and had a series of affairs, some strictly casual, some intense but not long-lasting (nor intended to be). He always enjoyed sex and the company of bright, attractive women, but it was clear to everyone who got to know him that his work came first, and he would make few concessions and no major breaks in his work routine to accommodate them.

Ellis joined Mensa, the organization of very bright people who have to achieve a high intelligence test score to become members. He is still a dues-paying member, though he attends neither meetings nor parties. He occasionally addresses the organization without charge. He found women companions in other ways, mainly through professional meetings and friends. Earlier he had wanted to found such an organization himself, largely to give financial help to smart but poor children to further their education.

Robert Harper was probably Ellis's best friend in the 1950s and 1960s, until Janet entered Ellis's life, but they have seldom seen each other in later years except at professional meetings. This raises an interesting point. Ellis has a hard time naming "closest friends." He had his brother, and his old friend and accountant Manny, both Institute board members whom he saw regularly and who were his lifelong companions. He has a friend of 24 years in California, Ted Crawford, whom he visits when he is there. Although primarily a businessman, this friend conducts RET workshops and actively collaborates with Ellis to promote RET in the fields of communication and conflict resolution. He has Janet, his companion of the past 22 years, whom he sees and talks with personally and professionally far more than anyone else. And he maintains friendships of 30 years with Paul Krassner and Lyle Stuart, who early publicized his views on sex. He also mentioned Gordon Derner, who died recently, ending their 40-year relationship, and Leonard Haber, who he still occasionally sees after 25 years. He has also known and interacted with many of the most notable psychologists of his lifetime, usually on professional issues. He also considers them friends, although they rarely see each other socially.

He and I have corresponded for almost 40 years and have visited at least once or twice a year during that period. We have probably talked more about his life during the past five or so years than anyone else has, except perhaps for Janet and him.

Earlier, Harper was his strongest advocate in professional circles, where he was active as the head of various committees and organizations. He was Ellis's friend at a time when Ellis might have been considered a liability. Some other colleagues agreed with Ellis, but often dissociated themselves from him because they thought his tactics were self-defeating. One colleague who was very active in professional organizations recalls that Ellis was anathema at early meetings of the American Academy of Psychotherapists.

He would tell people off and make blunt statements — for instance, that Freud had set psychotherapy back 50 years, that Carl Rogers helped people feel better rather than get better. He was, one colleague observed, most respected in the American Psychological Association in the early years of RET as a kind of clinical "Fearless Fosdick," directly confronting academicians, psychologists, and psychiatrists. Of notable professional or academic organizations, perhaps the Center for the Philosophy of Science at the University of Minnesota early provided him with his most respected public forum for his percolating new ideas.

At this time Ellis was at his peak as an outspoken rebel. His language became ever more vulgar, replete with words that perhaps had never been heard from a public professional platform before, but now, 25 years later, have become fairly common: f . . . , bull . . . , sh . . . and such. To some colleagues, he was a hero for cutting loose on his adversaries in ways that no one else dared. Yet sometimes his opponents gave back as good as they got, which often just egged him on to more acerbic responses.

Sometimes his outbursts were so insensitive and intolerant that friends became concerned and attributed them to overdoses of insulin. One colleague concluded that you couldn't count on Ellis to control his behavior, and that you'd better not plan "nice things with nice people" that included Albert. After his outbursts, Ellis would not mend fences even when that was clearly in his best interest.

Harper and Ellis would bandy outrageous comments about friends, sex, anything, with each other, and have thought of publishing their sprightly correspondence. They kidded with outlandish ideas and wild words, mainly about sex. They had fun that way, which was one of Ellis's few outlets for playfulness. At parties he'd often get bored quickly and quit talking, or leave early.

In 1965 Ellis moved into the lovely old building that had housed the Woodrow Wilson Institute, and gave his Institute its first real home outside of his apartment. It is at 45 East 65th Street, one and a half blocks from Central Park, on a well-kept residential street lined with brownstones, town houses, apartment buildings, and consulates.

A month after he moved into the Institute building, to live on the sixth floor (the other five were to be used for offices and lecture and meeting rooms), he sprained his ankle and needed help to get around, to shower, to prepare food. By this time, he had been going with Janet Wolfe for several months. He asked her to live with him on a more permanent basis, and she agreed to help care for him. They had been meeting for dinner, so he proposed that she use the money he would have spent on dinners to buy food and cook at the Institute. So began a loving friendship and professional partnership that has lasted for over 22 years and promises to continue indefinitely.

Janet is a very intelligent woman, tall, slender, and attractive, who is not highly sociable, though far more so than Ellis. She had an erratic academic career before finally completing her B.A. at Columbia in 1969 and had worked mainly in the publishing field.

She resembled Albert more than had his wives, both physically and in her acceptance of a rather hermitic life. She was drifting about a career, wanting to move ahead professionally but unsure of what direction. She also tended to be quite depressed, and was looking for stability and more certainty in her life. It did not seem very important to either of them that she was 28 years younger than he, that he was over twice her age and close to her father's age. Her parents objected to their relationship because of the age difference, and for a long time Albert and Janet did not tell them they were living together. Even now, when he is 74 and she is 47, the age discrepancy does not seem terribly important to either of them.

Janet is serious-minded about her work, but finds time for frequent visits with friends. She has adapted well to Albert's insistence that he stay home to work. He is there evenings, weekends, and holidays, to answer the phone and do other off-hours business for the Institute unless he is out of town giving talks and workshops. The only remuneration he receives for all of his work for the Institute, almost every day of the year, is his quarters.

Janet rather rapidly adopted Ellis's views on psychotherapy and decided with his encouragement, to become a clinical psychologist. She started graduate studies at New York University and acquired a Ph.D. there in 1975. She also became associate director of the Institute and director of clinical services in 1974. If ever Ellis had a close counterpart in habits, outlook, and values, besides his brother, it is Janet. She has expanded his views to specific women's liberation and feminist movement problems, and conducts a full practice of individual and group sessions, workshops, and lectures, as well as writing.

Janet has furnished their apartment as she wished. Ellis does not necessarily share her taste, but has not interfered and accepts it in good grace. She has her own office at the Institute, in which she spends much of her time, as he does in his. Most of the time they get together only late at night, when she fixes supper.

Their spacious, dark apartment is furnished in a mix of Victorian and baroque that she bought at thrift shops before those styles came back in vogue. There is a large attached greenhouse and a well-equipped kitchen. Rather than reflecting a particular style and personality, it is eclectic and comfortable.

Janet and Albert go out together perhaps once or twice a year, though it was somewhat more often earlier in their relationship. Then, as now, their main blocks of time together come when they attend conventions and other meetings, some of which they conduct jointly. In 1985, for example, they went to a major Evolution of Psychotherapy conference in Phoenix, where Albert was a main speaker. Incidentally, some acquaintances of his don't know of Janet, even though their living together has not been kept secret for many years.

When asked about the place of Janet Wolfe in his life, Ellis strongly felt that he had better be quoted directly. Here are his comments on their relationship.

People often ask me, "How have you managed to live for over two decades with Janet Wolfe after your previous checkered career of briefly loving and living with so many different women? Were you already growing old and crotchety, at the age of 51, and therefore decided to become a reformed lothario?"

Not at all. I first fell madly in love with Janet because she was young, attractive, and exceptionally bright and funny. That was *before* I asked her to live with me early in 1965. When I invited her to share my bed and board, it was because I knew she would be a caring companion and could help me with some of the work in getting the Institute started in its new building, as she was a skilled writer, editor, and organizer.

At that point I was not yet thinking that she would turn into my life partner. As we grew closer, she proved to be not only interesting and vital but really — and I mean really — warm and affectionate. Sex was also great — as good or better than I (or we) had ever had it.

What was more unusual, especially on a lasting basis, was the real endearment that blossomed — the steady looking out for each other, the mutual considerateness, the solid partnership in sharing problems and possible solutions, the anticipation of each other's desires, and the strong intent and sheer pleasure of fulfilling those desires.

Even better — if possible — has been our steadily maintained humor and fun. Sweet nothings — pre-Janet — had not exactly been my forte. Now I honestly tell Janet, at least five times a week, "I love you!" and I very much mean it and feel it. We warmly hug and kiss each other several times a day, at lunch and dinner time, which we try to schedule together. We often kid each other, converse in our private language, write each other comic cards and poems, play foolishly with our stuffed plush pig (which we take turns sleeping with), and do many other silly, fun-oriented things that were mainly missing from my previous love relationships. Not that I wasn't funny and outlandish; but my other mates simply did not give me the solid highs that I so often experience with Janet.

Does Janet have significant ideological influence over RET and my presentations of it? Indeed she does. She frequently surveys my articles, books, and talks, and importantly amends and adds to them. She suggests topics and recommends modifying others. She has especially worked out the RET approach to assertiveness training. Although I was a pioneering psychotherapist-feminist before I met her, she has helped deepen my profeminist attitudes and has contributed greatly, in her own right, to the application of RET to women's and men's sex role issues. She has also helped cement the ties between RET and other prominent feminists, such as Penelope Russianoff, Iris Fodor, Shere Hite, and Violet Franks. Under her guidance, the Institute for Rational-Emotive Therapy in New York has become one of the leading therapy centers specializing in women's problems.

Janet has not become an RET devotee to win and keep me in tow. In fact, at the beginning of our relationship, she believed in it mildly and practiced it less. And, when upset, she almost always resisted my "What are you telling yourself to make yourself disturbed?" "Don't use that stuff on me!" she would say, like many other mates of RETers. But as she became a clinical psychologist in her own right, experimented with other methods, and started seeing her own clients, she became an outstanding practitioner (and self-practitioner) of RET. Her own variations on rational-emotive themes have been widely quoted; and her supervisees at our Institute learn much from her that they do not learn from me and our other supervisors. I, too, have learned considerably from her and fully acknowledge her personal contributions to RET.

In many ways Janet has helped me to solve my prior problems in relating permanently to a woman. Most notably, she is one of the very few women I know who craves closeness, deep emotion, steady attachment, and expressed love feelings, who fully gives what she craves, but who asks for love in quality rather than in quantity. Most of my previous mates were what I have called "love slobs," who accepted themselves quite conditionally — because some lover (they thought) really cared for them and thereby gave them human worth. Janet, early in her life, had similar tendencies. Motivated, however, by my allergies to "love slobbism" and by her personal use of RET to overcome her own difficulties, she has developed herself into one of those rare women who strongly want (and enjoy) but do not absolutely need love. So the quantity of companionship and togetherness that she has wanted but often lacked because of my devotion to my multiple work activities she has very successfully managed to get elsewhere — with several close women friends, with her nieces, and with male friends who have other sexual involvements. Being much more "normal" than I in regard to going to the theater, museums, concerts, social affairs, and weekends in the country, she has managed to enjoy these activities with other companions, or at times quite happily alone.

For me to find someone else with similar self-strengths and accommodation to my peculiarities would indeed be miraculous. I "need" a woman who is truly her own person — and who relishes being just that. Janet is one of the damned few of that kind! Because of the specific woman she has evolved into, the two of us may well go down in history as a rare and inspiring example of busy and creative people who have worked and loved together free of most of the negativity that is rife with so many more demanding and needy couples.

Otherwise stated, I have always had powerful urges to be highly productive *and* intensely related. To the first of these impulsions I have not had any difficulty catering. With the second, prior to my relationship with Janet, I have succeeded mainly at the expense of the first. My mateships were enjoyable and romantic. But my work efficacy sadly suffered. Only with Janet have we both striven and achieved mutual nonneediness and been able to live together for 22 happy years in a state of amazing nonentrapment, with minimal stress and hurt, with double-barreled coadjustment, and with maximum freedom and productivity.

Finally — since I am trying to be brief here and will expand on my relationship with Janet in the autobiography I am now working on — let me say how much I truly appreciate her work at the Institute. Despite my diabetes, my health is unusually good so far — so she only occasionally nurses me back to health. But the executive role she takes over at the Institute is enormous and uniquely frees me to do scores of things for which I otherwise would never have the time.

Although I am technically the executive director of the IRET, she is the real principal who wears many vitally important hats, such as top administrator, outstanding member of the board of directors, publications and publicity specialist, director of clinical services, superintendent of documents, promulgator of new ideas, executrix of others' ideas, etc. Her name is Janet L. Wolfe, and the L seems to stand for Loyalty and devotion, not merely to me personally but especially to RET and the Institute. Without my financial support, clinical talks and workshops, and publication endeavors, our organization would certainly have a hard time maintaining its activities. Without Janet's brilliant and energetic administration, it would hardly keep its doors open at all.

These are some — yes, some — of the reasons why my mateship with Janet has been remarkably permanent. Do they sound reasonably rational? They do to me!

In 1965 Albert's father died of a stroke at the age of 80. In 1981 his sister died in California at the age of 64, also of a stroke. He did not grieve, but was much sadder, when his brother died at the age of 71. At a very young age he learned never to feel sorry for himself despite all his real physical misery, and he seems to have extended that attitude to others. To him death seems to be a natural event for which no depression is needed or felt. He is sorry when a friend or relative dies, but not depressed.

Ellis seldom expresses any deep feeling for people. I have heard or read none except for his recent statement about Janet, I have not, however, read his early love letters and diaries, which he says are replete with strong sentiments. His correspondence with friends is full of flippant and humorously sarcastic remarks. His strongest feelings seem to have been of desire, love, and longing for sexual partners. Kindly feelings for his mother can be inferred from his thoughtfulness to reassure her about her health and his, his interest in her activities. His letters to her, brief and vague but frequent, are full of "Please don't worry about . . . ," I'm feeling fine . . . gaining weight . . . enjoying life."*

While not expressing strong personal feelings of love or dislike for most of the many people he knows, Ellis is well known for his forceful sentiments, often openly stated during his talks and workshops, about the ideas and practices of other notable people. He was enthusiastic about the ideas of Bertrand Russell, Eric Hoffer, George Kelly, Karl Popper, among others. On the unfavorable side, he has shocked his audiences by declaring that "Sigmund Freud was a brilliant writer of fiction who had a gene for therapeutic inefficiency"; "Wilhelm Reich was always semi-psychotic and, though nicely liberal in his sex views, wrote one of the most idiotic books on women's sexuality ever written — *The Function of the Orgasm*"; "Carl Rogers really felt and gave his clients unconditional positive regard but, in his typical Boy Scout manner, he hadn't the slightest idea of how to actively and forcefully teach them to give it to themselves." In his therapy sessions, too, he frequently expresses his feelings strongly and directly, and, while giving unconditional acceptance to his clients, is often critical of their self-defeating behaviors.

His public talks attracted a lot of attention, and many feature articles with pictures appeared in the newspapers of cities where he talked. An article in the *Philadelphia Daily News* of September 7, 1967, was typical: "A New York psychologist believes that romance is not lasting and that to keep a marriage together,

---

*From numerous letters in Ellis's files author read over a 15-year period.

adultery may be a good thing for some couples." His theme was developed more cautiously than the lead sentence. What he said was that romantic love is not durable if both parties live closely under the same roof. If the mates agree, it is all right for each to have another partner, which can provide a great sexual experience. That can work out satisfactorily if they don't punish themselves with guilt or ignore home problems, and it can even make a mediocre marriage more tolerable.*

The *Detroit Free Press* on February 19, 1969, printed that

> Albert Ellis ... delivered a blunt and bawdy minority report on sexual freedom to students at Michigan State University.... His message: Marriage or not, don't feel guilty and ashamed about sex. If you like it, do it. Just don't hurt anyone, including yourself.... With the devilish humor of a man who enjoys being outrageous, Ellis lambasted "neo-puritan" views of mainstream theologians and moralists as damaging and foolish.... Just about anything man does has its joys and sorrows, its blessings and its regrets. Why should non-marital coition be any different? ... Not only do sexual feelings frequently stem from love emotions, but sex also begets love. (n p.)

He attracted great attention at that time. Mores were far more conservative than now. Kinsey, and Masters and Johnson had not yet been fully absorbed into the mainstream. He was blazing a trail that has resulted in the freedom of such counselors as Dr. Ruth Westheimer who repeats the same messages on television now without much public fuss, and a plethora of books not only repeats Ellis's original advice but illustrates it, and sells in respectable bookstores.

It was also in the 1960s that Ellis was investigated by the F.B.I. His Washington, D. C., file contains 187 pages, 17 of which were not released for unspecified reasons.† Mostly there are unverified charges made by disgruntled conservatives who didn't like his sexual views and seemed to associate them with communism, though his early days of political radicalism were never mentioned. His loyalty to the government was not questioned, and he was not known to hold any strong political beliefs. His credit rating was unsullied, and he had no police record.

What the F.B.I. uncovered, mostly as part of a routine investigation required for his clearance as a consultant to the

---

*Albert Ellis 1985: personal interview.

†The author obtained the complete file through Ellis's request.

Veterans Administration, was mild indeed. It referred to "DR. ALBERT ELLIS, the son of HAVELOCK ELLIS, famous psychologist," several times. (Author's note: they are not related.) It notes that "Dr. Ellis is described as a 'way out individual,' who believes in sexual freedom. He has been quoted in the past as an authority in this field by Playboy Magazine and other periodicals."

Ellis's name came up at a U.S. Senate subcommittee hearing in 1963* when Lyle Stuart, his publisher, was interviewed about a book he had published about Fidel Castro, and the chief counsel called the senators' attention to a mailing piece Lyle Stuart had printed stating that Ellis's *The Art and Science of Love* (1960) "tells you how to make every sex episode completely satisfying." Senator Thomas Dodd commented: "I don't think you have to read it all, do you?" It turns out that Stuart was being accused of using the same mailing list for Ellis's book on sex that he used for the volume on Castro.

F.B.I. records also reveal that Special Agent McLaughlin was invited to participate in a seminar on sexual deviates by the Tenafly, N.J., Board of Education, with Ellis and other sex experts, including Margaret Mead. He was not authorized to do so, since "this may be a controversial group."

Bureau files further disclose that Ellis had published an article titled "On the Cure of Homosexuality" (1952), which was reprinted by the Mattachine Society, a homosexual organization, but that he had no association with the society. There was "no reason to question character and reputation. Considered extremely blunt in his lectures and articles in the field of Sexology. . . . No credit or arrest record." He had "a MD Degree," was reported to be "completely void in the field of politics," and was "extremely blunt in his lectures and articles to the point of embarrassment even to other Psychologists."

The F.B.I. report continued: "Ellis takes extreme position in condoning homosexualism and pre-marital sexual experience, but knows of nothing reflecting on employee's personal moral conduct." But "In none of the books mentioned did Doctor ELLIS take any firm position in condoning homosexuality or recommending pre-marital sexual experiences." Additionally, "Dr. ELLIS is a man of good character, personal habits and moral conduct. [Blacked out] his personal life is conducted along

---

*Information that appeared in Ellis's F.B.I. file.

commonly accepted patterns and does not reflect the extreme liberal viewpoint on his psychological approach to homosexuality and pre-marital sexual experiences."

Aside from additional opinions elicited from many colleagues, neighbors, friends, and employers, which are within the boundaries of the above comments, one other F.B.I. file of eight pages is of interest. In 1973, a wild man had sent threatening letters to a number of people in New York City, including Ellis, and made an appointment to see Ellis after the F.B.I. was on his trail. Ellis got in touch with the F.B.I. and invited a special agent to sit in on the second session. Ellis thought the man was "a classical example of the paranoid schizophrenic," but that he seemed relieved after the session. The United States attorney declined to prosecute on the evidence at hand.

Maturing later than his sexual beliefs, Ellis's views on psychotherapy were more original, better integrated with theory, and taken more seriously by his profession. They attracted less attention from the public, but more from his colleagues. He held many consultantships, including several with the Veterans Administration, at various colleges and universities, and at state institutions.

A journal was started at the Institute in 1967; originally called *Rational Living*, the named was changed in January 1985 to *Journal of Rational-Emotive Therapy*. In 1983 it became a "refereed" academic publication "featuring theoretical, clinical and research articles on rational-emotive therapy and other forms of cognitive behavior therapy."* It has been improving in professional quality, and has published articles on research and theory as well as case descriptions. While it does not measure up to American Psychological Association journals in strength of research and reviews, it is more sprightly than most professional publications and helps knit together RET therapists around the world.

The Institute for Rational-Emotive Therapy was founded in 1968 primarily to offer professional training and clinical services, to supplement the Institute for Rational Living, whose original purpose was to educate and otherwise serve the public. Both were chartered by the State of New York as nonprofit educational organizations. In 1984, the two were brought together under the latter name. Staff, clients, and public activities proliferated over

---

*Quoted from the premier issue.

the years in various directions, including, in the 1970s, a lower-level school for children.

The Institute has flourished mainly through the subsidy of Ellis's large income, which has grown to more than a quarter of a million dollars a year, all of which is turned over to the Institute. It comes from the royalties on his many best-selling books and cassettes, his lectures and workshops around the world, and his heavy schedule of individual and group clients. There will be tough times when he is not there to inspire, direct, and help finance it.

Ellis was ever the propagandist, and during this time his language became a real attention getter. No longer was it offensive only to the rather formal academicians who dominated the American Psychological Association and university departments of psychology in the 1960s. It became part of the growing legend about him along with his sarcasm, his blatant message of sexual freedom, his personal sexual emancipation, his hardheaded assertiveness with patients.

It is hard to recapture the attitudes that produced shocked reactions and severe newspaper editing for newcomers to the Ellis presence. Seldom were his favorite words repeated in print. And it was not only the vulgarities that were skirted; it was also the outrageous inventions of words such as "must-urbation" (even in his *Marquis Who's Who in America* [1986-1987] text), "awfulize," "skullduggerist," "self-downing," "anti-fornicative," "necessitiz-ing," "love slobism." He did not hesitate to improvise new words on the spot. They did not set well with more formal, more polite, more inhibited professionals.

His mother had used a coarse vocabulary, but not his early friends. Neither did most of his early colleagues of whom I am aware, though later some did copy his vocabulary at symposia where his presence seemed to inspire it. In any case, he was offensive to many because of his language. The times, however, have overtaken him, and his so-called obscenities are now fairly common in movies, magazines, books, lectures, and discussions.

It is probably the rest of his demeanor and his background that have gained his language more attention than it would otherwise have drawn. Ellis did not grow up as a street person or even blue-collar. He has always had middle-class goals, manners, and friends — indeed, never used his special language until he was grown up. He was never much with people who used it; it did not come naturally to him from his environment.

It seems obvious that he adopted it for the purpose of gaining attention, not so much for himself as for his message. He determinedly used whatever lay at hand to influence others to his views about sex and therapy. Language surely was a powerful tool, and he had few inhibitions about how he applied it. He had always valued good literature, and in his late adolescence he had tried to write it. He did not use vulgar language in his novels.

Ellis really opened up when he became excited, trying to overwhelm his adversaries or to spark a neutral audience to his side by shaking them up, gaining their attention, stimulating them, in the most effective ways he could. Vivified language proved to be a useful tool. He ignored any adverse effect it might have on his reputation. He was simply not that interested in being respectable.

He does not write the way he talks. He still uses some of the invented words, but he usually does not — indeed, usually cannot — print the so-called obscene words. Publishers would print them in only one of his recent books, *The Sensuous Person* (1972), according to Ellis. Many of his friends object that such language is unnecessary to convey his message, that his importance does not depend upon his florid vocabulary, that his reputation may be trivialized. But no one has been able to budge him. He is convinced of its effectiveness in attracting immediate attention from an indifferent audience, in gaining empathy from the majority of listeners whom he believes think or talk that way, and in shocking the already sympathetic into becoming less inhibited.

The 1960s were good to Ellis. His voice was being heard not only as that of a leader in the exploding sexual liberation movement, which had acquired powerful support from the early Kinsey books of the late 1940s and early 1950s, and Masters and Johnson's work of the late 1960s; he was also, albeit more slowly, gaining importance as head of an increasingly important school of psychotherapy, Rational-Emotive Therapy.

Ellis with RET, Rogers with Non-Directive Therapy, Skinner with Behavior Modification, and Psychoanalysis in various versions were the major forms of psychological treatment. The roots of Cognitive (Behavioral) Therapy were also being planted, facilitated by RET. Ellis correctly perceives a close relationship, and feels grandfatherly toward the cognitive therapies variously also called cognitive restructuring, self-instructional training, rational behavior therapy, and multimodal therapy.

His Institute was firmly in place, and yearly turning out
students and practitioners by the dozens, treating clients by the
hundreds, and reaching public audiences by the thousands. Most
of them were influenced by his views of changing attitudes and
solving problems through rational methods in order to gain
control and direction of human behavior. He had achieved
celebrity status, and almost always got heavy coverage in
newspapers when he visited a city to conduct lectures, workshops,
or symposia.

Ellis's sessions at the annual meetings of the American
Psychological Association drew (draw) among the biggest
audiences. Not only were colleagues and students eager to hear of
his theory and methods, but he was good theater. He never
hesitated to illustrate his methods by inviting volunteers from the
audience to expose themselves to his techniques on stage. He once
competed with other major theorists, with three different
therapists interviewing the same patient. The film of it, *Three
Approaches to Psychotherapy* (1963), with Carl Rogers and Fritz
Perls, has become a classic in college psychology classes.

In a typical lecture-demonstration at an American
Psychological Association convention several years ago, a
volunteer from the audience told of her long-term therapy that
unsuccessfully tried to treat her difficulties with her sister. After
asking a few questions, Ellis devised a way for her to think about
and treat the sister that was a brilliantly simple and direct way to
handle the problem, taking into account sensitive and complex
material. The volunteer herself said it made excitingly good
sense.

This is not to suggest that stage, television, and radio
performers should be encouraged to solve difficult human
problems in 15 to 20 minutes. It is, rather, to suggest that a
sophisticated audience can differentiate among a huckster, a
confidante, and a professional doing a good job in a short time.
Ellis passes that test with flying colors.

12

The Later Years

By 1970, Ellis was in his late fifties, well settled in his Institute and with a program that was flowering with clients, staff, students, and public audiences for lectures, recordings, and workshops. He had set the pattern of his habits to maintain a high level of productivity, largely undistracted by social or personal events. He was concentrating on advancing his views and practices of therapy throughout the country and world. As Penelope Russianoff put it, he was operating with an acute sense of his mortality, and wanted to make the largest contribution he could to humankind in his limited lifetime.*

Both by being highly regular in his habits and by eliminating all unnecessary activities that were not productive for his mission, he ensured that he squeezed maximum professional output from himself. As one ages, it becomes increasingly evident that irregular habits reduce effectiveness, that regularity, even approaching rigidity, conserves one's powers to continue to produce in accustomed ways. This may not be true of artists and other innovators, for some of whom irregularity and dormant or disparate activities may trigger spurts of creativity.

By the sixties one's creative years usually are past, and one lives off the fat of skills and knowledge acquired in earlier years. While Ellis has been vital, alert, and energetic from 1970 to the present, he had earlier set the nature of his contributions to his profession and the public. Although he would add useful new

---

*Penelope Russianoff 1984: personal interview.

ideas and techniques, they did not contain the richness of invention and biting propaganda of his middle age, when he burst on the professional scene with his bright, enlightened views.

During the 1970s he strongly pursued the same ideas, but the times overtook him. His views were adopted and applied in sex therapy and psychotherapy by many who did not know where they originated, and did not acknowledge Ellis's pioneering presentations.

His theory and methods continued to arouse controversy, particularly from psychoanalysts, who still viewed him as superficial in his therapy; from Rogerians, who continued to criticize him as intrusive and demanding; from behavior modifiers, who believed that he placed too much emphasis on thoughts, attitudes, and words; and from the latest comers to the competition, the cognitive (behavioral) therapists, who often overlooked his original contributions to their use of images and perceptions to change behavior.

Lately Ellis has more often been credited with his contributions to cognitive therapy and more frequently included under that rubric. However, he continues to insist upon the unique power of his RET, and its prior embrace of the basic concepts of what is now called cognitive (behavioral) therapy. Only the historians of psychology need to know who came first and how. In any case, Ellis will stand out in this era as one of the most original and influential contributors to progress in the field.

RET has grown mightily since the early 1970s, mainly by expanding its activities in psychotherapy with individuals, in training psychologists, psychiatrists, and social workers in its methods, and in conducting sessions for the general public and for special groups, such as women and corporations.

There have been some innovations in recent years. One was a film series consisting of old movies shown at the Institute to illustrate how nonsensically romantic notions, mainly about sex, love, and marriage, can inspire subsequent muddle-headed thinking. They generate unreasonable expectations that are bound to be disappointed in real life. Discussions followed the showings to underscore how wrong-minded portrayals in the movies get people into personal trouble.

Also in the early 1970s the Institute conducted one of the more innovative measures in the history of preventive psychotherapy. It started what was called the "Living School," for children ages 6 to 14, where, along with a standard curriculum, they were also taught the principles of RET. Licensed teachers were hired and trained in the purposes and methods of RET, and around 30 students were enrolled in the classes. Charges were based on ability to pay. The school quarters were in the Institute building.

The purpose of the school was to demonstrate that children's thinking could be directed toward rational, efficient, socially desirable attitudes and solutions to their problems. All kinds of devices were used to this end — slogans on the walls, songs with an RET message, little talks, classroom discussions of common problems and solutions.

The school lasted for five years. It was adjudged a success by its directors and the parents involved. No systematic studies were conducted, however, and there has been no follow-up, because no adequate control group was developed. As with most research on psychotherapy, criteria were difficult to define, follow-up over a period of years was not done, and there was no adequate scientific design to assess results. But a noble experiment was undertaken without outside support which proved that such a school could be run in satisfactory academic ways along with a mental health purpose and a concrete therapeutic orientation, in this case RET.

It also illustrated the problems that would have to be confronted before another such experiment could meet scientific standards. One of the major difficulties was the mobility of the students. Some of them and their parents moved away. Or they wanted enriched resources, such as a gym, which the little school could not provide. Or they obtained enough of RET so they did not any longer want or need its special orientation. Or they didn't want to stay long. The major problem was to hold the students long enough, and retain communication with them afterward for sufficient time to determine the advantages, if any, of the education in RET for their subsequent mental health.

During this period Ellis expanded the range of techniques he recommended to influence his clients. He encouraged the use of diaries, and he used both group and individual sessions for the same clients. He experimented with marathon sessions, then decided that the inconvenience of keeping clients awake for 24 hours or more at a time was not justified by the results. He found instead that single days of 14-hour marathons worked well.

He also tried different forms of homework reports and assignments outside of the individual sessions. He had patients imagine different kinds of situations and what they might do in them, adapting Maultsby's (Maultsby & Ellis 1974) rational-emotive image to make it more forceful and effective. He started a program of 9-hour training sessions for 60 to 200 participants at a time.*

During his adolescence, Ellis had become an expert on musical comedies and operettas, and had hoped to become a famous composer and librettist. He never did, but neither did he relinquish the desire. He retains most of his past dreams, such as publishing novels, which he still hopes to do — someday. He did have his chance, though, to return to writing lyrics for an audience. He wrote them to advance the principles of RET, and set them to popular tunes (he never did learn how to write music). He became notable for these lyrics. The *St. Louis Post-Dispatch* reported in 1980 ("Albert Ellis Mixes Shown," 1980, p. 2D), "There is more than a tinge of showmanship in an Albert Ellis workshop . . . Ellis employed his Woody Allen-style voice to lead the group in singing . . . to the 'Whiffenpoof Song'":

> I cannot have all my wishes filled —
> Whine, whine, whine!
> I cannot have every frustration stilled —
> Whine, whine, whine!
> Life really owes me the things that I miss,
> Fate has to grant me eternal bliss!
> And if I must settle for less than this —
> Whine, whine, whine! (p. 2D)†

And so on. He wrote, and the Institute sells, an entire book of these songs, and he has led group singing at all kinds of meetings, including several annual conventions of the American Psychological Association. Hardly the elegance one might expect of a famous psychologist, but Ellis is a showman. He draws large audiences because of it, and that helps mightily to attract attention to RET.

But perhaps the greatest change in his attitude came with regard to homosexuals. Originally Ellis had been a hero to them, preaching powerfully for sexual freedom, for any sexual practices that were not harmful to the individual or others, for a wide range of sexual experimentation without irrational fear of what it might "mean" in some philosophical or theoretical sense. He addressed

---

*Albert Ellis 1985: personal interview.

†"Whine, Whine, Whine" From *A Garland of Rational Songs*. Copyright 1976 by the Institute for Rational Living, Inc., New York, New York.

many homosexual meetings, and was considered a leading advocate of sexual tolerance.

In 1965 he had written a book entitled *Homosexuality: Its Causes and Cure* (1965), in which he concluded that fixated homosexuality, like fixated heterosexuality, or fixated anything, did not permit full consideration of alternatives that might bring satisfaction. His major thrust was that if homosexuals wanted to enjoy heterosexual relationships, they could learn to do so through the principles of RET, that it was nonsense to believe one was born to be one way or the other and that a sexual orientation could not be changed.

This is a professionally legitimate view, as much as any other at least, and one held by many experts in the field. Many homosexuals, however, and homosexual organizations have become virulently opposed to this attitude. They insist that one is born homosexual, that it cannot be changed, and that therapy to produce change is invariably unsuccessful. Ellis cites many studies that indicate homosexuality has been changed via therapy to full heterosexuality or to bisexuality.

Lately, however, he has relented somewhat in his stance. He now believes that there may often be a strong genetic component in homosexuality and that change in such cases "is quite difficult to accomplish and often not worth working at."* Janet Wolfe disagrees with his notion of successful change. He is reluctant to stand by his book on the subject of "cure," since that implies a concept of sickness he does not hold. He still sees many gay clients — "almost always to help them lead happier homosexual lives."† It is probably the only major change in his theoretical views since he turned on psychoanalysis.

Despite his prominence in the field, his widespread memberships in all kinds of professional and humanistic organizations, his frequent professional and public presentations, his best-selling general and professional publications, and his large and devoted following, Ellis has never been elected president of the American Psychological Association. The 1970s would have been his time for it. He was at the peak of his impact and professional activity.

Years ago, the presidency of the American Psychological Association was an acknowledgment of its holder's scientific

---

*Albert Ellis 1985: personal interview.

†Janet Wolfe 1985: personal interview.

importance in the profession, and the solicitation of votes was considered vulgar. In recent years, however, election has required vigorous, dedicated campaigning, the expenditure of large amounts of money (setting a spending limit has been considered), and the direct wooing of votes. As a result, some of the most significant psychologists in the history of the field have not been anointed lately. Most conspicuously, Skinner, probably the most notable of living psychologists, and Ellis have never been elected to that office.

It is also likely that Ellis's emphasis on sex has turned off some colleagues, along with an imputed desire to make money in writing his best sellers and accepting so many lectureships and workshops. It is not generally known that he plows back all such money into his Institute. Also working against him are his occasional stylistic crudity and language, and his foot in the two doors of the profession, clinical and scientific-experimental, rather than just one. In 1985, however, the American Psychological Association (see "Awards for Distinguished Professional Contributions," 1986) belatedly gave Ellis its notable award for Distinguished Professional Contributions. The citation read:

> Dr. Albert Ellis' theoretical contributions have had a profound effect on the professional practice of psychology. His theories on the primacy of cognition in psychopathology are at the forefront of practice and research in Clinical Psychology. Dr. Ellis' theories have importantly encouraged an active-directive approach to psychological treatment, combined with a deep humanistic respect for the uniqueness of the individual. His early research in love and sexuality and his early practice . . . resulted in a deeper understanding of intimate human relationships as well as the expansion of our clinical knowledge and therapeutic techniques. . . . Dr. Ellis expanded his clinical work . . . into a comprehensive theory of psychological treatment, Rational-Emotive Therapy. . . . In addition to his scholarly contributions, Dr. Ellis has been a devoted clinician and teacher. . . . Few psychologists have nurtured and mentored as many clinicians. . . . As a teacher, he has always been a model, an inspiration, and a discerning . . . advisor. (p. 380)

In 1976 Ellis's mother died of a stroke at age 93. She was kicking up her heels, dancing and carrying on to the end, despite common ailments of old age. To the end, he showed her the only gentle touch I found in his latter-day correspondence — not intimacy, but kindliness and solicitude for her discomforts while reassuring her about his own health, spirits — and relations with women.

Until he wrote his section for this chapter, Ellis had publicly expressed no such solicitude for Janet, who is, of course, much younger than he and in good health. He quickly became, in the 1970s, the major influence in her life. He won her to RET, he encouraged her to pursue a doctorate in clinical psychology, he shared the administration of the Institute with her, he supported her efforts to make a place for herself in the profession, to the point that eventually she traveled throughout the country, on her own, to spread the gospel of RET, with particular application to women's emancipation.*

The nature of their relationship became solidified during the 1970s until it was obvious that this was no casual or short-term affair, but that it would probably be the longest-lasting one of his life. It seemed rather a practical situation at first, in which they needed each other: he, to enhance his physical health, activity, and comfort; she, to find a goal and way of life. She quickly adopted RET for her purposes and has not wavered since. She soon was playing a major role in running the Institute.

Rough spots between them were ironed out during this time. They did their work in separate quarters and seldom saw each other except late at night. Each traveled frequently without the other in an open relationship that accepted liaisons on the road. They presumably ruled out such relationships for New York City, where it could strain their affinity both by taking time from each other and by threatening to replace their long-term bond.

Each readily acknowledges the influence the other has had in his/her life. Albert thinks that Janet has largely had her way in furnishing their quarters, in running the Institute, in establishing a social life. He expresses no complaints, merely observing that she is free to establish and maintain her own life while making few demands of him, with which he "dutifully complies."

He acknowledges that he has influenced her substantially, but admits to no pressing need for her that might imply dependency. He has consistently disclaimed that he has craved anyone at all since he rejected any need for love while enduring the changeability of his first wife, Karyl. Sometimes this denial of any dependency seems unreasonable, since he has been temporarily deranged when overdosed on insulin and has had to be restrained

---

*Albert Ellis 1985: personal interview; Janet Wolfe 1985: personal interview.

by firm measures to keep him safe, and needed help when his ankle was damaged.

Janet looks up to him as the person who essentially directed her life when they first met and she was drifting in her activities and goals. RET then gradually determined her life, as it already had his. She acknowledges his profound influence on her and is grateful for it. She also knows that he has needed her at times despite his denial, that she has served as a devoted watchdog to safeguard his health, and that she has encouraged the growth of his affectional capacity.

In addition, she has grown to assert her own requirements, to lead enough of a social life to satisfy her even though she must do it almost entirely without him. She can occasionally wheedle a night out with him, but such an event is increasingly rare. It is possible that he has not been entirely comfortable about accepting affairs as readily as their oral understanding would imply.

The *Philadelphia Inquirer* ("The Know-It-All Sex Shrink," 1983) pointed out: despite his wisdom, Ellis has been divorced twice and quoted him as saying that ". . . now I live in sin for the last 18 years, with one woman. And, also we have a sort of open arrangement . . . ." (p. 9). Neither seems to care to be married, though recently they have agreed that he must make a will to provide for her in a way that might not be required if they were married. But marriage would seem to make a difference. His long-time friend Paul Meehl, for example, knew nothing of Janet until 1986.

Typical of their financial naiveté, it seems that neither Albert nor Janet initiated the question of inheritance. It was Ellis's brother, Paul, the businessman-manager of Albert's finances, who raised the issue and worked on it.

Since 1977 the Institute has charged modestly for lectures and workshops ($4.00 for the former). It submits insurance claims for therapy but requires payment in advance for services. Fees vary according to the seniority of the staff member, from $45 for 30 minutes with Ellis, about 20 percent lower for less experienced therapists, and much less for therapists in training. Individual clients are encouraged to participate in groups led by Janet and Albert for $60 per person per month.

All kinds of educational sessions are held continuously. A recent catalog (*Institute for Rational-Emotive Therapy* [*Catalogue*] 1986) lists weekly lectures and workshops for one month: "Self Renewal: Surviving Burnout and Mid-Life Crisis"; "Rational-Emotive Psychotherapy in Groups (for professionals)"; "Becoming

More Effective: A Workshop for Women"; "Primary Certificate Practicum for Professionals"; "Loving Yourself"; "Rational-Emotive Training, Intensive."

The same catalog lists 12 pages of books, pamphlets, films, and tapes — that are for sale. It describes five Institute leaders who are available to give lectures and conduct workshops. Fees for outside presentations are negotiable, but the Institute charges for Ellis's services essentially what he would earn working in New York, around $1,500 a day. He may combine engagements in the same area so that sponsors can split the cost.

His books and articles continue to pour forth. The most important are mentioned throughout this book (see References). His workshops have been held around the world, including, in one recent year, Bombay, Jerusalem, Sydney, and Montreal. Training is available at various locations in the United States, and through affiliates in Australia, England, Germany, Italy, Mexico, and the Netherlands.

Ellis has also been mellowing with regard to his adversaries. He never thought that his enemies were "out to get him," according to a friend; he dealt with them on intellectual grounds almost exclusively. Only once have I heard him speak deprecatingly of an acquaintance — one erstwhile friend who, when drunk, seemed to be trying to attack Janet.

Otherwise he has seldom commented personally on those who don't like him, and seems successfully to ignore that aspect of their attitudes. Two well-known colleagues (and doubtless others) think that he is unfeeling, and even unethical in his advocacy and practice of sexual freedom, and the informal way he writes some of his books, but such views seem not to bother him at all.

Ellis acknowledges that he occasionally cuts loose on friends with a quick irritability that he just as rapidly forgets. One friend reported that Ellis told him at times that he (the friend) was behaving like a "pain in the ass." He comments, "he was correct about that about half the time. . . . " He doesn't spare such rough words even with patients. He advised one to " . . . tell your crazy mother to drop dead." Patients as well as friends have generally reacted to him with respect, but sometimes " . . . kind of as if he's from another planet" as far as his feelings go, wrote a colleague.*

---

*Personal correspondence: 1984, 1985.

His language also has muted somewhat. The heyday when he sparked lots of attention with it has passed. Many use the same words today from public platforms, especially when they're on a program with him. Vulgarity in his speech has obviously become much less of an attention getter.

But Ellis would deny any diminution of his blunt language — and of any other form of vitality, for that matter. He's full of denial of any lack of feeling, the desire for approbation, any strong sense of hurt, guilt, disappointment, personal anger, grief, unfairness. He takes quick exception to most views of his personal life that differ from his own and, with less intensity, of his professional life. Nonetheless, he is exceptionally accepting of the fact that others may disagree with him, and does not get angry or maintain anger about it. He merely states his disagreement forcefully, which may have an intimidating effect.

He is occasionally reluctant to acknowledge his debt to contemporaries — for example, that Meehl may have called his attention to Epictetus who is so basic to RET. Nor does he readily admit to some contradictions or distorted recollections, even though he may later modify them, about his early family life: for example, his claim that he formulated the principles of RET when he was a young child, or that he may have mistreated his sister. He has minimized his misbehavior when overdosed on insulin. Friends believe that he does experience anxiety, especially over events he cannot always control, such as meeting schedules.

Ellis is often quick to admit to other contradictions and misinterpretations, and to correct them. Once, for example, he bit an ambulance driver when in insulin shock. At first he denied he was out of his head, but later agreed that he was. He has also reluctantly accepted his brother's interpretation that he may have been protected as a child because of his sickliness.

These are picky things such as involve almost all mortals. They contribute to a fuller description of him and do not diminish in any way his standing in his profession.

After the two institutes were merged into the Institute for Rational-Emotive Therapy, the structure of responsibility remained the same, with Ellis, as always, listed as executive director; Janet, as director of clinical services; Raymond DiGiuseppe, as director of training and research; and other directors and consultants heading more specialized services that change from time to time.

With Ellis funding most of its activities as well as being the founder, spiritual leader, and dominant force of the Institute, there has never been an organized rebellion. However, administrative staff members have left or, rarely, been fired, one major loss being the director of training several years ago. Ellis confronted him for criticizing RET in a paper delivered at a professional meeting. This was no small matter to Ellis. He believed it was a serious deviation from the fundamentals of RET, and that the man should no longer represent the Institute.

The departing director considered the difference with Ellis to be a matter of values. He adhered to what he considered "Christian values," and to a religiously based therapy that he believed diverged fundamentally from Ellis's atheism, which held (only) humanistic values. He also believed that Ellis often gave practical advice that had no foundation in RET.*

The directors of Institute activities have, except for Albert and Janet, been part-time, and not fully engaged only with the Institute. Thus they might not identify as closely with RET as those working there full time.

This problem also shows itself in the inadequacy of much of the research done at the Institute. Two ex-directors believe that research has never been sufficiently supported, largely because clinical work and training have had priority for the time and energy of staff and students. They believe that Ellis has not as keen a dedication to rigorous research as to clinical practice and training, so he will not sacrifice standard procedures in order to obtain control groups, follow-up data, statistical analysis, and other processes that would interfere with the free flow of therapy. Nor will he spend the money for analysis of the research. He did employ at least two persons to do research part time, but they never completed the work and eventually left.

Like his ex-wives, however, the ex-staffers expressed considerable respect for Ellis and his efforts to listen to and be fair with them, even though they disagreed with him. They believe they can still communicate well with him.

Ellis's personal regimen has changed very little over the past decade. Ellis (1983b) wrote about it:

> I still carry out my regular daily and weekly program, pretty much as I have been doing for the last 40 years, and almost exactly as I have been working since 1965 — when the Institute ... opened our present building. ... Believe it or not, here is one of my typical weekday working schedules:

---

*Personal interview with departing director in 1986.

8:30 to 9:00 A.M.: Rise within ten seconds after my alarm rings; wash, dress, eat, and take my daily shot of insulin.

9:00 to 9:30 A.M.: Confer with administrator on Institute affairs.

9:30 A.M. to 1:00 P.M.: Conduct individual therapy sessions. . . . Most . . . run for half an hour. . . . At 11:30 A.M., during one of my sessions, I eat my second meal of the day, a sandwich.

1:00 to 3:00 P.M.: Supervision of the Institute ['s] ten or twelve training Fellows. . . . Each . . . is in one of my seven regular therapy groups and assists me. . . . In the course of this . . . session, I usually eat another sandwich and some fruit. . . .

3:00 to 5:00 P.M.: Supervision of the individual psychotherapy sessions of three of our training Fellows . . . [or] therapists who come . . . to work for our Primary . . . or Associate . . . Certificate.

5:00 to 5:30 P.M.: Supper in my apartment . . . one of my two hot meals of the day sometimes cooked by me and sometimes by . . . Dr. Janet L. Wolfe. Oh, yes! — we also talk and share at this time.

5:30 to 6:00 P.M.: Individual psychotherapy session with one of my . . . clients.

6:00 to 7:30 P.M.: Leading one of my seven weekly regular therapy groups, with from ten to thirteen . . . members. . . .

7:30 to 9:00 P.M.: Leading another of my regular therapy groups (in the course of which I eat my fifth small meal of the day, usually a cheese sandwich).

9:00 to 11:00 P.M.: Final half-hour or hour-long individual psychotherapy sessions. . . .

11:00 to 11:30 P.M.: Another hot meal, usually cooked by Janet. Conversation with her about Institute and personal affairs.

11:30 P.M. to 12:15 A.M.: Return to my office. . . . Finish up Institute business for the day and dictate letters relating to my fairly voluminous world-wide correspondence.

12:15 to 1:00 A.M.: Return to . . . apartment for conversation with Janet, brief physical exercise program, and shower. Usually get to bed by 1:00 A.M.

1:00 to 1:15 A.M.: Final small sandwich. . . . Soon sound asleep.

3:00 to 4:10 A.M.: Spontaneously awake; go to the bathroom; eat my eighth and final sandwich of the day, brush and water-pik my teeth (for the eighth time), and go back to sleep.

8:30 A.M.: Here I go again for a new day! . . .

"A pretty hectic program!" people say. . . . Right! But I like it; my health is generally good in spite of my diabetes. . . consistently weigh my usual 150 pounds; and my blood pressure has been quite normal up to now, but [recently] slightly elevated (which is common with diabetics). I look forward to going on this way, and finally (I hope!) dying in the saddle, about fifty years from now. Well, we shall see! (pp. 47–49)

In case the reader is wondering when Ellis does his writing and reading, that is done Saturday nights and Sundays, when the above schedule is laid aside in favor of equally rigid periods dedicated to work on his manuscripts, his correspondence, and books and journals he orders. He meticulously answers all letters promptly, sometimes more fully than the writer anticipates. And in off hours, he can receive and make phone calls, although it is difficult to squeeze them in.

"What's new?" I asked Albert and Janet separately when I visited with them recently. The most major event was that he was designated to receive the American Psychological Association Award for Distinguished Professional Contributions to Knowledge plus a $500 prize and the honor of addressing the next annual convention. His nominator, Ray DiGiuseppe, told me, ". . . I can't imagine his biography being very interesting since all he does is work, but I am sure there must be some more exciting things in his past."*

He also has invited a number of colleagues to collaborate on books with him and to choose among these titles: *The Biological Basis of Human Disturbance; The Case against Religion and Religiosity; Transpersonal Psychology and Psychotherapy, The Enormous Harm That They Do; Psychotherapy as Disturbance; A History of Human Stupidity;* and *The Sex Lives of Famous People.* It should be a good bet that he will see at least some of these to completion.

Janet added that the Institute has expanded corporate services, with a specialist to run them. Workshops are scheduled for Australia, Canada, and Puerto Rico, as well as numerous places across the continental United States.

So neither Ellis nor the Institute is standing still. Their influence is still expanding in ripples from the rock he dropped into the psychotherapy pool 30 years ago. He seems to have latched on to a fundamental truth of this emerging science: that the human animal's best hope for solving its personal problems is to use its brain as effectively as possible, rationally, according to the dictates of science, without distraction by myths, conventions, or imperatives about behavior that have been taught as if they were necessities of human life.

There is this final footnote: After writing a review of a biography of Helene Deutsch that says almost as much significant about Freud's behavior as about hers (Roazen 1985), I was struck by the similarities between Freud and Ellis, and by how superficial the differences between them may have been in their actual conduct of psychotherapy.

---

*Raymond DiGiuseppe 1985: personal interview.

Both valued the intellect and rationality above all. Both considered themselves scientists carefully examining problems as basically and stripped of cant as possible. Both did excellent scientific work early in their careers: Freud with aphasia, childhood paralyses, and gold staining of brain tissue; Ellis, in his Ph.D. dissertation on questionnaires, and on sexual misconceptions. Neither, however, sustained his scientific standards for his later and most important work except for reviewing the literature, or produced rigorous research to substantiate his theory.

Both came to consider constitution and genetics as fundamental to human behavior, with cultural influences of limited effect and subject to change. Both tried to cleanse sex of its societal inhibitions and strictures.

Both were ruthless adversaries when crossed, both were strong atheists, both preached like Jewish prophets — fluent, prolific, and dedicated — to establish and gain acceptance for their beliefs. Both roused dedicated followers and bitter enemies with their views, and both could charm an audience when they wanted to. Both enjoyed "detectiving," as Ellis called it, searching for underlying reasons for human behavior.

They have their differences also. Freud surely had an elegance and grace in writing that Ellis would never cultivate; and in speech they differed sharply when Ellis purposely developed a vulgarity unnatural to him. Freud was in practice much more conservative (or guarded) in his way of life, grooming, and sexual behavior. Freud had many more petty personal quarrels with colleagues and friends, while Ellis's conflicts have practically never been personal and he has nurtured objectivity and continuity in relationships.

Ellis accepts the above parallels and agrees that perhaps the major difference between them as therapists is that Freud rather quickly became bored with therapy, perhaps sensing the limited applications of his theories for "cures" or behavior change. Freud came to believe that psychoanalysis was primarily a way to study human behavior, not to change it. Ellis finds his own views to be most useful in solving human problems, and thoroughly enjoys and flourishes in the clinical application of his theories.

In their practice of psychotherapy, however, at least some of Freud's work eerily resembled Ellis's despite the greatly different methods of psychoanalysis practiced by most of Freud's followers. At times, at least, he did something like RET. One of Freud's most famous patients has reported how he worked with her (Roazen

1985). He gave her direct, practical advice and terminated her after a year, telling her why she should stay with her husband, that he thought her goals were clear and rational, and that she could work effectively toward them on her own. He thought she needed no more therapy — even though she later took more analysis from a different therapist.

One other similarity particularly stands out. The young Freud wrote: "I am not really a man of science, not an observer, not an experimenter, and not a thinker. I am nothing but by temperament a conquistador — an adventurer — with the curiosity, the boldness, and the tenacity that belong to that type of being" (quoted in Malcolm 1984, p. 102).

I believe that the young Ellis might well have written similarly if he had possessed Freud's capacity to see himself in the broadest perspective. Above all, the young Ellis wanted to become famous, and he tried a variety of ways to do so. But he could not find within himself the key to originality, creativity, and freewheeling in any of them: light music, radical politics, fiction writing. Finally he did find it in psychotherapy with his creation of RET.

Hettie (mother) and Albert, 7, Paul, 5, and Janet, 3 — 1920

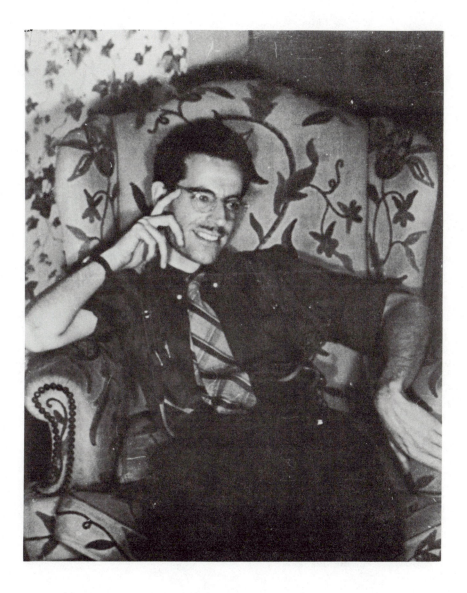

Albert — 1950

Albert — 1960

Rhoda Winter — 1957

Albert — 1965

Photograph of Albert Ellis and Janet Wolfe — 1974. Courtesy of
Jill Krementz, 228 E. 48th St., New York City

Albert — 1972

Workshop on RET and Stress Reduction — Kuwait, 1980

Epilogue

Just when the final editing of the manuscript had been completed, I received belated modifications proposed by Janet Wolfe which changed my perspective on her relationship with Al from the one he had recorded in our interviews, and others had substantiated.

Besides incorporating a few specific revisions, I have now included several pages of a long quotation from Ellis of his current version of their association. It represents a greater attention and sensitivity to their relationship.

I do believe that Janet exercises more effect on him than he originally conveyed, perhaps increasing as he grows older. Ellis remains, however, a committed antiromanticist and cool customer who constantly, in word and deed, asserts his independence and rationality.

At the last convention of the American Psychological Association in August, 1987, he was his usual self, speaking at meetings with certitude, fearlessness, and clarity. In addition, it was apparent at the party he and Janet threw for guests at the convention, that the Institute building had been spruced up. Perhaps this, like other changes occurring during the years I talked with him for this book, the act of being observed modestly changed the nature of that being described.

References

Adler, A. *The practice and theory of individual psychology.* London: Routledge & Kegan Paul, 1955.

Albert Ellis mixes shown. *St. Louis Post-Dispatch,* October 10, 1980, p. 2D.

American heritage dictionary, 1st ed., s.v. "romance"; "romantic."

Awards for distinguished professional contributions: 1985 — Albert Ellis. *American Psychologist,* 1986, *41,* 380–397.

Barber, B. Resistance by scientists to scientific discovery. *Science,* September 1, 1961, pp. 1–7.

Bayer, R. *Homosexuality and American psychiatry.* New York: Basic Books, 1981.

Beck, A. *Cognitive therapy and the emotional disorders.* New York: International Universities Press, 1976.

Bruner, J. Thoughts on thoughts. *New York Review of Books,* August 18, 1983, p. 36.

Detroit Free Press, February 19, 1969, n.p.

Ellis, A., The sexual psychology of human hermaphrodites. *Psychosomatic Medicine,* 1945, *7,* 108–125.

____. Towards the improvement of psychoanalytic research. *Psychoanalytic Review,* 1949, *36,* 123–143.

____. *The folklore of sex.* New York: Boni/Doubleday, 1951.

____. On the cure of homosexuality. *International Journal of Sexology,* 1952, *55,* 135–138.

____. Is the vaginal orgasm a myth? In A. P. Pillay & A. Ellis (eds.), *Sex, society and the individual.* Bombay: International Journal of Sexology, 1953. (a)

____. Recent reviews on sexual deviation. In A. P. Pillay & A. Ellis (eds.), *Sex, society and the individual.* Bombay: International Journal of Sexology, 1953. (b)

____. A study of 300 sex offenders. In A. P. Pillay & A. Ellis (eds.), *Sex, society and the individual.* Bombay: International Journal of Sexology, 1953. (c)

151

____. *The American sexual tragedy*. New York: Twayne, 1954. (a)

____. An operational reformulation of some of the basic principles of psychoanalysis. Paper presented at the Conference on Psychoanalysis and Philosophy of Science at the Center for the Philosophy of Science, University of Minnesota, 1954. (b)

____. *Sex life of the American woman and the Kinsey Report*. New York: Greenberg, 1954. (c)

____. New approaches to psychotherapy techniques. *Journal of Clinical Psychology Monograph Supplement*, 1955, *11*, 1–53.

____. *How to live with a neurotic*. New York: Crown, 1957. (a)

____. Rational psychotherapy and individual psychology. *Journal of Individual Psychology*, 1957, *13*, 38–44. (b)

____. Rational psychotherapy. *Journal of General Psychology*, 1958, *59*, 35–49. (a)

____. *Sex without guilt*. New York: Lyle Stuart, 1958. (b)

____. *The art and science of love*. New York: Lyle Stuart, 1960. (a)

____. An impolite interview with Albert Ellis. *Realist*, May 1960, pp. 1–18. (b)

____. *Reason and emotion in psychotherapy*. New York: Lyle Stuart, 1962.

____. *The intelligent woman's guide to man-hunting*. New York: Lyle Stuart, 1963. (a)

____. *Sex and the single man*. New York: Lyle Stuart, 1963. (b)

____. *Homosexuality: Its causes and cure*. New York: Lyle Stuart, 1965. (a)

____. *Suppressed: Seven key essays publishers dared not print*. Chicago: New Classics House, 1965. (b)

____. *The sensuous person: Critique and corrections*. New York: Lyle Stuart, 1972.

____. *Humanistic psychotherapy: The rational-emotive approach*. New York: Julian Press, 1973.

____. *Sex and the liberated man*. Secaucus, NJ: Lyle Stuart, 1976.

____. *The intelligent woman's guide to dating and mating*. Secaucus, NJ: Lyle Stuart, 1979.

____. The philosophical implications and dangers of some popular behavior therapy techniques. In M. Rosenbaum, C. M. Franks, & Y. Jaffe (eds.), *Perspectives on behavior therapy in the eighties*. New York: Springer, 1981.

____. New developments in rational-emotive therapy. *I'ACT Rationally Newsletter*, 1982, n.p.

____. Failures in rational-emotive therapy. In E. B. Foa & P. M. G. Emmelkamp (eds.), *Failures in behavior therapy*. New York: Wiley, 1983. (a)

____. My philosophy of work and love. *Psychotherapy in Private Practice*, Spring 1983, pp. 43–49. (b)

____. The origins of rational-emotive therapy (RET). *Voices*, 1983, *18*, 29–33. (c)

____. The evolution of rational-emotive therapy (RET) and cognitive behavior therapy (CBT). Paper presented at Evolution of Psychotherapy: A Conference, Phoenix, December 15, 1985.

Ellis, A., & Brancale, R. *The psychology of sex offenders*. Springfield, IL: Charles C. Thomas, 1956.

Ellis, A., & Conway, R. O. *The art of erotic seduction*. New York: Lyle Stuart, 1967.

Ellis, A., & Harper, R. A. *Creative marriage*. Secaucus, NJ: Lyle Stuart, 1961.

_____. *A new guide to rational living*. Englewood Cliffs, NJ: Prentice-Hall, 1975.

Ellis, A., Rogers, C., & Perls, F. (speakers). *Three approaches to psychotherapy: Gloria*. Orange, CA: Psychological Films, 1963. (Film)

Ellis, A., & Sagarin, E. *Nymphomania: A study of the oversexed woman*. New York: Gilbert Press, 1964.

Ellis, A., & Whitely, J. M. (eds.). *Theoretical and empirical foundations of rational-emotive therapy*. Monterey, CA: Brooks/Cole, 1979.

Epictetus. *The works of Epictetus*, T. W. Higginson, trans., vol. II. Boston: Little, Brown, 1897.

Ferenczi, S. *Final contributions to the theory and technique of psychoanalysis*. New York: Basic Books, 1955.

Freud, S. *The origins of psychoanalysis*. New York: Basic Books, 1954.

_____. Psychoanalysis. In *Encyclopaedia Britannica*, 14th ed.

Gardner, H. *Frames of mind*. New York: Basic Books, 1983.

Glasser, W. *Reality therapy*. New York: Harper, 1964.

Harris, F. *My life and loves*. New York: Grove Press, 1963.

Hathaway, S. R. Some considerations relative to non-directive therapy. *Journal of Clinical Psychology*, 1958, *4*, 226–231.

Heesacker, M., Heppner, P., & Rogers, M. Classics and emerging classics in counseling psychology. *Journal of Counseling Psychology*, 1982, *29*, 400–405.

Institute for rational-emotive therapy (Catalogue). September 1986–March 1987. Published by the Institute for Rational-Emotive Therapy, 45 East 65th St., New York, NY 10021.

Kazin, A. The exceptional William James. *New York Review of Books*, November 10, 1983, p. 4.

Kendall, P., & Bemis, K. M. Thought and action in psychotherapy: The cognitive behavioral approaches. In M. Herson, A. Kayden, & A. Bellak (eds.), *The clinical psychology handbook*. New York: Pergamon, 1983.

Kinsey, A., Pomeroy, W. B., & Martin, C. E. *Sexual behavior in the human male*. Philadelphia: W. B. Saunders, 1948.

The know-it-all sex shrink. *Philadelphia Inquirer*, May 15, 1983, p. 9.

"M." *The sensuous man*. New York: Lyle Stuart, 1971.

Malcolm, J. *In the Freud archives*. New York: Knopf, 1984.

Marquis who's who in America. Wilmette, IL: Macmillan Directory Division, 1986–1987.

Masters, W., & Johnson, V. *Human sexual inadequacy*. Boston: Little, Brown, 1970.

Maultsby, M. C., Jr., & Ellis, A. *Techniques for using rational-emotive imagery (REI)*. New York: Institute for Rational Living, 1974.

Miller, H. *Sexus*. New York: Grove Press, 1965.

Miller, R. C., & Berman, J. S. The efficacy of cognitive behavior therapies: A quantitative review of the research evidence. *Psychological Bulletin*, 1983, *94*, 39–53.

Paris, F. C. *Gestalt therapy verbatim*. Lafayette, CA: Real People Press, 1969.

Philadelphia Daily News, September 7, 1967, n.p.

Phillips, L. *Psychotherapy: A modern theory and practice*. Englewood Cliffs, NJ: Prentice-Hall, 1956.

_____. *A guide for therapists and patients to short-term psychotherapy*. Springfield, IL: C. C. Thomas, 1985.

Pillay, A. P., & Ellis, A. (eds.). *Sex, society and the individual*. Bombay: International Journal of Sexology, 1953.

Report of the presidential commission on obscenity and pornography. [No city] CA: William Hanling, 1970.

Reuben, D. *Everything you always wanted to know about sex but were afraid to ask*. New York: McKay, 1969.

Roazen, P. *Helene Deutsch: A psychoanalyst's life*. Garden City, NY: Anchor Press/Doubleday, 1985.

Rogers, C. *Counseling and psychotherapy*. Boston: Houghton, 1942.

_____. *Client-centered therapy*. Boston: Houghton-Mifflin, 1951.

Russianoff, P. (psychologist). *An unmarried woman*. Written and directed by Paul Mazursky. Made in United States (n.p.), 1978. (Film)

Sheldon, W. *The varieties of human physique*. New York: Harper & Brothers, 1940.

Skinner, B. F. *Cumulative record*. New York: Appleton-Century-Crofts, 1972.

Smith, D. Trends in counseling and psychotherapy. *American Psychologist*, 1982, *37*, 802–809.

Smith, M. What research says about the effectiveness of psychotherapy. *Hospital and Community Psychiatry*, 1982, *33*, 457–461.

Sprenkle, D., Keeney, B., & Sutton, P. Theorists who influence clinical members of AAMFT. *Journal of Marital and Family Therapy*, 1982, *8*, 367–369.

Village Voice, July 2, 1985, n.p.

Walen, S., DiGiuseppe, R. A., & Wessler, R. L. *A practitioner's guide to rational-emotive therapy*. New York: Oxford University Press, 1980.

Watson, J. B. Psychology as a behaviorist views it, *Psychology Review*. 1913, *20*, 158–177.

Wiener, D. N., & Raths, O. N. Contributions of the mental hygiene clinic team to clinic decisions. *American Journal of Orthopsychiatry*, 1959, *2*, 350–356.

Ellis Bibliography

1945

The case study as a research method. *Review of Educational Research, 15*, 352, 359.

Review of M. Hirschfeld, *Sexual anomalies. Psychosomatic Medicine, 7*, 382.

The sexual psychology of human hermaphrodites. *Psychosomatic Medicine, 7*, 108–125.

1946

Review of T. Reik, *A psychologist looks at love* and *Psychology of sex relations. Journal of Social Psychology, 24*, 121–126.

Review of G. H. Seward, *Sex and the social order. Journal of Social Psychology, 26*, 133–136.

The validity of personality questionnaires. *Psychological Bulletin, 43*, 385–440.

1947

A comparison of the use of direct and indirect phrasing in personality questionnaires. *Psychological Monographs, 61*, iii–41.

Discussion of Heinlein's comment on "The validity of personality questionnaires." *Psychological Bulletin, 44*, 83–86.

With J. Gerberich. Interests and attitudes. *Review of Educational Research, 17*, 64–67.

With H. H. Abelson. Other devices for investigating personality. *Review of Educational Research, 17*, 101–109.

Personality questionnaires. *Review of Educational Research, 17*, 56–63.

Questionnaire versus interview methods in the study of human love relationships. *American Sociological Review, 12*, 541–543.

Review of P. M. Symonds, *The dynamics of human adjustment. Journal of Genetic Psychology, 71*, 145–150.

With M. R. Hertz & P. M. Symonds. Rorshach methods and other projective techniques. *Review of Educational Research, 17,* 78–100.

Telepathy and psychoanalysis: A critique of recent findings. *Psychiatric Quarterly, 21,* 607–659.

1948

The application of scientific principles to scientific publications. *Scientific Monthly, 66,* 427–430.

The attitudes of psychologists toward psychological meetings. *American Psychologist, 3,* 511–512.

A critique of the theoretical contributions of non-directive therapy. *Journal of Clinical Psychology, 4,* 248–255.

Discussion of Mrs. Bernard's comments on research methods. *American Sociological Review, 13,* 219.

Questionnaire versus interview methods in the study of human love relationships. II. Uncategorized responses. *American Sociological Review, 13,* 62–65.

The relationship between personality inventory scores and other psychological test results. *Journal of Social Psychology, 26,* 287–289.

Review of A. C. Kinsey, W. B. Pomeroy, & C. E. Martin, *Sexual behavior in the human male. Journal of General Psychology, 39,* 299–326.

Review of P. Wylie, *An essay on morals. Journal of Social Psychology, 27,* 289–290.

A study of trends in recent psychoanalytic publications. *American Image, 5* (4), 3–13.

With H. Conrad. The validity of personality inventories in military practice. *Psychological Bulletin, 45,* 385–426.

Valuation in presenting scientific data. *Sociology and Social Research, 33*(2), 92–96.

The value of marriage prediction tests. *American Sociological Review, 13,* 710–718.

1949

With R. M. Beechley. Assortative mating in the parents of child guidance clinic patients. *American Sociological Review, 14,* 678–679.

With E. W. Fuller. The personal problems of senior nursing students. *American Journal of Psychiatry, 106,* 212–215.

Re-analysis of an alleged telepathic dream. *Psychiatric Quarterly, 23,* 116–126.

With H. S. Conrad. Reply to the Humm's "Notes on the validity of personality inventories in military practice." *Psychological Bulletin, 46,* 307–308.

Results of a mental hygiene approach to reading disability problems. *Journal of Consulting Psychology, 13,* 56–61.

Some significant correlations of love and family behavior. *Journal of Social Psychology, 30,* 3–16.

A study of human love relationships. *Journal of Genetic Psychology, 15,* 61–76.

A study of the love emotions of American college girls. *International Journal of Sexology, 3,*15–21.

Towards the improvement of psychoanalytic research. *Psychoanalytic Review, 36,* 123–143.

What kinds of research are American psychologists doing? *American Psychologist, 4,* 490–494.

1950

With G. Groves, M. Brown, & H. Lamson. Articles of interest to marriage and family life educators and counselors. *Marriage and Family Living, 12,* 106–110.

With R. Beechley. A comparison of matched groups of mongoloid and non-mongoloid feebleminded children. *American Journal of Mental Deficiency, 54,* 464–468.

With R. Beechley. Comparisons of Negro and white children seen at a child guidance clinic. *Psychiatric Quarterly Supplement, 24,* 93–101.

Discussion of L. M. Terman, "Predicting marriage failure from test scores." *Marriage and Family Living, 12,* 56–57.

An experiment in the rating of essay-type examination questions by college students. *Educational and Psychological Measurement, 10,* 707–711.

An introduction to the principles of scientific psychoanalysis. *Genetic Psychology Monographs, 41,* 147–212.

Love and family relationships of American college girls. *American Journal of Sociology, 55,* 550–558.

Requisites for research in psychotherapy. *Journal of Clinical Psychology, 6,* 152–156.

The sex, love and marriage questions of senior nursing students. *Journal of Social Psychology, 31,* 209–216.

1951

With R. Doorbar. Classified bibliography of articles, books, and pamphlets on sex, love and marriage, and family relations published during 1950. *Marriage and Family Living, 13*(2), 71–86.

With R. Beechley. A comparison of child guidance clinic patients coming from large, medium and small families. *Journal of Genetic Psychology, 79,* 131–144.

The folklore of sex. New York: Boni/Doubleday.

The influence of heterosexual culture on the attitudes of homosexuals. *International Journal of Sexology, 5,* 77–79.

Introduction to D. W. Cory, *The homosexual in America* (pp. ix–xi). New York: Greenberg Publishers.

Legal status of the marriage counselor: A psychologist's view. *Marriage and Family Living, 13,* 116–120.

Prostitution re-assessed. *International Journal of Sexology, 5,* 41–42.

Report on survey of members of the Division of Clinical and Abnormal Psychology who are presently engaged in paid private practice. *Supplement, Newsletter of the Division of Clinical Psychology of the American Psychological Association,* 1–4.

Review of A. Ellis, *The folklore of sex. Psychological Book Previews, 1,* 53–56.

Review of K. Horney, *Neurosis and human growth. Psychological Bulletin, 48,* 581–582.

Sex — the schizoid best seller. *Saturday Review of Literature, 34*(11), 42–44.

A study of 300 sex offenders. *International Journal of Sexology, 4,* 127–135.

A young woman convicted of manslaughter. *Case Reports in Clinical Psychology, 2*(1), 9–32.

1952

Applications of clinical psychology to sexual disorders. In D. Brower & L. A. Abt (eds.), *Progress in clinical psychology,* Vol. I (pp. 467–480). New York: Grune and Stratton.

Classified bibliography of articles, books, and pamphlets on sex, love, marriage, and family relations published during 1951. *Marriage and Family Living, 14,* 153–177.

A critique of systematic theoretical foundations in clinical psychology. *Journal of Clinical Psychology, 88,* 11–15.

With D. W. Cory (pseud.). In defense of current sex studies. *Nation, 174,* 250–252.

On the cure of homosexuality. *International Journal of Sexology, 55,* 135–138.

Perversions and neurosis. *International Journal of Sexology, 6,* 232–233.

With R. A. Harper, D. Dyer, S. Duvall, B. Timmons, R. Hill, & N. Kavinoky. Premarital sex relations: The facts and the counselor's role in relation to the facts. *Marriage and Family Living, 14,* 229–236.

With R. Brancale & R. Doorbar. Psychiatric and psychological investigations of convicted sex offenders. *American Psychiatry, 109,* 17–21.

The psychologist in private practice and the good profession. *American Psychologist, 7,* 129–131.

With R. Doorbar. Recent trends in sex, marriage and family research. *Marriage and Family Living, 14,* 338–340.

Review of E. Bergler, *The superego. Psychological Bulletin, 50,* 192.

Self-appraisal methods. In D. Brower & L. A. Abt (eds.), *Progress in clinical psychology,* Vol. II (pp. 67–90). New York: Grune and Stratton.

With R. Doorbar, H. Goze, & L. Clark. A study of sexual preferences: Preliminary report. *International Journal of Sexology, 6,* 87–88.

What is normal sex behavior? *Complex, 8,* 41–51. Revised in Ellis & Brancale, *The psychology of sex offenders* (pp. 120–132). Springfield, IL: Thomas, 1956.

1953

The Blacky Test used with a psychoanalytic patient. *Journal of Clinical Psychology, 9,* 167–172.

With R. Doorbar. Classified bibliography of articles, books, and pamphlets on sex, love, marriage, and family relations published during 1952. *Marriage and Family Living, 15,* 156–175.

Correspondence relating to "Marriage counseling with couples indicating sexual incompatibility." *Marriage and Family Living, 15,* 251–252.

Discussion of W. Stokes & D. Mace, "Premarital sexual behavior." *Marriage and Family Living, 15,* 248–249.

From the first to the second Kinsey report. *International Journal of Sexology, 12,* 64–72.

The International Journal of Sexology. *International Journal of Sexology, 6,* 180–181. Also Preface to A. P. Pillay and Albert Ellis (eds.), *Sex, society and the individual* (pp. vii–x). Bombay: International Journal of Sexology.

Is the vaginal orgasm a myth? In A. P. Pillay and A. Ellis (eds.), *Sex, society and the individual* (pp. 155–162). Bombay: International Journal of Sexology.

Marriage counseling with couples indicating sexual incompatibility. *Marriage and Family Living, 15,* 53–59.

Pros and cons of legislation for psychologists. *American Psychologist, 8,* 551–553.

Reactions of psychotherapy patients who resist hypnosis. *Journal of Clinical and Experimental Hypnosis, 1,* 12–15.

Recent research with personality inventories. *Journal of Consulting Psychology, 17,* 45–49.

Recent studies on the sex and love relations of young girls: Resume. *International Journal of Sexology, 6,* 161–163.

Recent views on sexual deviation. In A. P. Pillay & A. Ellis (eds.), *Sex, society and the individual* (pp. 337–349). Bombay: International Journal of Sexology.

Recommendations concerning standards for the unsupervised practice of clinical psychology. *American Psychologist, 8,* 494–495.

Review of E. Bergler, *The superego. Psychological Bulletin, 50,* 252.

With A. P. Pillay (eds.), *Sex, society and the individual.* Bombay: International Journal of Sexology.

Theoretical schools of psychology. In A. Weider (ed.), *Contributions toward medical psychology* (pp. 31–50). New York: Ronald.

1954

The American sexual tragedy. New York: Twayne Publishers.

With R. Doorbar & R. Johnston. Characteristics of convicted sex offenders. *Journal of Social Psychology, 40,* 3–15.

With R. Beechley. Emotional disturbance in children with peculiar given names. *Journal of Genetic Psychology, 85,* 337–399.

Female sexual response and marital relations. *Social Problems, 1,* 152–155.

Interrogation of sex offenders. *Journal of Criminal Law, Criminology and Police Science, 45*(1), 41–47.

Nineteen-fifty-three classified bibliography on human sex relations. *International Journal of Sexology, 7,* 228–239.

1953 classified bibliography on marriage and family relations. *Marriage and Family Living, 16,* 146–161; *lb,* 254–263.

With H. Benjamin. An objective examination of prostitution. *International Journal of Sexology, 8,* 100–105.

Private clinical practice. In E. A. Rubinstein & M. Lorr (eds.), *A survey of clinical practice in psychology* (pp. 186–196). New York: International Universities Press.

The psychology and physiology of sex. In A. Ellis (ed.), *Sex life of the American woman and the Kinsey report* (pp. 203–214). New York: Greenberg.

Psychosexual and marital problems. In L. A. Pennington & I. A. Berg (eds.), *An introduction to clinical psychology* (pp. 264–283). New York: Ronald.

Sex freedom in marriage. *Best Years, 1*(1), 3–7.

Sex life of the American woman and the Kinsey report (ed.). New York: Greenberg.

1955

Are homosexuals necessarily neurotic? *One, 3*(4), 8–12.

Masturbation. *Journal of Social Therapy, 1*(3), 141–143.

New approaches to psychotherapy techniques. *Journal of Clinical Psychology Monograph Supplement, 11,* 1–53.

With R. G. Anderson, I. A. Berg, J. McV. Hunt, O. H. Mowrer, H. E. O'Shea, C. H. Rush, Jr., R. B. Selover, & W. H. Wulfeck. Professional liability insurance for psychologists. *American Psychologist, 10,* 243–244.

Psychotherapy techniques for use with psychotics. *American Journal of Psychotherapy, 9,* 452–476.

With J. Nydes & B. Riess. Qualifications of the clinical psychologist for the practice of psychotherapy. *Journal of Clinical Psychology, 11,* 33-37.

Review of V. Sonnemann, *Existence and therapy. Psychological Bulletin, 52,* 275–276.,

Woman as sex aggressor. *Best Years, 1*(3), 25–29.

1956

Adultery: Pros and cons. *The Independent,* Issue *61,* 4.

Another look at sexual abnormality. *The Independent,* Issue *55,* 6.

A critical evaluation of marriage counseling. *Marriage and Family Living, 18,* 65–71.

The effectiveness of psychotherapy with individuals who have severe homosexual problems. *Journal of Consulting Psychology, 20,* 191–195.

Evolving standards for practicing psychologists. In M. H. Krout (ed.), *Psychology, psychiatry and the public interest* (pp. 186–200). Minneapolis: University of Minnesota Press.

How American women are driving American males into homosexuality. *Expose (The Independent),* Issue *52,* 4.

How males contribute to female frigidity. *The Independent,* Issue *56,* 4.

New light on masturbation. *Expose (The Independent),* Issue *51,* 4.

On premarital sex relations. *The Independent,* Issue *59;* Issue *60,* 4.

On the myths about love. *The Independent,* Issue *58,* 6.

An operational reformulation of some of the basic principles of psychoanalysis. In H. Feigl and M. Scriven (eds.), *The foundations of science and the concepts of psychology and psychoanalysis* (pp. 131–154). Minneapolis: University of Minnesota Press. Also published in *Psychoanalytic Review, 43,* 163–180.

With R. Brancale & R. Doorbar. *The psychology of sex offenders.* Springfield, IL: Thomas.

The roots of psychology and psychiatry. In H. Krout (ed.), *Psychology, psychiatry and the public interest* (pp. 9–13). Minneapolis: University of Minnesota Press.

Sex: Fad and opinion. Review of J. F. Oliven, *Sexual hygiene and pathology: A manual for the physician. Contemporary Psychology, 2,* 86–87.

Sexual inadequacy in the male. *The Independent,* Issue *57,* 4.

Use of psychotherapy with homosexuals. *Mattachine Review, 2,* 14–16.

When are we going to quit stalling about sex education? *The Independent,* Issue *54,* 4.

Why Americans are so fearful of sex. *The Independent,* Issue *53,* 4.

1957

Adultery reconsidered. *The Independent,* Issue *68,* 4.

Adventures with sex censorship. *The Independent,* Issue *62,* 4; Issue *63,* 4.

Deviation, an ever-increasing social problem. In Fairchild, (ed.), *Personality problems and psychological frontiers* (pp. 138–151). New York: Sheridan House.

How do I love thee? Let me count the ways. Review of V. W. Grant, *The psychology of sexual emotion: The basis of selective attraction. Contemporary Psychology, 2,* 188–189.

How homosexuals can combat anti-homosexualism. *One, 5*(2), 7–8.

How to live with a neurotic. New York: Crown Publishers. Paperback edition: New York: Award Books.

"I feel so guilty." *True Story, 78*(6), 18–29.

The justification of sex without love. *The Independent,* Issue *64,* 4; Issue *65,* 4; Issue *66,* 4.

On sex fascism. *The Independent,* Issue *69,* 4; Issue *70,* 4; Issue *21,* 4.

Outcome of employing three techniques of psychotherapy. *Journal of Clinical Psychology, 13*(4), 344–350.

Rational psychotherapy and individual psychology. *Journal of Individual Psychology, 13*(1), 38–44.

The right to sex enjoyment. *The Independent,* Issue *22,* 4.

Sex problems of couples seen for marriage counseling. *Journal of Family Welfare, 3,* 81–84.

The sexual element in non-sex crimes. *Psychology Newsletter, 8,* 122–125.

Thoughts on petting. *The Independent,* Issue *68,* 4.

1958

Are suburban wives af-fair game? *New York Mirror Magazine,* July 28, 4–5.

Case histories: Fact and fiction. *Contemporary Psychology, 3,* 318–319.

Comments on J. Crist, "Marriage counseling involving a passive husband and an aggressive wife." *Marriage and Family Living, 20,* 126–127.

Helping troubled people. *Pastoral Psychology, 9*(82), 33–41.

How to live with a neurotic. *Family Living,* August 17, 8–9.

How you can get along with a neurotic. *Today's Living. New York Herald Tribune,* August 3, 4–5.

Hypnotherapy with borderline schizophrenics. *Journal of General Psychology, 59,* 245–253.

With S. Kosofsky. Illegal communication among institutionalized female delinquents. *Journal of Social Psychology, 48,* 155–160.

A marriage of two neurotics. In American Association of Marriage Counselors (ed.), *Marriage counseling: A casebook* (pp. 197–204). New York: Association Press.

Neurotic interaction between marital partners. *Journal of Counseling Psychology, 5,* 24–28.

New hope for homosexuals. *Sexology, 25,* 164–168.

The private practice of psychotherapy: A clinical psychologist's report. *Journal of General Psychology, 58,* 207–216.

Rational psychotherapy. *Journal of General Psychology, 59,* 35–49. Reprinted: New York: Institute for Rational-Emotive Therapy.

Sex without guilt. New York: Lyle Stuart 200. Paperback eds.: New York: Hillman; New York: MacFadden Books; New York: Grove Press.

With L. David. Should men marry older women? *This Week,* July 6, 8–9. Reprinted: R. S. Cavan (ed.), *Marriage and family in the modern world* (pp. 157–160). New York: Crowell.

Ten indiscreet proposals. *Pageant, 14*(5), 6–15.

1959

Case presentation and critical comments on the cases of other authors. In S. W. Standal & R. J. Corsini (eds.), *Critical incidents in psychotherapy* (pp. 88–91 and passim). Englewood Cliffs, NJ: Prentice-Hall.

Critique of "The homosexual in our society." *Mattachine Review, 5*(6), 24–27.

Does morality require religious sanctions? *Controversy Magazine, 1*(2), 16–19.

Guilt, shame, and frigidity. *Quarterly Review of Surgery, Obstetrics & Gynecology, 16,* 259–261.

A homosexual treated with rational psychotherapy. *Journal of Clinical Psychology, 15,* 338–343.

Homosexuality and creativity. *Journal of Clinical Psychology, 15,* 376–379.

How neurotic are you? *True Story, 79*(6), 34–35.

Introduction to Allen Edwardes, *The jewel in the lotus: A historical survey of the sexual culture of the east* (pp. xv-xxi). New York: Julian Press.

Overaggressiveness in wives. *King Features Syndicate, Inc.,* July 26.

Overcoming sexual incompatibility. *Realife Guide, 2*(4), 6–15.

The place of value in the practice of psychotherapy (ed.). *Annals of Psychotherapy,* Monograph no. 2. New York: American Academy of Psychotherapists.

Premarital relations — pro. *Controversy, 1*(4), 24, 26–27.

Psychological aspects of discouraging contraception. *Realist, 1*(7), 11–13.

Rationalism and its therapeutic applications. In A. Ellis (ed.), *The place of value in the practice of psychotherapy* (pp. 55–64). *Annals of Psychotherapy* Monograph no. 2. New York: American Academy of Psychotherapists.

Requisite conditions for basic personality change. *Journal of Consulting Psychology, 23,* 538–540.

The seven secrets of sexual satisfaction. *Pageant, 14*(12), 26–31.

With H. Lehfeldt (eds.). Symposium on aspects of female sexuality. *Quarterly Review of Surgery, Obstetrics, & Gynecology, 16,* 217–258.

The treatment of a psychopath with rational psychotherapy. *Quaderni di Criminologia Clinica, 2,* 1–11. Also in *Journal of Psychology,* 1961, *51,* 141–150. Revised with addendum: In S. J. Morse & R. I. Watson, Jr. (eds.), *Psychotherapies: A comparative casebook* (pp. 258–267). New York: Holt, Rinehart, & Winston, 1977.

What is normal sex behavior? *Realife Guide, 2*(3), 36–41.

What is psychotherapy? (ed.). *Annals of Psychotherapy* Monograph no. 1. New York: American Academy of Psychotherapists.

What is psychotherapy? — Varied approaches to the problem. In A. Ellis (ed.), *What is psychotherapy?* (pp. 5–7). *Annals of Psychotherapy* Monograph no. 1. New York: American Academy of Psychotherapists.

Why married men visit prostitutes. *Sexology, 25,* 344–347.

1960

With R. Felder, A. Levitsky, I. Progoff, C. Rogers, & J. Rosen. *American Academy of Psychotherapists research tape.* Cassette recording. Salt Lake City: American Academy of Psychotherapists Tape Library.

The art and science of love. New York: Lyle Stuart. Paperback eds.: New York: Dell; New York: Bantam.

A brief for sex honesty. *Realife Guide, 3*(4), 31–38.

A case for polygamy. *Nugget, 5*(1), 19, 24, 26.

With P. Krassner & R. A. Wilson. An impolite interview with Albert Ellis. *Realist,* Issue *16,* 1, 9–14; Issue *17,* 7–12. Reprinted: New York: Institute for Rational-Emotive Therapy.

Introduction to R. Anthony, *The Housewife's Handbook for Promiscuity.* Tucson, AZ: Seymour Press. Also: New York: Documentary Books.

The Institute for Rational Living, Inc. New York: Institute for Rational Living.

Introduction to R. Wood, *Christ and the homosexual* (pp. iii–iv). New York: Vantage Press.

Letter on the suspension of Dr. Leo F. Koch. *Balanced Living, 16,* 175.

Letter to Norman Cousins on sex censorship. *The Independent,* November 3, 5.

With R. Felder & C. Rogers (speakers). *Loretta.* Cassette recording. Salt Lake City: American Academy of Psychotherapists Tape Library.

Marriage counseling with demasculinizing wives and demasculinized husbands. *Marriage and Family Living, 22,* 13–21.

Mowrer on "sin." *American Psychologist, 15,* 713–714.

The psychology of sex. *Realife Guide, 3*(3), 6–13.

Research in psychotherapy. *Newsletter of Psychologists in Private Practice, 1*(1), 2.

Sexual intercourse: Psychological foundations. New York: Institute for Rational-Emotive Therapy.

There is no place for the concept of sin in psychotherapy. *Journal of Counseling Psychology, 7,* 183–192.

What should you do about an unfaithful husband? *Pageant, 15*(9), 6–11.

1961

Art and sex. In A. Ellis & A. Abarbanel (eds.), *The encyclopedia of sexual behavior* (pp. 161–179). New York: Hawthorn Books.

Coitus. In A. Ellis & A. Abarbanel (eds.), *The encyclopedia of sexual behavior* (pp. 284–292). New York: Hawthorn Books.

With R. A. Harper. *Creative Marriage*. Secaucus, NJ: Lyle Stuart. Paperback eds.: *The marriage bed*. New York: Tower Publications; *A guide to successful marriage*. North Hollywood: Wilshire Books.

With A. Abarbanel (eds.). *The encyclopedia of sexual behavior*. 2 vols. New York: Hawthorn Books. Rev. ed.: New York: Aronson, 1967. Paperback ed.: New York: Ace Books.

Frigidity. In A. Ellis & A. Abarbanel (eds.), *The encyclopedia of sexual behavior* (pp. 450–456). New York: Hawthorn Books.

Fried and Freud [Review of E. Fried, *The ego in love and sexuality*]. *Contemporary Psychology, 6*, 38–39.

With R. A. Harper. *A guide to rational living in an irrational world*. Englewood Cliffs, NJ: Prentice-Hall. Paperback ed.: North Hollywood: Wilshire Books.

How much sex freedom in marriage? *Sexology, 28*, 292–296.

Introduction to A. Bentham, *Sex crimes and sex criminals* (pp. i–xii). New York: Wisdom House.

Myths about sex. *Cosmopolitan*, February, 82–85.

A new sex code for modern Americans. *Pageant, 17*(6), 110–116.

On Riess and Durkin on Ellis on Fried on Freud. [Review of E. Fried, *The ego in love and sexuality*]. *Contemporary Psychology, 6*, 382.

The psychology of sex offenders. In A. Ellis & A. Abarbanel (eds.), *The encyclopedia of sexual behavior* (pp. 949–955). New York: Hawthorn Books.

A rational approach to premarital counseling. *Psychological Reports, 8*, 333–338.

Rational therapy applied. *Balanced Living, 17*, 273–278.

With T. Arnold, R. Ginzburg, M. Girodias, N. Mailer, O. Preminger, B. Rosset, & P. Krassner. Sex and censorship in literature and the arts. *Playboy*, July, 27–28, 74–99.

The sex offender and his treatment. In H. Toch (ed.), *Legal and criminal psychology* (pp. 400–416). New York: Holt, Rinehart & Winston.

1962

The American sexual tragedy. Revised ed. New York: Lyle Stuart. Paperback ed.: Grove Press.

The anatomy of a private practitioner. *Newsletter of the Division of Consulting Psychology of the American Psychological Association, 7*, 26–28.

Are homosexuals really creative? *Sexology, 29*, 88–93.

The case against religion: A psychotherapist's view. *The Independent*, Issue *126*, 4–5. Reprinted: New York: The Institute for Rational-Emotive Therapy.

(Speaker). *Fifteen year old boy avoiding schoolwork; 14 year old hospitalized boy who molested a young girl; 15 year old angry at himself and critical stepfather; 8 year old bedwetter.* Cassette recording. New York: Institute for Rational-Emotive Therapy.

How to live with a sex deviate. *Sexology, 28*, 580–583.

Introduction to Fanny Hill — condensed. *Eros, 1*(3), 82–83.

Introduction to Larry Maddock, *Single and pregnant* (pp. 5–7). Hollywood: Genell Corp.

Is nudism anti-sexual? *Eden,* Issue *11,* 6–9.
The lesbian. *Rogue,* September, 17–18, 28, 76.
Morality and therapy. *Columbia University Forum, 5*(2), 47–48.
Myths about sex compatibility. *Sexology, 28,* 652–655.
Psychotherapy and atomic warfare. *The Realist,* Issue *38,* 1–4.
Reason and emotion in psychotherapy. New York: Lyle Stuart. Paperback: Citadel Press.
The seven-year itch. *Dude, 6,* 8–10, 71–72.
Sex and summer violence. *This Month, 1*(6), 46–52.
Teen-age sex relations. *The Realist,* Issue *31,* 30–31.
Twelve true versus false ideas. *Balanced Living, 18,* 140–141.
What is normal sex behavior? *Sexology, 28,* 364–369.

1963

Constitutional factors in homosexuality: A re-examination of the evidence. In H. G. Beigel (ed.), *Advances in sex research* (pp. 161–186). New York: Harper & Row.
Diane David on sex. *Realist,* Issue *42,* 11–12, 16.
Dr. Albert Ellis on fantasies during intercourse. *Liaison, 1*(12), 1–6.
Foreword to H. Beigel (ed.), *Advances in sex research* (pp. xi–xii). New York: Harper & Row.
If this be sexual heresy . . . New York: Lyle Stuart. Paperback ed.: New York: Tower Publications.
Instinct, reason, and sexual liberty. *A Way Out, 19,* 332–335.
The intelligent woman's guide to man-hunting. New York: Lyle Stuart. Paperback ed.: New York: Dell.
Is the vaginal orgasm a myth? *Liaison, 1*(9), 2–4.
With R. Felder & C. Rogers. *Loretta.* [Three interviews with the same hospitalized schizophrenic patient.] Orlando, FL: American Academy of Psychotherapists.
The myth of nymphomania. *Gent, 7*(6), 31–33, 74–80.
A new sex code for modern Americans. *Mattachine Review, 9*(2), 4–10.
Nudity and love. *The Independent,* Issue *135,* 3, 6.
Orgasm and health. *A Way Out, 19,* 240–242.
The origins and the development of the incest taboo. [Bound together with Emile Durkheim, *Incest: The nature and origin of the taboo.*] New York: Lyle Stuart.
A psychologist looks at adultery. *Rogue,* February, 15–16.
The psychology of assassination. *The Independent,* Issue *139,* 1, 4, 5. Reprinted: New York: Institute for Rational-Emotive Therapy.
Rational-emotive psychotherapy. New York: Institute for Rational-Emotive Therapy.
Rational-emotive psychotherapy: A critique of three critiques. *Bulletin of the Essex County Society of Clinical Psychologists in Private Practice,* 7–11.
Sex and the single man. New York: Lyle Stuart. Paperback ed.: Dell.
Sex: Love or hate? *The Independent,* Issue *131,* 4, 6.
Sick and healthy love. *The Independent,* Issue *132,* 1, 8, 9; Issue *133,* 4–6.
With C. Rogers & F. Perls (speakers). *Three approaches to psychotherapy: Gloria.* Film. Orange, CA: Psychological Films.

To thine own psychotherapeutic self be true. *Psychologists in Private Practice Newsletter,* 4(1), 8.

Toward a more precise definition of "emotional" and "intellectual" insight. *Psychological Reports, 13,* 125–126.

The truth about nudity and sexuality. *Bachelor,* 4(5), 18–20, 67–68.

With D. Susskind, A. L. Kinsolving, M. David, R. Ginzburg, H. Hefner, & M. Lerner. Banned program: The sexual revolution in America. *Mademoiselle,* October, 112–113, 158–164.

1964

The American Academy of Psychotherapists. New York: American Academy of Psychotherapists.

The essence of sexual morality. Issue 2(1), 20–24. Reprinted: New York: Institute for Rational-Emotive Therapy.

A guide to rational homosexuality. *Drum: Sex in Perspective,* 4(8), 8–12.

How to have an affair and end it with style. *Saga,* 29(1), 44–45, 89.

How to keep boredom out of the bedroom. *Pageant,* 20(2), 14–18.

In defense of *The American sexual tragedy.* Dr. Ellis answers the charges of Dr. Levin. *Current Medical Digest, 31,* 518–522.

With R. Wolf. An interview with Dr. Albert Ellis. *Campus Voice,* Issue *19,* 6–11.

Introduction to D. W. Cory, *The lesbian in America* (pp. 11–20). New York: Citadel Press.

Introduction to A. Maddaloni, *To be fully alive* (pp. 15–16). New York: Horizon Press.

Introduction to V. Morhaim, *Casebook: Nymphomania* (pp. 7–9). New York: Dell.

Is pornography harmful to children? *The Realist,* Issue *47,* 2–3.

(Speaker). *John Jones: Interview with a male homosexual.* Cassette recording. Salt Lake City: American Academy of Psychotherapists Tape Library.

Marriage counseling. In E. Harms (ed.), *Handbook of counseling techniques* (pp. 147–153). New York: Pergamon.

Must we be guilty about premarital sex? *Modern Sex,* 1(1), 66–75.

New dynamics in contemporary petting. *Nugget,* 9(2), 16–20.

With E. Sagarin. *Nymphomania: A study of the oversexed woman.* New York: Gilbert Press. Paperback ed.: New York: MacFadden-Bartell.

Postscript to J. Z. Eglinton (pseud.), *Greek love* (pp. 429–438). New York: Oliver Layton Press.

The pressures of masculinity and femininity. *The Independent,* Issue *143,* 1, 4, 6–7.

With J. C. Weaver & W. Thomas. Religion and moral philosophy in a manifesto [Pan Humanist manifesto of Ralph Borsodi]. *A Way Out, 20,* 73–76.

Should we ban war toys? *The Realist,* Issue *48,* 1, 29–31.

With C. Averitt & L. Lipton. A talk with Dr. Ellis. *Los Angeles Free Press,* September 10, 3.

Thoughts on theory vs. outcome in psychotherapy. *Psychotherapy, 1,* 83–87.

What creates sex hostility? *Sexology, 30,* 592–594.

Wife swapping. *The Realist,* Issue *50,* 19–21.

1965

An answer to some objections to rational-emotive psychotherapy. *Psychotherapy: Theory, Research and Practice, 2,* 108–111.
The case for sexual liberty. Tucson, AZ: Seymour Press.
Homosexuality: Its causes and cure. New York: Lyle Stuart.
How to beat the antisex laws. *Innovator, 2,* 33.
How to vary your sex techniques. *Sex Guide,* Issue *103,* 26–35.
Introduction to N. Chorier, *Dialogues of Luisa Sigea* (pp. iii–xiv). North Hollywood: Brandon House.
Introduction to M. M. Grossack, *You are not alone* (pp. 15–16). Boston: Christopher Publishing House.
Introduction to *Guild dictionary of homosexual terms* (pp. 3–4). Washington, DC: Guild Press.
Introduction to *The love pagoda* (pp. 3–8). North Hollywood: Brandon House.
Introduction to P. Reage, *The story of O* (pp. iii–xi). North Hollywood: Brandon House.
Introduction to K. Thornley, *Oswald* (pp. 5–12). Chicago: New Classics House.
Is the "Myth of negro superiority" a myth? *Fact,* September, 1–7.
With R. Nathan. The legitimate pickup. *Mademoiselle,* May, 88, 94, 126.
Morality and rational therapy [Letter to the editor]. *Journal of Marriage and the Family, 19,* 417.
Rational-emotive psychotherapy. New York: Institute for Rational-Emotive Therapy.
Review of P. & E. Kronhausen, The sexually responsive woman. *Marriage & Family Living, 18,* 101.
Sex and violence in society. *Independent,* Issue *157,* 1, 4, 6.
Showing the patient that he is not a worthless individual. *Voices, 1*(2), 74–77. Reprinted in *Showing clients they are not worthless individuals.* New York: Institute for Rational-Emotive Therapy.
Some uses of the printed, written, and recorded word in psychotherapy. In L. Pearson (ed.), *The use of written communications in psychotherapy* (pp. 23–36). Springfield, IL: Thomas.
Suppressed: Seven key essays publishers dared not print. Chicago: New Classics House.
The treatment of psychotic and borderline psychotic patients with rational-emotive psychotherapy. In *Symposium on therapeutic methods with schizophrenics* (pp. 5–32). Battle Creek, MI: Veterans Administration Hospital. Reprinted: New York: Institute for Rational-Emotive Therapy.

1966

Books on marriage. *Voices, 2*(3), 83–85.
Continuing personal growth of the psychotherapist. *Journal of Humanistic Psychology, 6,* 156–169.
With J. Wolfe & S. Moseley. *How to prevent your child from becoming a neurotic adult.* New York: Crown. Paperback ed.: *How to raise an emotionally healthy, happy child.* North Hollywood: Wilshire Books.
Introduction to V. Howard, *Secret techniques of erotic delight* (pp. i–vii). New York: Lyle Stuart.

The nature of disturbed marital interaction. *Rational Living, 1* (1), 22–26. Also in H. L. Silverman (ed.), *Marital counseling: Psychology, ideology, science* (pp. 91–96). Springfield, IL: Thomas, 1967.

New kooky (but workable) cures for frigidity. *Cosmopolitan, 160*(1), 30–35. Reprinted in *New cures for frigidity.* New York: Institute for Rational-Emotive Therapy.

With R. Nathan. Our soaring suicide rate. *Long Island Press,* January 18, 37, and January 19, 28.

Preface to J. Wilmot, Earl of Rochester, *Sodom* (pp. iii–ix). North Hollywood: Brandon House.

Psychosexual and marital problems. In I. A. Berg & L. A. Pennington (eds.), *An introduction to clinical psychology,* 3rd ed. (pp. 248–269). New York: Ronald Press.

Recorded interview: Example of a session of rational-emotive therapy. In C. H. Patterson (ed.), *Theories of counseling and psychotherapy* (pp. 117–129). New York: Harper & Row.

The requisites of the sexual revolution and their relation to nudism. *Sol,* Issue 7, 30–31.

Review of L. Ullerstam, *The erotic minorities. Journal of Marriage and the Family, 20,* 378.

Rules for group psychotherapy sessions. New York: Institute for Rational-Emotive Therapy.

The search for sexual enjoyment. New York: Macfadden Bartell.

Sex and civilization. *The Independent,* Issue *167,* 1, 8; Issue *168,* 5–6, 8.

Sex without guilt. Revised ed. Secaucus, NJ: Lyle Stuart. Paperback eds.: New York: Lancer Books; North Hollywood: Wilshire Books.

Should non-professionals be trained to do psychotherapy? *Newsletter of the Divsion of Clinical Psychology of the American Psychological Association, 19*(2), 10–11.

(Speaker). *Thirty-five year old man angry at self for picking a disturbed wife; fifty year old woman with brain-injured husband and unhappy daughter; forty-four year old male librarian unable to relate to co-workers.* Cassette recording. New York: Institute for Rational-Emotive Therapy.

(Speaker). *Twenty year old college student with study problems; male student with dating anxiety; thirty-five year old woman who can't stand her boss.* Cassette recording. New York: Institute for Rational-Emotive Therapy.

Who killed Kennedy? *Fact, 3*(6), 13.

(Speaker). *Woman angry at husband for overinvolvement with relative; woman in love with non-reciprocating male; woman angry at boss.* Cassette recording. New York: Institute for Rational-Emotive Therapy.

(Speaker). *Young schizophrenic male, afraid of groups; middle-aged paranoid female, hurt by daughter's behavior; thirty-five year old depressed female.* Cassette recording. New York: Institute for Rational-Emotive Therapy.

1967

With R. O. Conway. *The art of erotic seduction.* New York: Lyle Stuart. Paperback ed.: New York: Ace.

Counseling adolescents with problems of sex and values. *Rational Living, 2*(1), 7–12.

With D. Sandler & R. Liswood. Doctors tell you the best time to love. *Pageant,* August, 148–154.

Goals of psychotherapy. In A. R. Mahrer (ed.), *The goals of psychotherapy* (pp. 206–220). New York: Meredith.

Introduction to W. Braun, *The cruel and the meek* (pp. ix–xiv). New York: Lyle Stuart.

Introduction to A. Mol, *The memoirs of an Amsterdam streetwalker* (pp. 7–23). New York: Award Books.

Masturbation by sexually isolated individuals. In R. E. L. Masters, ed., *Sexual self-stimulation* (pp. 221–231). Los Angeles: Sherbourne.

The new sexual freedoms. *Rogue, 12*(6), 12–13, 17, 83–85.

Objectivism, the new religion. *Rational Living, 2*(2), 1–6.

Phobia treated with rational-emotive psychotherapy. *Voices, 3*(3), 34–40.

With H. Hefner. Phone dialogue: The American sex revolution. *Voices, 3,* 88–97.

A psychologist looks at the Warren report dissenters. *Cincinnati Pictorial Enquirer,* November 19, 5, 18, 20–26.

Psychotherapy and moral laxity. *Psychiatric Opinion, 4*(5), 18–21.

Rational-emotive psychotherapy. In D. S. Arbuckle (ed.), *Counseling and psychotherapy: An overview* (pp. 78–99). New York: McGraw-Hill.

With M. L. Blum. Rational training: A new method of facilitating management and labor relations. *Psychological Reports, 20,* 1267–1284. Reprinted: New York: Institute for Rational-Emotive Therapy.

Reply to D. L. Stedding. *Rational Living, 2*(1), 30.

Review of A. Low, *Lectures to relatives of former patients. Rational Living, 2*(2), 29–30.

Review of A. H. Maslow, *The psychology of science: A reconnaissance. Salmagundi, 2*(1), 97–101.

Review of W. Masters & V. Johnson, *Human sexual response. New York State Psychologist, 19*(2), 38–39.

Review of F. Wertham, *A sign for Cain: An exploration of human violence. Annals of the American Academy of Political and Social Science,* Issue 370, 181–182.

Self acceptance and successful human relations. *Newsletter of the Institute for Marriage and Friendships,* Winter, 8–9.

Should some people be labeled mentally ill? *Journal of Consulting Psychology, 31,* 435–446.

State's adopted "Kinsey" reports. *Los Angeles Free Press,* January 20, 16.

Structure and psychotherapy. [Review of E. L. Phillips & D. N. Wiener, *Short-term psychotherapy and structured behavior change*]. *Psychiatry and Social Science Review, 1*(7), 4–6.

Talking to adolescents about sex. *Rational Living, 2*(1), 7–12.

(Speaker). *Thirty-nine year old woman afraid of failure on new job; twenty-one hear old teacher with compulsion to finish all tasks; forty year old male teacher afraid of failing orals.* Cassette recording. New York: Institute for Rational-Emotive Therapy.

(Speaker). *Twenty year old female college student, upset at not getting straight A's and angry at father for his treatment of her; twenty-four year old girl in love with two men and demeaning herself for her lack of education.* Cassette recording. New York: Institute for Rational-Emotive Therapy.

Why one out of every five wives is having an affair. *Pageant, 23*(3), 112–117.

1968

Biographical information form. New York: Institute for Rational-Emotive Therapy.
Discussion of C. Jackson, "In praise of inadequacy." *Voices, 4*(3), 88–89.
Fifteen ways to get more out of sex. *Sexology, 35,* 148–151.
Havelock Ellis. In D. Sills (ed.), *International Encyclopedia of the Social Sciences,* Vol. 5 (pp. 29–31). New York: Macmillan.
Homosexuality: The right to be wrong. *Journal of Sex Research, 4,* 96–107.
Is objectivism a religion? Secaucus, NJ: Lyle Stuart.
Is psychoanalysis harmful? *Psychiatric Opinion,* January, *5*(1), 16–24. Reprinted: New York: Institute for Rational-Emotive Therapy.
Let's change our marriage system. *Sexology, 34*(7), 436–439.
Objectivism, the new religion. Part II. *Rational Living, 3*(1), 12–19.
Objectivism, the new religion. Part III. *Rational Living, 3*(2), 9–19.
Personality data form: Parts 1–4. New York: Institute for Rational-Emotive Therapy.
A rational approach to interpretation. In E. Hammer (ed.), *The use of interpretation in treatment* (pp. 232–239). New York: Grune & Stratton. Reprinted: New York: Institute for Rational-Emotive Therapy.
Review of A. S. Neil, *Freedom — not license! Rational Living, 3*(1), 35–36.
Rules for individual therapy, marriage, and family therapy sessions. New York: Institute for Rational-Emotive Therapy.
Sex and revolution. *Modern Utopian, 2*(5), 3.
Sex and the young adult. *Twenty-five, 1*(1), 36–39, 50–51.
A sexologist looks at sexual love. *The Independent,* Issue *184,* 5; Issue *186,* 1, 4, 6; Issue *188,* 7–8.
Sexual manifestations of emotionally disturbed behavior. *Annals of the American Academy of Political and Social Science,* Issue *376,* 96–105.
Sexual promiscuity in America. *Annals of the American Academy of Political and Social Science,* Issue *378,* 58–67.
(Speaker). *Twenty-three year old male teacher who has trouble getting up in the morning; twenty-five year old female compulsive eater; forty year old woman recently operated on for breast cancer.* Cassette recording. New York: Institute for Rational-Emotive Therapy.
What really causes psychotherapeutic change? *Voices, 4*(2), 90–97. Reprinted: New York: Institute for Rational-Emotive Therapy.

1969

Are you secretly afraid of being touched? *Pageant, 10*(4), 132–137.
A cognitive approach to behavior therapy. *International Journal of Psychiatry, 8,* 896–900.
Comments on C. H. Patterson's "Current view of client-centered or relationship therapy." *Counseling Psychologist, 1*(2), 37–42.
Emotional problems of the young adult. In Forest Hospital Foundation (ed.), *The young adult* (pp. 83–102). Des Plaines, IL: Forest Hospital Foundation. Also in *Rational Living,* 1971, *5*(2), 2–11.

The essence of rational psychotherapy: A comprehensive approach to treatment. New York: Institute for Rational-Emotive Therapy.

(Speaker). *First and second sessions with twenty-nine year old teacher guilty about doing things her mother disapproves of and anxious in the presence of interesting men; twenty-eight year old truck driver with problem of early ejaculation and fear of wife abandoning him.* Cassette recording. New York: Institute for Rational-Emotive Therapy.

Healthy and disturbed reasons for having extramarital relations. In G. Neubeck (ed.), *Extra-marital relations* (pp. 153–161). Englewood Cliffs, NJ: Prentice-Hall.

How to increase sexual enjoyment in marriage. In B. N. Ard & C. Ard (eds.), *Handbook of marriage counseling* (pp. 375–378). Palo Alto, CA: Science and Behavior Books.

How to participate effectively in a marathon weekend of marital encounter. Rev. ed. New York: Institute for Rational-Emotive Therapy.

Introduction to L. R. O'Conner, *The photographic manual of sexual intercourse* (pp. 9–13). New York: Pent-R Books.

With J. Elliot. Irrational ideas. *Explorations,* Issue *17,* 13–16.

Mothers are too good for their own good. *Boston Sunday Globe Magazine,* May 11, 26–31. Syndicated article.

(pseud. Arnold Green). Nine power seduction tips. *Wildcat, 54,* 8–10, 59–60.

Orality and psyche. [Review of F. Perls, *Ego, hunger and aggression: The beginning of gestalt therapy*]. *Catholic World, 210* (no. 1255), 36–38.

Preface to M. DeMartino, *The new female sexuality* (pp. ix–xi). New York: Julian Press.

Rational-emotive theology?! *Rational Living, 4*(1), 9–14.

Rational-emotive therapy. *Journal of Contemporary Psychotherapy, 1,* 82–90. Also in *Explorations,* Issue *17,* 5–12.

Rationality in sexual morality. *Humanist, 29*(5), 17–21. Reprinted: New York: Institute for Rational-Emotive Therapy.

Review of J. Peterson & M. Mercer, *Adultery for adults. Psychology Today, 3*(2), 12–62.

Sex, frustration and aggression. *Rogue,* Issue *18,* 27–30.

(Speaker). *Sex, sanity, and psychotherapy.* Cassette recording. New York: Institute for Rational-Emotive Therapy.

Suggested procedures for a weekend of rational encounter. New York: Institute for Rational-Emotive Therapy.

Teaching emotional education in the classroom. *School Health Review,* November, 10–13.

(Speaker). *Thirty-four year old housewife upset at not doing anything "worthwhile" and wasting her life; thirty-nine year old programmer who is self-downing in relations with men.* Cassette recording. New York: Institute for Rational-Emotive Therapy.

Toward the understanding of youthful rebellion. In R. Frank (ed.), *A search for the meaning of the generation gap* (pp. 85–111). San Diego: San Diego County Department of Education.

With D. Mace. The use of sex in human life: A dialogue. *Journal of Sex Research, 5,* 41–49.

A weekend of rational encounter. In A. Burton (ed.), *Encounter* (pp. 112–127). San Francisco: Jossey-Bass. Also in *Rational Living,* 1970, *4*(2), 1–8.

What else is new? Me! *Voices, 5*(3), 33–35.
Where can we go from here? *Psychology Today, 2*(8), 38.

1970

With J. Baez, J. Campbell, & P. Goodman. The authentic man: A symposium. *Humanist, 30*(1), 19–26.
The case against religion. *Mensa Bulletin,* Issue *38,* 5–6. Reprinted: New York: Institute for Rational-Emotive Therapy.
The cognitive element in experiential and relationship psychotherapy. *Existential Psychiatry, 7*(28), 35–52.
Ellis on Kinsey, Part 1. *Penthouse, 2*(4), 115–121.
The emerging counselor. *Canadian Counselor, 4*(2), 99–105.
(Speaker). *Excerpts from 2nd to 7th sessions with 54 year old woman with job anxiety and difficulties handling underachieving teenage son; 26 year old woman guilty about mistakes and fearful of rejection.* Cassette recording. New York: Institute for Rational-Emotive Therapy.
With J. Henderson, D. Murray, & R. Seidenberg (speakers). *Four psychotherapies.* Cassette recording. Salt Lake City: American Academy of Psychotherapists Tape Library.
Frigidity. In P. Gillette (ed.), *The layman's explanation of sexual inadequacy* (pp. 192–209). New York: Award Books.
Group marriage: A possible alternative? In H. A. Otto (ed.), *The family in search of a future* (pp. 85–97). New York: Meredith.
Humanism, values, rationality. In tribute to Alfred Adler on his 100th birthday. *Journal of Individual Psychology, 26*(1), 11–12.
Intellectual fascism. *Journal of Human Relations, 18*(1), 700–709.
Introduction to P. Gillette, *The big answer book about sex* (pp. v–x). New York: Award Press.
(Speaker). *Marriage: Hotbed of neurosis.* Cassette recording. New York: Institute for Rational-Emotive Therapy.
(Speaker). *Rational-emotive psychotherapy.* Cassette recording. New York: Institute for Rational-Emotive Therapy.
Rational-emotive therapy. In L. Hersher (ed.), *Four psychotherapies* (pp. 47–83). New York: Appleton-Century-Crofts.
With D. Wholey. *Rational-emotive therapy.* Cassette recording. New York: Institute for Rational-Emotive Therapy.
Review of N. Branden, *The psychology of self-esteem. Rational Living, 4*(2), 31.
Sex and the family. In I. A. Falk (ed.), *Prophecy for the year 2000* (pp. 176–178). New York: Julian Messner.
The sexual criminal. *Penthouse, 1,* 83–86, 93.
What you should know about the sensuous man. *Coronet, 8*(10), 18–24.

1971

The case for sexual latitude. In H. Hart (ed.), *Sexual latitude: For and against* (pp. 67–83). New York: Hart Publishing Company. Reprinted: New York: Institute for Rational-Emotive Therapy.

Critique of A. DiLoreto's *Comparative psychotherapy*. In A. DiLoreto (ed.), *Comparative psychotherapy, an experimental analysis* (pp. 213–221). Chicago: Aldine-Atherton.

With D. Casriel. Debate: Albert Ellis vs. Daniel Casriel on anger. *Rational Living*, 6(2), 2–21.

With M. Cohen. Dr. Albert Ellis answers the 17 most asked questions about sex. *Pageant*, 26(7), 46–58.

Ellis on Kinsey: Part 2: The other side of Kinsey. *Penthouse*, 2(5), 71–73.

Emotional disturbance and its treatment in a nutshell. *Canadian Counselor*, 5(3), 168–171. Reprinted: New York: Institute for Rational-Emotive Therapy.

An experiment in emotional education. *Educational Technology*, 11(7), 61–63. Reprinted: New York: Institute for Rational-Emotive Therapy.

Fifteen ways to get more out of sex. *Sexology*, 38, 4–7.

With B. N. Ard, H. J. Geis, Jr., J. M. Gullo, P. A. Hauck, & M. C. Maultsby, Jr. *Growth through reason*. Palo Alto, CA: Science and Behavior Books. Paperback ed.: North Hollywood: Wilshire Books.

How to learn to relax and enjoy women's lib. *Chicago Tribune Sunday Magazine*, January 10, 38–39, 44.

Homework report. New York: Institute for Rational-Emotive Therapy.

With A. Karlen. Interview. In A. Karlen, *Sexuality and homosexuality: A new view* (pp. 223–227). New York: Norton.

With R. Liswood. Is premarital chastity desirable? *Sexual Behavior*, 1(3), 42–52.

Is there any cure for nymphomania? *Sexual Behavior*, 1(5), 13–14.

Letter to the editor on religion. *Logorrhea*, pp. 2–3.

With J. Gullo. *Murder and assassination*. New York: Lyle Stuart.

Penthouse Casebook. *Penthouse*, 2(10), 60–63.

Penthouse Casebook: Ego, sex and the great I am. *Penthouse*, 3(1), 66–67.

Penthouse casebook: Me, myself and I: Ego and the male. *Penthouse*, 3(3), 40–46.

With P. Lehman. Practical applications of rational-emotive technique. *Rational Living*, 6(2), 36–38.

Problems of daily living workshop. In R. J. Menges & F. Pennington (eds.), *A survey of nineteen innovative educational programs for adolescents and adults* (pp. 49–51). Minneapolis: Youth Research Center.

Rational-emotive therapy and its application to emotional education. New York: Institute for Rational-Emotive Therapy.

Rational-emotive treatment of impotence, frigidity and other sexual problems. *Professional Psychology*, Fall, 346–349.

A rational sex morality. In L. A. Kirkendall & R. N. Whitehurst (eds.), *The new sexual revolution* (pp. 47–61). New York: Donald W. Brown and Prometheus Books.

Reason and emotion in the individual psychology of Adler. *Journal of Individual Psychology*, 27(1), 50–64.

Review of A. A. Lazarus, *Behavior therapy and beyond*. *Behavior Therapy*, 2, 300–302.

The role of coital positions in sexual relations. *Sexual Behavior*, 1(4), 12–13.

(Speaker). *Sex therapy sessions: Fifty-eight year old male with ejaculatory problems; thirty-six year old woman with depression, anxiety and low sexual arousal; forty year old male with work anxiety and low sexual arousability.* Cassette recording. New York: Institute for Rational-Emotive Therapy.

Sex without guilt. In D. L. Grummon & A. M. Barclay (eds.), *Sexuality, a search for perspective* (pp. 226–255). New York: Van Nostrand Reinhold.

Sexual adventuring and personality growth. In H. Otto (ed.), *The new sexuality* (pp. 94–108). Palo Alto, CA: Science and Behavior Books. Reprinted: New York: Institute for Rational-Emotive Therapy.

Twenty-two ways to stop putting yourself down. *Rational Living, 6*(1), 8–15.

Was Mudchen tun mussen, damit ihnen Manner hunderte von Kilometern nachreisen [What girls must do to have men chase them for hundreds of miles]. *Jasmin,* January 4, 38–39.

Which intercourse position or positions are best for a woman to reach orgasm? *Sexual Behavior, 1*(8), 2–4.

1972

Answer to question on aggression by M. R. Edelstein. *Rational Living, 7*(1), 12–13.

The civilized couple's guide to extramarital adventure. New York: Peter Wyden. Paperback ed.: New York: Pinnacle Books.

The contribution of psychotherapy to school psychology. *School Psychology Digest,* Spring, 6–9.

Emotional education in the classroom: The living school. *Journal of Clinical and Child Psychology, 1*(3), 19–22. Also in G. J. Williams & S. Gordon (eds.), *Clinical child psychology: Current practices and future perspectives* (pp. 242–251). New York: Behavioral Publications, 1974.

Executive leadership: A rational approach. New York: Citadel Press.

Helping people get better rather than merely feel better. *Rational Living, 7*(2), 2–9.

How does an affair affect a marriage? It all hinges on the guilt quotient. *Sexual Behavior, 2*(9), 48–49.

How to master your fear of flying. New York: Curtis Books.

Humanistic psychotherapy: A revolutionary approach. *Humanist, 32*(1), 24–28. Reprinted: New York: Institute for Rational-Emotive Therapy.

Instant therapy for erotic hangups. *Penthouse, 3*(6), 48–52.

Is there any difference between "vaginal" and "clitoral" orgasm? *Sexual Behavior, 2*(3), 42.

With P. Lehman. New developments and techniques in RET. *Rational Living, 7*(1), 34–35, 40.

Open letter to Nathaniel Branden. *Reason, 13*(12), 33.

Philosophy and rational-emotive therapy. *Counseling and Values, 16,* 158–161.

Psychotherapy and the value of a human being. In J. W. Davis (ed.), *Value and valuation: Axiological studies in honor of Robert S. Hartman* (pp. 117–139). Knoxville: University of Tennessee Press. Reprinted: New York: Institute for Rational-Emotive Therapy.

Psychotherapy without tears. In A. Burton (ed.), *Twelve therapists* (pp. 103–126). San Francisco: Jossey-Bass.

Rational-emotive psychotherapy: A comprehensive approach to therapy. In G. D. Goldman & D. S. Milman (eds.), *Innovations in psychotherapy* (pp.

147–163). Springfield, IL: Thomas.

Rebuttal of my supposed views on gay liberation. In L. Smith, Rebuttal. *Harper's Bazaar*, December.

Review of H. Hart, *The complete Immortalia. Rational Living, 7*(2), 38.

Review of E. Shostrom, *Caring relationship inventory*. In O. Buros (ed.), *Seventh mental measurements yearbook* (pp. 560–561). New Brunswick, NJ: Gryphon Press.

A revolutionary approach. *Humanist*, January-February, 25–27.

The sensuous person: Critique and corrections. New York: Lyle Stuart. Paperback ed.: New York: New American Library.

With F. C. Seruya & S. Losher. *Sex and sex education: A bibliography.* New York and London: R. R. Bowker Co.

Sexperts — do we really need them? *Forum, 1*(4), 6–9.

Sexual spontaneity. *Forum, 1*(9), 12–15.

(Speaker). *The theory and practice of rational-emotive psychotherapy.* Videotape. New York: Institute for Rational-Emotive Therapy.

What does transpersonal psychology have to offer the art and science of psychotherapy? *Voices, 8*(3), 10–20. Revised version in *Rational Living*, 1973, *8*(1), 20–28.

What kinds of reinforcement can cognitive-behavior therapists receive from B. F. Skinner? *Behavior Therapy, 3*(2), 263–274.

Why can't I bring myself to kiss a woman when I want to very much? *Sexual Behavior*, 7.

Why I am opposed to censorship of pornography. *Osteopathic Physician, 39*(10), 40–41.

1973

Afterword to L. Casler, *Is marriage necessary?* (pp. 181–184). New York: Human Sciences Press.

Albert Ellis bibliography 1945–1973. New York: Institute for Rational-Emotive Therapy.

Albert Ellis' rationality score. *Rational Living, 8*(2), 31.

With W. Knaus and E. Garcia (speakers). *Anxiety and phobias: Twenty-four year old male with fear of urinating in public restrooms and severe masculinity preoccupation; thirty-one year old woman fearful of leaving manfriend and being on own; woman with fear of death and anxiety about job, sex.* Cassette recording. New York: Institute for Rational-Emotive Therapy.

Are cognitive behavior therapy and rational therapy synonymous? *Rational Living, 8*(2), 8–11.

Autobiography. In M. M. Ohlsen (ed.), *Counseling children in groups* (pp. 79–80). New York: Holt, Rinehart & Winston.

Can there be a rational concept of healthy personality? *The Counseling Psychologist, 4*(2), 45–48.

Comment on Judge Tyler's decision to cut the throat of *Deep throat. Clinical Social Work Journal, 1*(3).

Commentary on "The bisexual." *Humanist, 33*(4), 18–19.

With *Practical Psychology*. Conversations with Albert Ellis, *Practical Psychology*, September, 11–18.

Definition of rational-emotive therapy. In B. B. Wolman (ed.), *Dictionary of behavioral science*. New York: Van Nostrand Reinhold.

(Speaker). *A demonstration with a woman fearful of expressing emotions*. Film. Arlington, VA: American Association for Counseling and Development.

(Speaker). *A demonstration with a young divorced woman*. Film. Arlington, VA: American Association for Counseling and Development.

(Speaker). *A demonstration with an elementary school child*. Film. Arlington, VA: American Association for Counseling and Development.

Emotional education at the living school. In M. M. Ohlsen (ed.), *Counseling children in groups* (pp. 79–94). New York: Holt, Rinehart & Winston. Reprinted: New York: Institute for Rational-Emotive Therapy.

How to experiment in bed. *Sexology, 39*(12), 6–10.

(Speaker). *How to stubbornly refuse to be ashamed of anything*. Cassette recording. New York: Institute for Rational-Emotive Therapy.

(Speaker). *Human sexuality concepts*. Videotape. Austin: Audio-Visual Resource Center, School of Social Work, University of Texas.

Humanistic psychotherapy: The rational-emotive approach. New York: Julian Press. Paperback ed.: New York: McGraw-Hill.

Introduction to M. W. Emmett, *I love the person you were meant to be* (pp. i–vii). New York: Warner.

Is transpersonal psychology humanistic? *Newsletter of the Association for Humanistic Psychology*, May-June, 10–13.

Life must be easy! *Rational Living, 8*(2), 18.

Mad people may eat improperly — but a good diet won't cure them! *Sexual Behavior, 3*(3), 8.

(Speaker). *Marital and relationship problems: Twenty-six year old male with problem of anger and lack of openness with woman-friend; woman who is suicidal because husband has left her; forty-two year old man making progress with jealousy of wife*. Cassette recording. New York: Institute for Rational-Emotive Therapy.

My philosophy of psychotherapy. *Journal of Contemporary Psychotherapy, 6* (1), 13–18. Reprinted: New York: Institute for Rational-Emotive Therapy.

The no cop-out therapy. *Psychology Today, 7*(2), 56–62. Reprinted: New York: Institute for Rational-Emotive Therapy.

With D. Riesman, D. Viscott, T. S. Szasz, L. B. Ames, & E. J. Lieberman. The psychological fallout [of Watergate]: How other professionals see it. *Today's Health, 51*(8), 19, 64–66.

(Speaker). *Rational-emotive psychotherapy: A comprehensive approach to personality change*. Two cassette recordings. New York: Institute for Rational-Emotive Therapy.

With T. Allen (speakers). *Rational-emotive psychotherapy: Interview with Tom Allen*. Film. Arlington, VA: American Association for Counseling and Development.

With T. Allen (speakers). *Rational-emotive psychotherapy applied to groups*. Interview with Tom Allen. Film. Arlington, VA: American Association for Counseling and Development.

Rational-emotive therapy. In R. J. Corsini (ed.), *Current psychotherapies* (pp. 167–206). Itasca, IL: F. E. Peacock.

Rational emotive therapy. In R. M. Jurjevich (ed.), *Direct psychotherapies,* Vol. 1 (pp. 295–327). Miami: University of Miami Press.

(Speaker). *Recession and depression: Or how not to let the economy get you down.* Cassette recording. Philadelphia: American Academy of Psychotherapists Tape Library.

(Speaker). *RET and marriage and family counseling.* Cassette recording. New York: Institute for Rational-Emotive Therapy.

Review of W. Kaufman, *Without guilt and justice: From decidophobia to autonomy. Rational Living, 8*(2), 34.

Review of O. S. Rachleff, *The occult concept: A new look at astrology, witchcraft and sorcery. Rational Living, 8*(2), 36.

Review of E. Shostrom & J. Kavanaugh, *Between man and woman: The dynamics of intersexual relationships. Rational Living, 8*(1), 43.

Sexual mores a quarter of a century from now. *Psychiatric Opinion, 10*(3), 17–21.

So verlangere ich meine Erektion [So prolonged is my erection]. *Animus,* Issue 8, 8–9.

Think your way to happiness. *Rational Living, 8*(2), 18.

With W. Block. This way for Doctor Ellis. Interview with Albert Ellis. *Outlook, 3*(11), 12–15.

Toward a new humanist manifesto. *Humanist, 33*(1), 17–18.

(Speaker). *Treatment of sexual dysfunction.* Videotape. Austin: Audio-Visual Resource Center, School of Social Work, University of Texas.

(Speaker). *Twenty-five ways to stop downing yourself.* Cassette recording. Philadephia: American Academy of Psychotherapists Tape Library.

(Speaker). *Twenty-one ways to stop worrying.* Cassette recording. New York: Institute for Rational-Emotive Therapy.

Unhealthy love: Its causes and treatment. In M. E. Curtin (ed.), *Symposium on love* (pp. 175–197). New York: Behavioral Publications. Reprinted: New York: Institute for Rational-Emotive Therapy.

1974

Are self-help books helpful? [Review of R. S. Parker, *Emotional common sense: How to avoid self-destructiveness*]. *Contemporary Psychology, 19,* 307–308.

Barnum was right. *Rational Living, 9*(2), 2–6.

Cognitive aspects of abreactive therapy. *Voices, 10*(1), 48–56. Reprinted: New York: Institute for Rational-Emotive Therapy.

(Speaker). *Cognitive behavior therapy.* Cassette recording. New York: Institute for Rational-Emotive Therapy.

With G. Clanton. A conversation with Albert Ellis. *Alternative Life-Styles, 2,* 243–253.

With H. Greenwald, V. Satir, & A. Seagull. (Speaker). *Dealing with sexual material* [Ellis: Premarital sex]. Cassette recording. Orlando, FL: American Academy of Psychotherapists.

(Speaker). *Demonstration of rational-emotive therapy.* Cassette recording. Saratoga, CA: Cognetics, Inc.

(Speaker). *A demonstration with a woman fearful of expressing emotions.*
Videotape. New York: Institute for Rational-Emotive Therapy.

Disputing irrational beliefs. New York: Institute for Rational-Emotive
Therapy.

With S. Moore. *Dr. Albert Ellis, in his own words: "Sex is the worst reason to
marry — or divorce." People Weekly, 1*(4), 28–31.

The education and training of a rational-emotive therapist. *Voices, 10*(3),
35–38.

Epilogue to M. F. de Martino (ed.), *Sex and the intelligent woman* (pp.
266–286). New York: Springer.

Experience and rationality: The making of a rational-emotive therapist.
Psychotherapy: Theory, Research and Practice, 11, 194–198.

Foreword to D. Goodman & M. C. Maultsby, Jr., *Emotional well-being through
rational behavior training* (pp. 5–6). Springfield, IL: Thomas.

Foreword to J. M. Lembo, *Help yourself* (pp. vii–xii). Niles, IL: Argus.

Foreword to D. G. Tosi, *Youth: Toward personal growth* (pp. iii–iv). Columbus,
OH: Merrill.

The group as agent in facilitating change toward rational thinking and
appropriate emoting. In A. Jacobs & W. F. Spradlin (eds.), *The group as
agent of change* (pp. 100–115). New York: Behavioral Publications.

With R. A. Harper. *Interview with Dr. Albert Ellis.* Cassette recording. Salt
Lake City: American Academy of Psychotherapists.

Introduction to E. Garcia & N. Pellegrini, *Homer the homely hound dog* (p.
iii). New York: Institute for Rational-Emotive Therapy.

Introductory remarks to symposium on homosexuality (pp. 1–3). *Proceedings
of the international congress of medical sexology.* Paris.

Is nudity anti-sexual? *Ace Annual, 16,* 44, 66.

With A. Elkin and M. Edelstein (speakers). *Male with low self-worth and
relationship problems at home and work; man angry at woman friend for
not being rational enough; young woman angry at patronizing attitudes of
her male employers.* Cassette recording. New York: Institute for Rational-
Emotive Therapy.

One hundred million Americans *are* wrong: If the stars rule your life you were
born under the sign of ignorance. *Scene Magazine of the Dallas Sunday
News,* June 23, 21–24. Also in *American Atheist,* 1979, *21*(2), 13–14.

Preface to W. Knaus, *Rational-emotive education* (p.xi–xiii). New York:
Institute for Rational-Emotive Therapy.

The prevalence of mystical nonsense. *St. Louis Globe-Democrat Sunday
Magazine,* June 2, 10–16.

Questions and answers on patients' problems. *Medical Tribune, 15*(35), 24–25.

Rational-emotive revisited. *Professional Psychology, 5,* 111.

Rational-emotive theory: Albert Ellis. In A. Burton (ed.), *Operational theories
of personality* (pp. 308–344). New York: Brunner/Mazel.

Rational-emotive therapy: A few corrections. *Humanist, 34*(5), 35–36.

Rational emotive therapy in groups. *Rational Living, 9*(1), 15–22.

(Speaker). *Rational-emotive therapy with individuals and groups.* Videotape.
Austin: Audio-Visual Resource Center, School of Social Work, University of
Texas.

Rationality and irrationality in the group therapy process. In D. S. Milman &

G. D. Goldman (eds.), *Group process today* (pp. 78–96). Springfield, IL: Thomas.

(Speaker). *Rational living in an irrational world.* Cassette recording. New York: Institute for Rational-Emotive Therapy.

A rational voice. *Newsletter of the American Academy of Psychotherapists,* p. 1.

Review of H. Greenwald, *Decision therapy. Psychoanalytic Review, 61,* 486–487.

Review of J. L. Shelton & J. M. Ackerman, *Homework in counseling and psychotherapy. Behavior Therapy, 6,* 582–583.

(Speaker). *Sessions with two different middle-aged alcoholic males with social anxiety and low self-esteem; fifty-two year old woman with anxiety about finding a job.* Cassette recording. New York: Institute for Rational-Emotive Therapy.

With A. Lazarus, L. Myers, & H. Lehfeldt (speakers). *Sex therapy: Cognitive/behavioral approaches.* Three cassette recordings. New York: Institute for Rational-Emotive Therapy.

Techniques for disputing irrational beliefs (DIBS). New York: Institute for Rational-Emotive Therapy.

With M. C. Maultsby, Jr. *Techniques for using rational-emotive imagery.* New York: Institute for Rational-Emotive Therapy.

(Speaker). *Theory and practice of rational-emotive psychotherapy.* Cassette recording. New York: Institute for Rational-Emotive Therapy.

The theory and practice of rational-emotive psychotherapy. Videotape. New York: Institute for Rational-Emotive Therapy.

With E. Shostrom & H. Greenwald (speakers). *Three approaches to group psychotherapy. Part 2: Rational-emotive therapy.* Film. Orange, CA: Psychological Films.

The treatment of sex and love problems in women. In V. Franks & V. Burtle (eds.), *Women in therapy* (pp. 284–306). New York: Brunner/Mazel.

What rational-emotive therapy is and is not. *Counselor Education and Supervision, 14,* 140–144.

What signs does an RET therapist consider most prognostically favorable in an initial interview? *The Stoic,* Issue *1,* 2.

1975

With *Practical Psychology.* Albert Ellis: The physician and RET. *Practical Psychology for Physicians, 2*(4), 20–27.

Albert's answers. *The Stoic,* Issue 2, 2.

Bibliography [of articles and books by Albert Ellis]. In H. Mosak & B. Mosak, *A bibliography for Adlerian psychology* (pp. 88–99). Washington, DC: Hemisphere; New York: Wiley.

Comments on Frank's "The limits of humanism." *The Humanist, 35*(5), 43–45.

Controversial issues. In K. T. Morris & K. McCinnamon, *Controversial issues in human relations training groups* (pp. 3–4, 20–21, 30–31, 42–43, 52–53, 63–65, 73–74, 82–84, 93–94, 100–101, 107–110). Springfield, IL: Thomas.

Creative joy and happiness: The humanistic way. *The Humanist, 35*(10), 11–13.

With H. Greenwald, V. Satir, & A. Seagull (speakers). *Dealing with sexual material.* Cassette recording. Salt Lake City: American Academy of Psychotherapists Tape Library.

(Speaker). *Demonstration with a family.* Videotape. New York: Institute for Rational-Emotive Therapy.

(Speaker). *Demonstration with woman with sexual and weight problems.* Videotape. New York: Institute for Rational-Emotive Therapy.

Do sex deviants have a readipus complex? [Review of M. J. Goldstein, H. S. Kant, & J. J. Hartman, *Pornography and sexual deviance*]. *Contemporary Psychology, 20,* 621–622.

Does rational-emotive therapy seem deep enough? *Rational Living, 10*(2), 11–14. Reprinted: New York: Institute for Rational-Emotive Therapy.

Foreword to V. A. Church, *Behavior, law and remedies* (pp. vii–viii). Iowa: Kendall & Hunt.

Foreword to M. C. Maultsby, Jr., *Help yourself to happiness* (pp. ix–xiv). New York: Institute for Rational-Emotive Therapy.

Foreword to K. T. Morris & H. M. Kanitz, *Rational emotive therapy* (pp. vii–viii). Boston: Houghton Mifflin.

How might I best turn one of my new year's resolutions into a practiced commitment? *The Stoic,* Issue *3,* 2.

(Speaker). *How to be happy though mated.* Cassette recording. New York: Institute for Rational-Emotive Therapy.

How to get along with neurotics without going crazy yourself. *Glamour, 73*(9), 194–195, 210, 216.

How to live with a "neurotic." Revised ed. New York: Crown Publishers. Paperback ed.: North Hollywood: Wilshire Books.

An informal history of sex therapy. *Counseling Psychologist, 5*(1), 9–13.

(Speaker). *Interview with a man with fear of failure in love relations.* Videotape. New York: Institute for Rational-Emotive Therapy.

Life without any kind of magic. Cassette recording. Orlando, FL: American Academy of Psychotherapists.

Minimizing irrational pronto-thinking. *Journal of the International Academy of Preventive Medicine, 2*(4), 38–40.

Myths and other sexual nonsense you can forget right now. *Brides, 42*(2), 120–121, 124.

With R. A. Harper. *A new guide to rational living.* Englewood Cliffs, NJ: Prentice-Hall. Paperback ed.: North Hollywood: Wilshire Books.

With K. Morris. The Perls perversion. *Personnel Guidance Journal, 54,* 91–93.

The physician and RET. *Practical Psychology for Physicians, 2*(4), 20–27.

(Speaker). *Raising an emotionally healthy, happy child.* Videotape. Austin: Audio-Visual Resource Center, School of Social Work, University of Texas.

A rational approach to leadership. In R. N. Cassel & R. L. Helchberger (eds.), *Leadership development: Theory and practice* (pp. 22–54). North Quincy, MA: Christopher.

The rational-emotive approach to sex therapy. *Counseling Psychologist, 5*(1), 14–22. Reprinted: New York: Institute for Rational-Emotive Therapy.

Rational-emotive group therapy. In G. M. Gazda (ed.), *Basic approaches to group therapy and counseling* (pp. 287–316). Springfield, IL: Thomas.

Rational-emotive psychotherapy. In D. Bannister (ed.), *Issues and approaches in psychological therapies* (pp. 163–186). New York: Wiley.

Rational-emotive therapy and the school counselor. *School Counselor, 22,* 236–242.

(Speaker). *Rational-emotive therapy: Four interviews.* Cassette recording. Salt Lake City: American Academy of Psychotherapists Tape Library.

With K. Morris & H. M. Kanitz. Reactions to RET. In K. T. Morris & H. M. Kanitz, *Rational-emotive therapy* (pp. 33–55). Boston: Houghton-Mifflin.

(Speaker). *RET and assertiveness training.* Cassette recording. New York: Institute for Rational-Emotive Therapy.

(Speaker). *RET group therapy demonstration.* Videotape. New York: Institute for Rational-Emotive Therapy.

Review of M. J. Goldstein, S. Kant, & J. Hartman, *Pornography and sexual deviance. Contemporary Psychology, 20,* 621–622.

Review of H. H. Mosak & B. Mosak, *A bibliography for Adlerian psychology. Rational Living, 10*(2), 38.

Review of J. L. Shelton & J. M. Ackerman, *Homework in counseling and psychotherapy. Behavior Therapy, 6,* 582–583.

With M. Edelstein (speakers). *Second and fifth sessions with sexually-blocked homosexual, ashamed of his orientation and fantasies; methadone client with severe job anxiety.* Cassette recording. New York: Institute for Rational-Emotive Therapy.

The treatment of sexual disturbance. *Journal of Marriage and Family Counseling, 1,* 111–121.

With J. Wolfe, L. Lowndes, J. Richardson, C. Gurevich, M. Rick, & N. Shapiro. You and your fantasy on film. *Galley, 5*(6), 95–97, 114–118.

1976

After Masters and Johnson — where is sex research going? *Village Voice,* p. 32.

Answering a critique of rational emotive therapy. *Canadian Counsellor, 10,* 56–59.

(Speaker). *Anxiety and phobias: Woman with fear of flying; severely disturbed male factory worker with defecation fears and incapacitating anxiety about what others think; male fearful of expressing feelings.* Cassette recording. New York: Institute for Rational-Emotive Therapy.

The biological basis of human irrationality. *Journal of Individual Psychology, 32,* 145–168. Reprinted: New York: Institute for Rational-Emotive Therapy.

(Speaker). *The certification of sex therapists.* Cassette recording. Baltimore: Hallmark Films.

(Speaker). *Dealing with conflicts in parent-child relationships.* Videotape. Austin: Audio-Visual Resource Center, School of Social Work, University of Texas.

With R. Harris. (Speaker). *Eighth session with man who drinks to avoid being lonely and dealing with his problems; male with depression over business failure; woman depressed and anxious about job problems.* Cassette recording. New York: Institute for Rational-Emotive Therapy.

With R. Oliver. (Speaker). *Fifty-six year old depressed woman with "empty-nest" syndrome and fear of being alone; woman depressed over rejection by manfriend; compulsive handwasher who believes she is a dirty person.* Cassette recording. New York: Institute for Rational-Emotive Therapy.

Foreword to A. J. Lange & P. Jakubowski, *Responsible assertive behavior* (pp. xiii–xv). Champaign, IL: Research Press.

Hazards in practicing RET: An answer. *Rational Living, 11*(1), 19–23.

Healthy and unhealthy aggression. *Humanitas, 12*(2), 239–254. Reprinted: New York: Institute for Rational-Emotive Therapy.

How I made the success trip. In R. Firestone, *The success trip* (passim). Chicago: Playboy Press.

The influence of therapists' image of humans upon their therapeutic approach. *Rational Living, 11*(2), 2–7.

(Speaker). *Life without any kind of magic.* Cassette recording. Salt Lake City: American Academy of Psychotherapists Tape Library.

A message from Albert Ellis. *Newsletter of the American Association of Sex Educators and Counselors, 8*(3), 6.

In V. Binder, A. Binder, & B. Rimland (eds.), *Modern Therapies* (pp. 21–34). Englewood Cliffs, NJ: Prentice Hall.

Nobody need feel ashamed or guilty about anything. In S. Kopp (ed.), *The naked therapist* (pp. 59–72). San Diego: Edits Publishers.

With D. Bloch. (Speaker). *The pros and cons of extramarital sexual relationships.* Cassette recording. Logan, UT: American Association of Marriage and Family Counselors.

With J. Barry & K. Heiser. Questions, issues and comments regarding continuing education for consulting psychologists. *Newsletter of the Division of Consulting Psychologists of the American Psychological Association, 28*(1), 27–52.

A rational-emotive approach to behavioral change. In A. Burton (ed.), *What makes behavior change possible?* (pp. 177–196). New York: Brunner-Mazel.

Rational-emotive psychotherapy. In W. S. Sahakian (ed.), *Psychotherapy and counseling,* 2nd ed. (pp. 272–285). Chicago: Rand McNally.

With R. J. Murphy. *Rational-emotive psychotherapy outcome studies: A bibliography.* New York: Institute for Rational-Emotive Therapy.

(Speaker). *Rational-emotive self-help techniques.* Cassette recording. New York: BMA Audio Tapes.

(Speaker). *Rational-emotive therapy: Clinician's guide.* Cassette recording. New York: BMA Audio Tapes.

Rational self-help form. New York: Institute for Rational-Emotive Therapy.

RET abolishes most of the human ego. *Psychotherapy: Theory, Research and Practice, 13,* 343–348. Reprinted: New York: Institute for Rational-Emotive Therapy.

(Speaker). *An RET approach to the treatment of possessiveness and jealousy.* Cassette recording. New York: Institute for Rational-Emotive Therapy.

With H. Greenwald. (Speaker). *RET vs. DDT.* Cassette recording. Salt Lake City: American Academy of Psychotherapists.

Review of M. I. Friedman, *Rational behavior: An explanation of behavior that is especially human. Rational Living, 11*(1), 39.

Review of M. R. Goldfried & G. C. Davison, *Clinical behavior therapy. Rational Living, 11*(1), 38–39.

Review of R. A. Harper, *The new psychotherapies. Rational Living, 11*(1), 38.

Review of R. M. Jurjevich, *The hoax of Freudism: A study of brainwashing the American professionals and laymen. Psychotherapy Bulletin, 9*(1), 19–20.

Review of D. H. Olson, *Treating relationships. Rational Living, 11*(1), 38.

Sex and the liberated man. Secaucus, NJ: Lyle Stuart.

Sex Differences. *New Dawn, 1*(3), 83–87.

Techniques of handling anger in marriage. *Journal of Marriage and Family Counseling, 2,* 305–316.

The what and how of psychotherapy: The rational-emotive view. *Journal of Contemporary Psychotherapy, 8*(1), 20–28.

Which, if any, of the Freudian concepts have you found useful within the RET system? *The Stoic,* Issue *4,* 2.

Yes, we seem to always think before we act: A reply to Warren Thorngate. Unpublished manuscript.

1977

Achieving emotional health. In W. R. Johnson (ed.), *Human health and action* (pp. 110–147). New York: Holt, Rinehart & Winston.

Becoming more becoming by coming. [Review of J. Heiman, L. LoPiccolo, & J. LoPiccolo, *Becoming orgasmic: A sexual growth program for women*]. *Contemporary Psychology, 22,* 763–764.

Can we change thoughts by reinforcement? A reply to H. Rachlin. *Behavior Therapy, 8,* 666–672.

Certification for sex therapists. In R. Genne & C. Wheeler (eds.), *Progress in sexology* (pp. 251–258). New York: Plenum.

Characteristics of psychotic and borderline individuals. In A. Ellis & R. Grieger (eds.), *Handbook of rational-emotive therapy* (pp. 177–186). New York: Springer.

Comments on C. Curran, "Values revisited." *Voices, 13*(3), 26–28.

Comments on R. A. Harper, "RET's place and influence in contemporary psychotherapy." In J. L. Wolfe & E. Brand (eds.), *Twenty years of rational therapy* (pp. 48–51). New York: Institute for Rational-Emotive Therapy.

(Speaker). *Dealing with sexuality and intimacy.* Cassette recording. New York: BMA Audio Cassettes.

Does the sex of the RET counselor affect the efficacy of RET procedures? *The Stoic,* Issue *5,* 3.

(Speaker). *Existentialism and rational psychotherapy.* Cassette recording. New York: Institute for Rational-Emotive Therapy.

Foreword to B. L. Little, *This will drive you sane* (pp. iii–vii). Minneapolis: Compcare Publications.

Fun as psychotherapy. *Rational Living, 12*(1), 2–6.

A garland of rational songs. New York: Institute for Rational-Emotive Therapy.

(Speaker). *A garland of rational songs. Lyrics by Albert Ellis sung to popular tunes.* Cassette recording. New York: Institute for Rational-Emotive Therapy.

Getting shrunk: Then and now. *Village Voice,* 31.

With R. Grieger (eds.). *Handbook of rational-emotive therapy.* New York: Springer.

How to be efficient though humanistic. *Dawnpoint, 1*(1), 38–47.

How to live with — and without — anger. New York: Reader's Digest Press. Paperback: *Anger: How to live with and without it.* Secaucus, NJ: Citadel Press.

In memory of Paul Frisch. *American Academy of Psychotherapists Newsletter,* p. 5.

The incredible shrinking plan. *Village Voice,* 6.

Intimacy in psychotherapy. *Rational Living, 12*(2), 13–19.

Introduction to D. Abelow, *Total sex* (pp. ix–xxv). New York: Ace Books.

Listen to Albert Ellis, Ph.D. In J. Fanelli, *National family sex education week notebook* (no paging). Syracuse, NY: Institute for the Family.

With W. Knaus. *Overcoming procrastination.* New York: Institute for Rational-Emotive Therapy. Paperback ed.: New York: New American Library.

The possibilities for human happiness. [Review of P. Kurtz, *Exuberance: A philosophy of happiness*]. *Humanist, 37*(5), 51.

With L. Eckstein. The psychology of political deviance. In E. Sagarin (ed.), *Deviance and social change* (pp. 195–218). Beverly Hills: Sage.

Rational-emotive therapy: Ellis' method. In B. Wolman (ed.), *International encyclopedia of psychiatry, psychology, psychoanalysis & neurology.* New York: Human Sciences Press.

Rational-emotive therapy: Research data that supports the clinical and personality hypotheses of RET and other modes of cognitive therapy. *Counseling Psychologist, 7*(1), 2–42. Also in A. Ellis & J. M. Whiteley (eds.), *Theoretical and empirical foundations of rational-emotive therapy* (pp. 101–103). Monterey, CA: Brooks/Cole, 1979.

Rational-emotive workshop. Cassette recordings. New York: BMA Audio Cassettes.

Rational love songs. *Mphasis, 14*(2), 19.

Rational thinking: An interview with Dr. Albert Ellis. *New Sun, 1*(10), 28–31.

Rejoinder: Elegant and inelegant RET. *Counseling Psychologist, 7*(1), 73–82. Also in A. Ellis & J. M. Whiteley (eds.), *Theoretical and empirical foundations of rational-emotive therapy* (pp. 240–267). Monterey, CA: Brooks/Cole, 1979.

Religious belief in the United States today. *Humanist, 37*(2), 38–41.

RET as a personality theory, therapy approach and philosophy of life. In J. L. Wolfe & E. Brand (eds.), *Twenty years of rational therapy* (pp. 16–31). New York: Institute for Rational-Emotive Therapy.

Review of A. T. Beck, *Cognitive therapy and the emotional disorders. Behavior Therapy, 7,* 295–296.

Review of H. J. Clinebell, Jr., & C. H. Clinebell, *The intimate marriage. American Journal of Orthopsychiatry, 41,* 186–187.

Review of S. B. Cotler & J. J. Guerra, *Assertion training: A humanistic-behavioral guide to self-dignity. Behavior Therapy, 8,* 516–517.

Review of individual education. *Journal of Individual Psychology, 33*(2a), 391–396.

Review of A. Senoussi, *Sexual development scale for females.* In O. Buros (ed.), *Seventh mental measurements yearbook* (pp. 571–572).

Skill training in counseling and psychotherapy. *Canadian Counsellor, 12*(1), 30–35.

Techniques of handling anger in marriage. *Journal of Marriage and Family Counseling, 2,* 305–315.

The what and how of psychotherapy: The rational-emotive view. *Journal of Contemporary Psychotherapy, 8*(1), 20–28. Reprinted: *Experiential therapy vs. rational therapy.* New York: Institute for Rational-Emotive Therapy.

What was the absolute worst mistake you ever made in your entire life? *Extra,* June, p. 8.

Why "scientific" professionals believe mystical nonsense. *Psychiatric Opinion, 14*(2), 27–30.

1978

(Speaker). *Albert Ellis on rational-emotive therapy: The development of his theories and practice and the application of his procedures.* Cassette recording. New York: Harper & Row Audio Colloquies.

Atheism: A cure for neurosis. *American Atheist, 20*(3), 10–13.

With E. Abrahms. (Speaker). *Brief psychotherapy and crisis intervention: Relationship breakups; disasters; job loss/retirement; betrayal; terrorism; fatal illness.* Six cassette recordings. New York: Institute for Rational-Emotive Therapy.

With E. Abrahms. *Brief psychotherapy in medical and health practice.* New York: Springer.

(Speaker). *Cognitive methods of sex therapy.* Cassette recording. Washington, DC: American Association of Sex Educators, Counselors, and Therapists.

Critical reaction to personal mastery group counseling. *Journal for Specialists in Group Work, 3,* 160–164.

(Speaker). *Dealing with conflicts in parent-child relationships.* Videotape. Austin: Audio-Visual Resource Center, School of Social Work, University of Texas.

(Speaker). *Dealing with sexuality and intimacy.* Cassette recording. New York: BMA Audio Cassettes.

With E. Abrahms. (Speaker). *Dialogues on RET.* Two cassette recordings. New York: Psychotherapy Tape Library.

Family Therapy: A phenomenological and active directive approach. *Journal of Marriage and Family Counseling, 4*(2), 43–50.

Feedback: A genius for lousing up. *Wharton Magazine, 2*(3), 72.

Foreword to M. DeMartino, *Human autoerotic practices* (pp. 9–18). New York: Human Sciences Press.

(Speaker). *I'd like to stop, but . . . Dealing with addictions.* Cassette recording. New York: Institute for Rational-Emotive Therapy.

Introduction to *The Forum man* (p. 3). New York: *Forum* Magazine.

Is cognitive-behavior modification sufficiently cognitive? [Review of D. Meichenbaum, *Cognitive behavior modification: An integrative approach*]. *Contemporary Psychology, 23,* 736–737.

Letter to the editor. *Forum, 7*(6), 56.

The male as a sex object. *Playgirl, 6*(1), 47–51.

Myths concerning autoeroticism. In M. F. DeMartino (ed.), *Human autoerotic practices* (pp. 55–57). New York: Human Sciences Press.

Personality characteristics of ratonal-emotive therapists and other kinds of therapists. *Psychotherapy: Theory, Research and Practice, 15,* 329–332.

Preface to Ben N. Ard, Jr., *Rational sex ethics* (pp. ix–xi). Washington, DC: University Press of America.

The problem of achieving scientific cognitive-behavior therapy. *Counseling Psychologist, 7*(3), 21–23. Also in C. E. Thoresen (ed.), *The behavior therapist* (pp. 42–46). Monterey, CA: Brooks/Cole, 1980.

With J. Marcano. *Un psicologo puertoriqueno entrevista a Albert Ellis.* San Juan: Taller de Communicaciones.

A rational approach to divorce problems. In S. M. Goetz (ed.), *Breaking asunder: Before, during and after divorce* (pp. 27–33). Greenvale, NY: C. W. Post Center, Long Island University.

A rational-emotive approach to family therapy. Part 1: Cognitive therapy. *Rational Living, 13*(2), 15–19. Reprinted: New York: Institute for Rational-Emotive Therapy.

Rational-emotive guidance. In L. E. Arnold (ed.), *Helping parents help their children* (pp. 91—101). New York: Brunner/Mazel.

Rational-emotive therapy. In R. J. Corsini (ed.), *Current psychotherapies*, 2nd ed. (pp. 158–229). Itasca, IL: Peacock.

(Speaker). *Rational-emotive therapy.* Cassette recording. New York: BMA Cassettes.

(Speaker). *Rational-emotive therapy — an overview.* Videotape. Austin: Audio-Visual Resource Center, School of Social Work, University of Texas.

Rational-emotive therapy and self-help therapy. *Rational Living, 13*(1), 2–9.

With E. Abrahms. (Speaker). *Rational-emotive therapy in the treatment of severe mental disorders: Introduction; severe depression; manic depression; schizophrenia; severe anxiety; dysfunctional habits.* Six cassette recordings. New York: Institute for Rational-Emotive Therapy.

(Speaker). *Rational-emotive workshop.* Cassette recording. New York: BMA Audio Cassettes.

With H. Greenwald. (Speaker). *RET vs. DDT: Rational emotive therapy vs. direct decision therapy.* Cassette recording. Salt Lake City: American Academy of Psychotherapists Tape Library.

Review of G. P. Sholevar, *Changing sexual values and the family. Journal of Marriage and Family Counseling, 4,* 152.

Review of S. Walen, N. Hauserman, & P. Lavin, *Clinical guide to behavior therapy. Rational Living, 13*(1), 37.

Self-help and sex therapy. *Sexual Medicine Today, 2*(11), 34.

Sex magazines as vehicles for sex education. *Humanist, 38*(6), 47–48.

Sexual violence. *Penthouse, 1*(8), 83–86, 96.

So-called alienation of sex in America. *Psychiatric Opinion, 15*(2), 25–27.

Solving your sex problems the rational-emotive way. *Interaction, 6*(2), 1–5; *6*(3), 1, 4, 5.

Swinging and affairs: Their place in marriage. In D. S. Milman & G. D. Goldman (eds.), *Man and woman in transition* (pp. 141–161). Dubuque, IA: Kendall/Hunt.

With R. Wessler. (Speaker). *Thirty year old woman with great fear of criticism which prevents her from exploring new paths; young man angry with wife for her spending habits.* Cassette recording. New York: Institute for Rational-Emotive Therapy.

Toward a theory of personality. In R. J. Corsini (ed.), *Readings in current personality theories* (pp. 298–311). Itasca, IL: Peacock.

(Speaker). *Treatment of sexual dysfunction.* Videotape. Austin: Audio-Visual Resource Center, School of Social Work, University of Texas.

With E. Abrahms. (Speaker). *TUse of rational-emotive therapy.* Cassette recording. Glendale, CA: Audio-Digest Foundation and American Psychiatric Association.

With J. L. Wolfe. The vaginal-clitoral orgasm controversy re-examined. In H. A. Otto (ed.), *The new sex education* (pp. 313–324). Chicago: Association Press and Follet Publishing Co.

What people can do for themselves to cope with stress. In C. L. Cooper & R. Payne (eds.), *Stress at work* (pp. 209–222). New York: Wiley.

1979

Accepting men the way they are. *Cosmopolitan,* December, 32.

(Speaker). *An interview with Albert Ellis.* Cassette recording. New York: Harper & Row Media Program.

The biological basis of human irrationality: A reply to McBurnett and La Pointe. *Individual Psychology, 35*(1), 111–116.

With J. Marmor, H. Kaplan, J. Wolpe, & C. Socarides. Can homosexuals change in fourteen days? Differing perspectives on Masters and Johnson. *Behavioral Medicine, 6*(6), 23–25.

With G. Clanton. A conversation with Albert Ellis. *Alternative Life-Styles, 2,* 243–253.

Dialogue and quotations on sex and *mus*turbation. In B. Avedon (ed.), *Ah men!* (passim). New York: A & W Publishers.

Discomfort anxiety: A new cognitive-behavioral construct (Part I). *Rational Living, 14*(2), 3–8.

(Speaker). *Discomfort anxiety: A new construct in cognitive behavior therapy.* Cassette recording. New York: BMA Audio Cassettes and Association for Advancement of Behavior Therapy.

Foreword to F. MacNab, *Change* (pp. v–vii). Melbourne: Hill of Content.

The intelligent woman's guide to dating and mating. Secaucus, NJ: Lyle Stuart.

Is rational-emotive therapy stoical, humanistic or spiritual? *Journal of Humanistic Psychology, 19*(3), 89–92.

The issue of force and energy in behavioral change. *Journal of Contemporary Psychotherapy, 10*(2), 83–97.

Negative linking of RET to positive thinking. *Contemporary Psychology, 24,* 1058–1059.

A note on the treatment of agoraphobics with cognitive modification versus prolonged exposure in vivo. *Behavior Research and Therapy, 17,* 162–164.

On Joseph Wolpe's espousal of cognitive-behavior therapy. *American Psychologist, 34,* 98–99.

The practice of rational-emotive therapy. In A. Ellis & J. M. Whiteley (eds.), *Theoretical and empirical foundations of rational-emotive therapy* (pp. 61–100). Monterey, CA: Brooks/Cole.

The rational-emotive approach to counseling. In H. M. Burks, Jr., & B. Stefflre (eds.), *Theories of counseling,* 3rd ed. (pp. 172–219). New York: McGraw-Hill.

A rational-emotive approach to family therapy. Part II: Emotive and behavioral therapy. *Rational Living, 14*(1), 23–27. Reprinted: New York: Institute for Rational-Emotive Therapy.

Rational-emotive psychotherapy. In W. S. Sahakian (ed.), *Psychopathology today,* 2nd ed. (pp. 439–448). Itasca, IL: Peacock.

Rational-emotive therapy. In A. Ellis & J. M. Whiteley (eds.), *Theoretical and empirical foundations of rational-emotive therapy* (pp. 1–6). Monterey, CA: Brooks/Cole.

Rejoinder: Elegant and inelegant RET. In A. Ellis & J. M. Whiteley (eds.), *Theoretical and empirical foundations of rational-emotive therapy* (pp. 240–267). Monterey, CA: Brooks/Cole.

Review of K. Meiselman, *Incest: A psychological study of cause and effects with treatment recommendations. Society, 16*(6), 87–88.

A reviewer sees familiar landmarks in E/R therapy. *Patient Care, 13*(14), 100–101.

Sex and the liberated man. In G. D. Goldman and D. S. Milman (eds.), *Modern man* (pp. 69–104). Dubuque, IA: Kendall/Hunt.

The sex offender. In H. Toch (ed.), *Psychology of crime and criminal justice* (pp. 405–426). New York: Holt, Rinehart & Winston.

With J. M. Whiteley (eds.). *Theoretical and empirical foundations of rational-emotive therapy.* Monterey, CA: Brooks/Cole.

The theory of rational-emotive therapy. In A. Ellis & J. M. Whiteley (eds.), *Theoretical and empirical foundations of rational-emotive therapy* (pp. 33–60). Monterey, CA: Brooks/Cole.

A too-brief look at the briefer psychotherapies [review of L. Small, *The briefer psychotherapies,* rev. ed.]. *Contemporary Psychology, 14,* 999–1000.

Toward a new theory of personality. In A. Ellis & J. M. Whiteley (eds.), *Theoretical and empirical foundations of rational-emotive therapy* (pp. 7–32). Monterey, CA: Brooks/Cole.

The untired rational-emotive therapist. *Voices, 15*(2), 34–35.

With E. Abrahms. (Speaker). *Use of rational-emotive therapy by psychiatrists.* Two cassette recordings. New York: American Psychiatric Association and Audio-Digest Foundation.

1980

With D. Meichenbaum, M. Goldfried, M. Beck, A. T. Beck, F. Kanfer, & P. Wachtel (speakers). *Cognitive behavior therapy and research.* Eight cassette recordings. New York: Institute for Rational-Emotive Therapy.

Comments on M. Gottesfeld, "When the therapist wants to terminate." *Voices, 16*(2), 16–17.

(Speaker). *The control of stress in everyday living.* Hauppauge, NY: Alison Audio Products.

Discomfort anxiety: A new cognitive behavioral construct (Part II). *Rational Living, 15*(1), 25–30.

The fact of mental illness. *Rational Living, 15*(2), 13–19.

Foreword to J. A. Bard, *Rational-emotive therapy* (pp. vii–x). Champaign, IL: Research Press.

Foreword to L. Losoncy, *You can do it!* (pp. xiii–xvi). Englewood Cliffs, NJ: Prentice-Hall.

Foreword to S. R. Walen, R. DiGiuseppe, & R. L. Wessler, *A practitioner's guide to rational-emotive therapy* (pp. vii–xii). New York: Oxford University Press.

Foreword to R. A. & R. L. Wessler, *The principles and practice of rational-emotive therapy* (pp. ix–xii). San Francisco: Jossey-Bass.

With T. Szasz (speakers). *Is mental illness a myth?* Cassette recording and videotape. New York: Institute for Rational-Emotive Therapy.

An overview of the clinical theory of rational-emotive therapy. In R. Grieger & J. Boyd (eds.), *Rational-emotive therapy: A skills based approach* (pp. 1–31). New York: Van Nostrand Reinhold.

Psychotherapy and atheistic values: A response to A. E. Bergin's "Psychotherapy and religious values." *Journal of Consulting and Clinical Psychology, 48,* 635–639.

The rational-emotive approach to children's and adoelscents' sex problems. In J. M. Sampson (ed.), *Childhood and sexuality: Proceedings of the international symposium* (pp. 513–524). Montreal: Editions Etudes Vivantes.

(Speaker). *Rational emotive psychotherapy.* Cassette recording. Washington, DC: Psychology Today Tapes.

Rational emotive therapy. In R. Herick (ed.), *The psychotherapy handbook* (pp. 380–386). New York: New American Library.

Rational-emotive therapy and cognitive behavior therapy: Similarities and differences. *Cognitive Therapy and Research, 4,* 325–340.

(Speaker). *Rational emotive therapy: Cognition. Workshop in RET.* Five cassette recordings. San Diego: Professional School for Humanistic Studies.

Review of E. S. Gomberg & V. Franks, *Gender and disordered behavior: Sex differences in psychopathology. Journal of Marital and Family Therapy, 6,* 94.

Review of H. S. Kaplan, *Disorders of sexual desire. Archives of Sexual Behavior, 10,* 395—397.

Sex in the 80's. *Penthouse Variations,* December-January, 6–7.

Sexual abuse by therapists — Part II. *The NOW NY Woman,* October, 3.

Some cognitive additions to Eysenck's "The conditioning model of neurosis." *Behavioral and Brain Sciences, 3,* 459–482.

The treatment of erectile dysfunction. In S. R. Leiblum & L. A. Pervin (eds.), *Principles and practice of sex therapy* (pp. 240–258). New York: Guilford.

The value of efficiency in psychotherapy. *Psychotherapy: Theory, Research and Practice, 17,* 414–419.

1981

With A. Lazarus, S. Gordon, C. Franks, P. Russianoff, R. Diekstra, H. Greenwald, & R. Harper (speakers). *Albert Ellis "roast".* Two cassette recordings. New York: Institute for Rational-Emotive Therapy.

Dr. Albert Ellis' list of 21 irrational beliefs that lead to sex problems and disturbances. In A. B. Gerber (ed.), *The book of sex lists* (pp. 46–48). Secaucus, NJ: Lyle Stuart.

(Speaker). *Intelligent person's guide to dating and mating.* Cassette recording. New York: Institute for Rational-Emotive Therapy.

Is RET ethically untenable or inconsistent? A reply to Paul E. Meehl. *Rational Living, 16*(1), 10–11.

Misrepresentation of behavior therapy by psychoanalysis. *American Psychologist, 36,* 798–799.

Personal and professional views on aging. In Jewish Ys and Center of Greater Philadelphia (ed.), *Creating aging* (pp. 3–5). Philadelphia: Jewish Ys and Center of Greater Philadelphia.

The philosophic implications and dangers of some popular behavior therapy techniques. In M. Rosenbaum, C. M. Franks, & Y. Jaffe (eds.), *Perspectives of behavior therapy in the eighties* (pp. 138–154). New York: Springer.

The place of Immanuel Kant in cognitive psychotherapy. *Rational Living, 16*(2), 13–16.

The rational-emotive approach to thanatology. In H. V. Sobel (ed.), *Behavior therapy in terminal care* (pp. 151–176). Cambridge, MA: Ballinger.

Rational-emotive family therapy. In A. M. Horne & M. M. Ohlsen (eds.), *Family counseling and therapy* (pp. 302—307). Itasca, IL: Peacock.

Review of H. S. Kaplan, *Disorders of sexual desire. Archives of Sexual Behavior, 10,* 395–397.

Science, religiosity and rational emotive psychology. *Psychotherapy: Research and Practice, 18,* 155–158.

Teoria e prassi della RET (rational-emotive therapy) [Theory and practice of RET (rational-emotive therapy)]. In A. F. Guidano & M. A. Reda (eds.), *Cognitivismo e psicoterapia* (pp. 219–237). Milan: Franco Angeli Editore.

Too much piz-Szasz? [Review of T. Szasz, *Sex by prescription*]. *Contemporary Psychology, 26,* 676–677.

The use of rational humorous songs in psychotherapy. *Voices, 16*(4), 29–36.

1982

Albert Ellis' list of the greatest Jewish psychotherapists. In R. Landau, *The book of Jewish lists* (pp. 191–193). New York: Stein & Day.

Becoming self-directed: Notes from Albert Ellis' workshop. In T. Orlick, J. T. Partington, & J. H. Salmela (eds.), *Mental health for coaches and athletes* (pp. 37–42). Ottawa: Coaching Association of Canada.

Comment. In V. deFoggia & L. Murray, "How much is too much sex?" *Forum, 12*(3), 52.

Dream watch. *Penthouse, 13*(5), 167–170; *13*(6), 159–162; *13*(7), 155–159; *13*(8), 151–154; *13*(9), 153–156; *13*(10), 155–158; *13*(11), 155–158; *13*(12), 149–152.

With I. Becker. *A guide to personal happiness.* North Hollywood: Wilshire Books.

The honesty of Laura Perls and the basic dishonesty of Gestalt therapy. *Voices, 18*(2), 49–50.

Intimacy in rational-emotive therapy. In M. Fisher & G. Striker (eds.), *Intimacy* (pp. 203–218). New York: Plenum.

Major systems. *Personnel and Guidance Journal, 61,* 6–7.

Must most psychotherapists remain as incompetent as they now are? *Journal of Contemporary Psychotherapy, 13*(1), 17–28.

Notes from Albert Ellis' workshop: Self-determination. In T. Orlick, J. T. Partington, & J. H. Salmela (eds.), *Mental health for coaches and athletes* (pp. 110–121). Ottawa: Coaching Association of Canada.

Psychoneurosis and anxiety problems. In R. Grieger & I. Z. Grieger (eds.), *Cognition and emotional disturbance* (pp. 17–45). New York: Human Sciences Press.

Rational-emotive family therapy. In A. M. Horne & M. H. Ohlsen (eds.), *Family counseling and therapy* (pp. 381–412). Itasca, IL: Peacock.

Rational-emotive group therapy. In G. M. Gazda (ed.), *Basic approaches to group psychotherapy and group counseling* (pp. 381–412). Springfield, IL: Thomas.

(Speaker). *Rational-emotive therapy: A documentary film featuring Dr. Albert Ellis.* Champaign, IL: Research Press.

A reappraisal of rational-emotive therapy's theoretical foundations and therapeutic methods: A reply to Eschenroeder. *Cognitive Therapy and Research, 6,* 393–398.

Review of P. Schiller, *The sex profession: What sex therapy can do. Journal of Sex Research, 18*(10), 84.

Self-direction in sport and life. *Rational Living, 17*(10), 26–33. Also in T. Orlick, J. T. Partington, & J. H. Salmela (eds.), *Mental health for coaches and athletes.* Ottawa: Coaching Association of Canada.

(Speaker). *Solving emotional problems.* Cassette recording. New York: Institute for Rational-Emotive Therapy.

The treatment of alcohol and drug abuse: A rational-emotive approach. *Rational Living, 17*(2), 15–24.

(Speaker). *Twenty-two ways to brighten up your love life.* Cassette recording. New York: Institute for Rational-Emotive Therapy.

1983

Albert Ellis' opinion. *American Academy of Psychotherapists Newsletter,* June/July, 2.

Al responds to Allyn. *American Academy of Psychotherapists Newsletter,* September, 2.

Comment [on Erika Wick, "Psychotherapy focus: Old and new"]. *Voices, 18*(4), 40–41.

The case against religiosity. New York: Institute for Rational-Emotive Therapy.

With R. Wessler (speakers). *Conversations with Albert Ellis.* Two videotapes. New York: Institute for Rational-Emotive Therapy.

Dream watch. *Penthouse, 14*(1), 145–148; *14*(2), 149–152; *14*(3), 159–162; *14*(4), 169–172; *14*(5), 171–174; *14*(6), 145–148.

Failures in rational-emotive therapy. In E. B. Foa & P. M. G. Emmelkamp (eds.), *Failures in behavior therapy* (pp. 159–171). New York: Wiley.

The future of rational-emotive therapy (RET). *I'Act Rationally, News and Views,* February, 2–4.

How to deal with your most difficult client — you. *Journal of Rational-Emotive Therapy, 1*(1), 2–8. Also in *Psychotherapy in Private Practice,* 1984, *2*(1), 25–35.

With P. Krassner & R. A. Wilson. *An impolite interview with Albert Ellis.* Rev. ed. New York: Institute for Rational-Emotive Therapy.

Letter to editor. *Recovery, 1*(4), 5.

With S. Keleman, R. Felder, & E. C. Brown (speakers). *Living one's life well: American Academy of Psychotherapists 1983 Conference.* Salt Lake City: American Academy of Psychotherapists Tape Library.

My philosophy of work and love. *Psychotherapy in Private Practice, 1*(1), 43–49.

With M. Spodak & J. Groebel (speakers). *Occupational stress: The counselor's role as consultant.* Cassette recording. Arlington, VA: American Association for Counseling and Development.

The origins of rational-emotive therapy (RET). *Voices: The Art and Science of Psychotherapy, 18*(4), 29–33.

With M. E. Bernard. An overview of rational-emotive approaches to the problems of childhood. In A. Ellis & M. E. Bernard (eds.), *Rational emotive approaches to the problems of childhood* (pp. 3–43). New York: Plenum.

With M. E. Bernard (eds.), *Rational-emotive approaches to the problems of childhood.* New York: Plenum.

Rational-emotive therapy (RET) approaches to overcoming resistance. 1: Common forms of resistance. *British Journal of Cognitive Psychotherapy, 1*(1), 28–38.

Rational-emotive therapy (RET) approaches to overcoming resistance. 2: How RET disputes clients' irrational resistance-creating beliefs. *British Journal of Cognitive Psychotherapy, 1*(2), 1–16.

(Speaker). *Stress management: The rational-emotive approach.* Cassette recording. Arlington, VA: Association of Counseling and Development.

With R. Wessler. Supervision in counseling: Rational-emotive therapy. *Counseling Psychologist, 11*(1), 43–49.

Two's company, three's a crowd. In R. L. Spitzer, A. E. Skodol, M. Gibbon, & J. B. W. Williams, *Psychopathology: A casebook* (pp. 99–104). New York: McGraw-Hill.

The use of rational-emotive therapy (RET) in working for a sexually-sane society. In G. W. Albee, S. Gordon, & H. Leitenberg (eds.), *Promoting sexual responsibility and preventing sexual problems* (pp. 402–411). Hanover, NH: University Press of New England.

1984

Autocontrol: El metodo de la terapia racional-emotiva. *Advances en Psicologia Clinica Latinoamericana, 3,* 35–43.

Curing hyperbole. *APA Monitor, 15*(7), 5.

Current psychotherapies. In R. J. Corsini (ed.), *Encyclopedia of psychology* (pp. 339–341). New York: Wiley.

The essence of RET — 1984. *Journal of Rational-Emotive Therapy, 2* (1), 19–25. Also foreword to W. Dryden, *Rational-emotive therapy: Fundamentals and innovations* (pp. vii–xvi). London: Croom Helm.

Foreword to M. E. Bernard & M. R. Joyce, *Rational-emotive therapy with children and adolescents* (pp. ix–x). New York: Wiley.

Foreword to W. Dryden, *Rational-emotive therapy: Fundamentals and innovations* (pp. vii–xxvi). London: Croom Helm.

Foreword to L. L. Sank & C. S. Shaffer (eds.), *A therapist's manual for cognitive behavior therapy in groups* (pp. vii–ix). New York: Plenum.

(Speaker). *How to be happy though human.* New York: Institute for Rational-Emotive Therapy.

How to maintain and enhance your rational-emotive therapy gains. New York: Institute for Rational-Emotive Therapy.

(Speaker). *Intelligent person's guide to dating and mating.* Cassette recording. New York: Institute for Rational-Emotive Therapy.

Introduction to the work of Howard S. Young. *British Journal of Cognitive Psychotherapy, 2,* 1–5.

Is the unified-interaction approach to cognitive-behavior modification a reinvention of the wheel? *Clinical Psychology Review, 4,* 215–218.

Maintenance and generalization in rational-emotive therapy (RET). *The Cognitive Behaviorist, 6*(1), 2–4.

The place of meditation in cognitive-behavior therapy and rational-emotive therapy. In D. H. Shapiro, Jr., & R. N. Walsh (eds.), *Meditation: Classic and contemporary perspectives* (pp. 671–673). New York: Aldine.

With C. Baldwin. Rational-emotive therapy. In C. Baldwin, *Instructor's manual to current psychotherapies,* 3rd ed. (pp. 33–38). Itasca, IL: Peacock.

Rational-emotive therapy. In R. J. Corsini (ed.), *Current psychotherapies,* 3rd ed. (pp. 196–238). Itasca, IL.

Rational-emotive therapy (RET) and pastoral counseling: A reply to R. Wessler. *The Personnel and Guidance Journal, 12,* 266–267.

Rational-emotive therapy (RET) approaches to overcoming resistance. 3: Using emotive and behavioral techniques of overcoming resistance. *British Journal of Cognitive Psychotherapy, 2*(1), 11–26.

The responsibility of counselors and psychologists in preventing nuclear warfare [comment on Gearhart's "The counselor in a nuclear world: A rationale for awareness and action"]. *Journal of Counseling and Development, 63,* 75–76.

With J. Sichel. *RET self-help form.* New York: Institute for Rational-Emotive Therapy.

Review of B. N. Ard, Jr., *Living without guilt and/or blame. Journal of Rational-Emotive Therapy, 2*(2), 35.

Review of W. Dryden, *Rational-emotive therapy: Fundamentals and innovations. Journal of Rational-Emotive Therapy, 2*(10), 36.

Sex therapies. In R. J. Corsini (ed.), *Encyclopedia of psychology* (p. 308). New York: Wiley.

Treating the abrasive client with rational-emotive therapy (RET). *The Psychotherapy Patient, 1*(1), 21–25.

With R. A. Wakefield. Use [of personal computers] in rational-emotive therapy. In R. A. Wakefield (ed.), *The home computer, families, and the mental health professions* (pp. 18–20). Washington, DC: American Family, Inc.

1985

Anxiety about anxiety. The use of hypnosis with rational-emotive therapy. In E. T. Dowd & J. M. Healey (eds.), *Case studies in hypnotherapy* (pp. 1–11). New York: Guilford.

Approaches to overcoming resistance. 4: Handling special kinds of clients. *British Journal of Cognitive Psychotherapy, 3*(1), 26–42.

With M. E. Bernard (eds.). *Clinical applications of rational-emotive therapy.* New York: Plenum.

Cognition and affect in emotional disturbance. *American Psychologist, 40,* 471–472.

Conceptual thinking and the criminal personality. *Journal of Counseling and Development, 63,* 589.

Critique of D. B. Wile's critique of Albert Ellis' method of cognitive restructuring in couple's therapy. *British Journal of Cognitive Therapy, 3* (1), 81–83.

Expanding the ABCs of RET. In M. J. Mahoney & A. Freeman (eds.), *Cognition and psychotherapy* (pp. 313–323). New York: Plenum. Also in *Journal of Rational-Emotive Therapy,* 1984, 2(2), 20–24.

Foreword to H. H. Barrish & I. J. Barrish, *Managing parental anger: The coping parent series* (pp. v–vi). Shawnee Mission, KS: Overland Press.

(Speaker). *A guide to personal happiness.* Cassette recording. Washington, DC: Psychology Today Tapes.

Intellectual fascism. *Journal of Rational-Emotive Therapy, 3*(1), 3–12. Reprinted: New York: Institute for Rational-Emotive Therapy.

With M. Nystul. An interview with Dr. Albert Ellis. *Individual Psychology, 41,* 243–254.

Love and its problems. In A. Ellis & M. E. Bernard (eds.), *Clinical applications of rational-emotive therapy* (pp. 32–53). New York: Plenum.

With D. Tascher & L. McGehee. *Manual for RET/EAP workshop.* New York: Institute for Rational-Emotive Therapy.

(Speaker). *The mind of addiction.* Cassette recording. Van Nuys, CA: On-site Tape Services and Institute for Integral Development.

Overcoming resistance: Rational-emotive therapy with difficult clients. New York: Springer.

(Speaker). *The practice of rational-emotive therapy.* 2 cassette recordings, No. L330-W21a, W21b. Garden Grove, CA: InfoMedix.

A rational-emotive approach to acceptance and its relationship to EAPs. In S. H. Klarreich, J. L. Francek, & C. E. Moore (eds.), *The human resources management handbook: Principles and practice of employee assistance programs* (pp. 325–330). New York: Praeger.

Rational-emotive therapy. In A. S. Bellack & M. Hersen (eds.), *Dictionary of behavior therapy techniques* (pp. 177–181). New York: Pergamon.

Review of W. Dryden, *Rational-emotive therapy: Fundamentals and innovations. Journal of Rational-Emotive Therapy,* 2(1), 36.

With M. E. Bernard. What is rational-emotive therapy (RET)? In A. Ellis & M. E. Bernard (eds.), *Clinical applications of rational-emotive therapy* (pp. 1–30). New York: Plenum.

(Speaker). *Workshop on rational-emotive therapy and addiction.* Two cassette recordings. Van Nuys, CA: On-site Tape Services and Institute for Integral Development.

1986

Bibliography. *American Psychologist, 41,* 382–397.

Can scientific psychotherapy save us from a nuclear holocaust? In P. Bollen (ed.), *Nuclear voices* (pp. 171–172). Lynnfield, MA: Highland/Hillside Books.

Clinical exchange: Ken. *International Journal of Eclectic Psychotherapy, 5,* 276–278.

Comments on Gloria. *Psychotherapy, 23,* 647–648.

Comments on the evolution of psychotherapy conference. *International Journal of Eclectic Psychotherapy, 5,* 239–241.

Do some religious beliefs help create emotional disturbance? *Psychotherapy in Private Practice, 4*(4), 101–106.

With L. B. Gschwandtner. Dr. Albert Ellis: The rational way to sell. *Personal Selling Power, 6*(5), 16–18.

An emotional control card for inappropriate and appropriate emotions in using rational-emotive imagery. *Journal of Counseling and Development, 65,* 205–206.

Fanaticism that may lead to a nuclear holocaust: The contributions of scientific counseling and psychotherapy. *Journal of Counseling and Development, 65,* 146–151.

Foreword (to R. E. McMullin, *Handbook of Cognitive Therapy Techniques*). New York: Norton.

With R. Grieger. *Handbook of rational-emotive therapy. Vol. 2.* New York: Springer.

(Speaker). *Incorporating hypnosis in RET.* Cassette recording. Phoenix, AZ: Milton H. Erickson Foundation and InfoMedix.

With B. Hoellen. An interview with Albert Ellis, *Psychotherapy in Private Practice, 4*(2), 81–98.

Introduction (to W. J. Knaus and C. Hendricks, *The illusion trap,* pp. ix–xi). New York: World Almanac Publications.

Letter to Paul Rifkin. In P. Rifkin (ed.), *The God letters* (p. 204). New York: Warner.

The nuclear threat. In D. Paulson (ed.), *Voices of survival in the nuclear age* (pp. 142–143). Santa Barbara: Capra Press.

Rational-emotive therapy. In I. L. Kutash & A. Wolf (eds.), *Psychotherapist's casebook: Theory and technique in the practice of modern therapies* (pp. 277–287). San Francisco: Jossey-Bass.

With W. Dryden. Rational-emotive therapy (RET). In W. Dryden & W. L. Golden (Eds.), *Cognitive-behavioral approaches to psychotherapy* (pp. 129–168). London: Harper & Row.

Rational-emotive therapy applied to relationship therapy. *Journal of Rational-Emotive Therapy, 4*(1), 4–21.

Review of M. L. Weiner, *Cognitive-experiental therapy. Readings: A Journal of Reviews and Commentary in Mental Health, 1*(3), 29.

Thoughts on supervising counselors and therapists. *Association for Counselor Education and Supervision Newsletter,* pp. 3–5.

1987

With R. Warren & R. W. McLellarn. Albert Ellis' personal responses to the survey of rational-emotive therapists. *Journal of Rational-Emotive Therapy, 5*(2), 92–101.

Ask Dr. Ellis. *Journal of Rational-Emotive Therapy, 5*(2), 135–137.

Critical incidents in group therapy: Rational-emotive therapy. In J. Donigan & R. Malnati (eds.), *Critical incidents in group therapy* (pp. 87–91, 105–109, 123–128, 141–146, 166–172, 189–192). Monterey, CA: Brooks/Cole.

Discussion [of C. Whitaker, The dynamics of American family life as deduced from twenty years of family therapy: The family unconscious]. In J. K. Zeig (ed.), *The evolution of psychotherapy* (pp. 84–90). New York: Brunner/Mazel.

(Speaker). *The enemies of humanism — What makes them tick?* Cassette recording, No. 108. New York and Alexandria, VA: Audio Transcripts.

The evolution of rational-emotive therapy (RET) and cognitive behavior therapy (CBT). In J. K. Zeig (ed.), *The evolution of psychotherapy* (pp. 107–133). New York: Brunner/Mazel.

Four decades of experience with the media. Cassette recording, No. 19. New York and Alexandria, VA: Audio Transcripts.

The impossibility of achieving consistently good mental health. *American Psychologists, 42,* 364–375.

On the origin and development of rational-emotive therapy. In W. Dryden (ed.), *Key cases in psychotherapy* (pp. 148–175). London: Croom Helm.

(Speaker). *Practical applications of rational-emotive therapy.* 3 cassette recordings. Indianapolis, IN: Access.

With W. Dryden. *The practice of rational-emotive therapy.* New York: Springer.

With W. Dryden & W. Back. Problems in living: The Friday night workshop. In W. Dryden, *Current issues in rational-emotive therapy* (pp. 154–170). London and New York: Croom Helm.

With W. Dryden. Rational-emotive therapy: An excellent counseling theory for NPS. *Nurse Practitioner, 12*(7), 16–37.

Rational-emotive therapy: Current appraisal and future directions. *Journal of Cognitive Psychotherapy, 1*(2), 73–86.

A sadly neglected cognitive element in depression. *Cognitive Therapy and Research, 11,* 121–146.

Self-control: The rational-emotive therapy method. *Southern Psychologist, 3*(1), 9–12.

Testament of a humanist. *Free Inquiry, 7*(2), 21.

(Speaker). *The theory and practice of rational-emotive therapy and practical applications of rational-emotive therapy.* 4 cassette recordings. Indianapolis, IN (P.O. Box 30006): Access.

The use of rational humorous songs in psychotherapy. In W. F. Fry Jr. & W. A. Salamen (eds.), *Handbook of humor and psychotherapy* (pp. 265–286). Sarasota, FL: Professional Resource Exchange.

In Press

With R. Yeager. *The enormous dangers of transpersonal psychology and psychotherapy.* Buffalo, NY: Prometheus.

How to stubbornly refuse to be miserable about anything — yes, anything! New York: Lyle Stuart.

With J. F. McInerney, R. DiGiuseppe & R. J. Yeager. *Rational-emotive therapy with alcoholics and substance abusers.* New York: Pergamon.

Index

About the Author

Daniel Wiener is clinical professor of psychiatry and of psychology at the University of Minnesota. He also has a private practice in Minneapolis.

Dr. Wiener has published many articles on clinical psychology in such professional journals as *American Psychologist, American Journal of Orthopsychiatry,* and *American Journal of Psychiatry;* book reviews; and seven books alone and in collaboration, including *Practical Guide to Psychotherapy* (Harper & Row), *Dimensions of Psychotherapy* (Aldine), and *Short-term Psychotherapy and Structured Behavior Change* (McGraw-Hill).

He holds B.A., M.A., and Ph.D. degrees from the University of Minnesota, is a fellow of the American Psychological Association, and a diplomate in clinical psychology of the American Board of Professional Psychology.